HOW
"GOD"
WORKS

HOW "GOD" WORKS

A LOGICAL INQUIRY

ON FAITH

· · ·

MARSHALL BRAIN

FOUNDER OF HOWSTUFFWORKS.COM

STERLING
New York

An Imprint of Sterling Publishing
1166 Avenue of the Americas
New York, NY 10036

ISBN 978-1-4549-1061-9

Distributed in Canada by Sterling Publishing
c/o Canadian Manda Group, 664 Annette Street
Toronto, Ontario, Canada M6S 2C8
Distributed in the United Kingdom by GMC Distribution Services
Castle Place, 166 High Street, Lewes, East Sussex, England BN7 1XU
Distributed in Australia by Capricorn Link (Australia) Pty. Ltd.
P.O. Box 704, Windsor, NSW 2756, Australia

For information about custom editions, special sales, and premium and
corporate purchases, please contact Sterling Special Sales at 800-805-5489
or specialsales@sterlingpublishing.com.

Manufactured in the United States of America

2 4 6 8 10 9 7 5 3 1

www.sterlingpublishing.com

DEDICATION

Dedicated to all of us, as members of the human race, with the hope that we can abandon irrationality, tribalism, and superstition, unify as an intelligent species, and work together to create heaven on earth for every human being on the planet.

And to

All of the rational, inspiring, scientific, mathematical, and engineering minds who have come before us, and upon whose shoulders we stand today here in the modern world.

CONTENTS

1:

WHAT HAPPENED
AT BANDA ACEH?

IMAGINE THAT YOU AND I ARE SITTING POOLSIDE AT A BEAUTIFUL RESORT NEAR BANDA ACEH, A CITY IN NORTHERN SUMATRA. The beach is nearby and we are enjoying drinks as our children splash happily in the shallows. It is a stunning, sunny day with a light, balmy breeze rustling the palm trees—a perfect day to be on vacation in this little slice of paradise. It is also the day after Christmas. Everyone is happy and smiling with the joy that surrounds the Christmas season.

Then we feel the earthquake. It rattles the furniture, shakes the buildings, knocks things over in the bar, and causes ripples to form on the surface of the pool. It lasts for what seems like an eternity but in reality is just a minute or two. There is something completely unnatural about the earth itself shuddering underneath you. And then it is over, as though nothing has happened. The sun is still out. The children return to their play. The birds continue singing. Earthquakes happen and life goes on. This one does not seem to have been that destructive.

Unfortunately, this has been no normal earthquake. It is so powerful that, over a thousand miles away, buildings are shaking in Bangkok, Thailand. It is one of the most powerful earthquakes ever recorded, and it has caused a gigantic tectonic plate deep under the ocean off the coast of Indonesia to quickly shift upward by as much as six feet (two meters). This shift will force many cubic miles of seawater upward as well, and in just a few seconds. All of that displaced water has to go somewhere. It spreads out in all directions and, over time, will crash upon many shores in the form of tsunamis.

Banda Aceh is the closest major city to the epicenter of the quake, and about twenty-five minutes later it is the first to feel the impact of all of this uplifted water. In the distance, the oncoming wall of brine is easy to see. Several waves, one as high as thirty feet (nine meters), will rush onto the shore, flooding inland up to two miles (four kilometers). Over 150,000 people in the city will die on December 26, 2004. There are many videos available on the Internet to help you understand what a disaster like this looks like if you are on the ground to witness it. What the videos cannot do is convey how horrific it is to actually be there as a participant.

If you and I are Christians or Muslims or members of another organized religion that advocates the belief in a higher power, and if we happen to be lucky enough to survive the tsunami with our families intact, we may sit down together afterward feeling a combination of shock, nausea, and anguish. We will feel relief because of our survival, certainly, but given that 150,000 fellow human beings are dead all around us, it may be impossible to feel any gratitude. If we were to become philosophical and ponder the utter destruction we have just witnessed, a disaster like this may cause us to ask legitimate questions. We are smart, rational people after all, and it is impossible to ignore such immense tragedy when we are located right in the middle of it. A catastrophe like this should logically raise questions about the God whom we pray to and worship. We would legitimately want to know: How does God work?

For example: Why would any loving God allow an unmitigated disaster like this to occur? It is an obvious question and anyone in such a situation would ask it. Since our God is all-knowing and prayer-answering, surely He knew this tsunami was coming and had the ability to prevent it. So why did He allow such an amazing cataclysm to unfold? The unfortunate thing about a question like this is that God will not answer directly. God will never sit down beside us and offer a clear, definitive explanation for why 150,000 people died in Banda Aceh. We know and accept that God does not materialize to do interviews when requested. But the questions remain.

Therefore, an alternative is to turn to some proxy for God Himself. We might, for example, open a holy book like the Bible or the Qur'an. God may offer some insight here. Or we might ask religious leaders for their interpretation of events and God's reasoning. We might try praying, with the hope that God will speak to us internally with answers. Or we might rely on introspection and speculation to arrive at answers to our questions. Using the information available, we might try to develop several different explanations to help us cope with the disaster that has unfolded before us.

It could be that this truly is an "Act of God." That is how insurance companies and many commentators are going to classify it. Perhaps God, in his infinite wisdom, may have decided that a tsunami needed to take place and that hundreds of thousands of people needed to die for some reason on that day in Indonesia. Or perhaps, as some believe, an event like this is a precursor to the end of time. It really isn't possible to argue with a supreme being, and there is not currently a way for human beings to stop a natural disaster of this magnitude. Whether it is a hurricane, a tornado, a volcano, a blizzard, a massive hailstorm, a flooding river, a drought, a monsoon, or an earthquake/tsunami like this one, any "Act of God" that arrives in the form of a natural disaster can cause a huge amount of suffering, pain, and death. Perhaps someone or something upset God? Maybe God needed to smite a person, a city, or an entire nation for some reason? Or perhaps the tsunami is God's punishment for a social evil festering in the region? God is known to snuff out entire cities in the Bible. For that matter, in the book of Genesis, God flooded the entire planet at one point. If God has His reasons, who are we to question Him?

Another potential explanation: Is it possible that this tsunami is part of God's plan? The Bible indicates, and prominent Christian leaders like Rick Warren tell us, that God has specific intentions for each individual human being He creates—for example, planning the exact times of our births and our deaths. Maybe God has preordained the tsunami as part of His plan. Maybe, as this unknowable plan unfolds, there will be a tremendous amount of good to be delivered from the deaths of so many people. There is nothing you can do to change things and it must be all for the good if God planned it.

Perhaps someone prayed to God and asked for the tsunami, and God answered the prayer. That doesn't really fit with our common vision of a loving God, but who knows? God appears to be answering prayers all the time, and maybe He sometimes answers ones that we would interpret as disastrous. After all, God must frequently get prayers that contradict each other—prayers where one person or the other is going to experience pain no matter what God chooses to do. What if a Christian festival organizer is praying for a month of sunshine to maximize his festival's attendance, while a nearby farmer is praying for a month of pouring rain to snap a long dry spell that is killing crops and livestock and draining the region's lakes? God might need to bring pain to someone; God might face this sort of dilemma constantly. Even though it brings immense pain to one group, perhaps another group experiences great happiness from the same event.

No matter what we hypothesize, however, we are still left with a hollow feeling because we are sympathetic to the suffering of fellow human beings. God is all-powerful and all-loving, and hundreds of thousands of deaths, along with untold billions of dollars in property damage, feels incredibly uncomfortable if they happened on His watch. Even more uncomfortable is the fact that this kind of thing happens all the time. The Japan earthquake and tsunami in 2011 killed over 10,000 people and damaged or destroyed over a million buildings. It also caused one of the largest nuclear accidents in the history of humankind. Hurricane Katrina in 2005 nearly wiped out an entire city in the United States, displacing over 200,000 people from their flooded homes. In 2003, a heat wave in Europe killed 40,000 people and a Russian heat wave in 2010 killed another 56,000. In 2008, a Chinese earthquake in the Sichuan province killed 69,000 people, while the 2008 cyclone in Myanmar killed nearly 150,000. The 2010 earthquake in Haiti killed over 300,000 people—something like 3 percent of the country's populace. Going back in history, there are events that are unimaginable today. The Black Death in the fourteenth century, for example, may have killed as many as 200 million people—roughly half of all the human beings alive at the time. If these truly are Acts of God—if God caused them through His direct and divine actions—they are agonizing. It is painful and depressing to think that this much death, suffering, and destruction comes at the hand of a loving God. If God was not the cause, but instead He sat by and watched these disasters unfold without preventing them—that is agonizing as well.

When we are discussing all of these disasters, we may eventually arrive at an important train of thought: How does God work? What is God doing? Why is He doing it? What is He thinking? What is the truth about God and His actions, many of which can seem capricious if not downright monstrous? If we believe that God is interacting with our planet every day in order to answer millions of prayers, why is He not also interacting with the planet to avert these catastrophes and save millions of people from such immense tragedy?

There is one other explanation that is possible. Believers discount this explanation, but it should not hurt anything to put it on the table. Could it be that the God described in our holy books like the Bible and the Qur'an is imaginary, and that these mass tragedies happen with such regularity because there is no God to intercede? What if all of the gods conceived by human beings, theologians, and philosophers were imaginary? Interestingly, this idea explains why no God ever materializes in the living room or on TV to answer questions of the sort we are asking right now.

Depending on your level of religiosity and your intellectual honesty, the act of raising this possibility might strike you in a number of different ways. At one end of the spectrum, it is possible that you find this sort of question to be intellectually stimulating and an appropriate area of examination. If God is real, questions like this should pose no problem whatsoever. At the other end of the spectrum is the staunch believer who considers such a question to be blasphemy. One part of the Bible goes so far as to suggest that a person who asks questions like this should be stoned to death. Parts of the Qur'an also prescribe death for infidels.

If we open up the conversation more broadly, we may also arrive at a related question: What is truth? How do people decide whether anything is true or false? This is one of the most interesting questions we can ask as human beings, because we are compelled to discover the truth all the time.

Think about all of the situations that you face every day where you are trying to discover the truth. For example, are the people whom we know and love being honest or lying? Are the advertisements and product descriptions that we see in the marketplace all around us truthful? Are our politicians and military leaders revealing true information about the economy or about an enemy in a foreign land? Does an expensive medicine truly heal a disease, or are we seeing a placebo effect? Without the truth, it is very difficult to make accurate decisions and it can be impossible to understand the reality of the world we live in.

It is the same with God and religion. What is the truth about God and His actions in our world today? It is an incredibly important question for us to examine.

UNDERSTANDING THE TRUTH

Human beings have to make decisions about the truth of information constantly. Every day we are sorting through situations trying to understand what is true and what is false. Some of these situations are trivial, while others can be matters of life and death for millions of people.

For example, imagine that a good friend of yours sends you an e-mail explaining that flying reindeer are real. Surely he is joking, right? But you question him about it and he appears to be serious. He has seen them with his own eyes and there can be no doubt about the reality of flying reindeer. You have not detected any signs of insanity in your friend previously, and have even trusted his advice on several occasions. How would a person decide whether your friend's claim is true or false?

Or imagine that you are reading about a court case in the newspaper. A man has been arrested as a suspect in a heinous murder in your city. All evidence points to him: The murder was captured on video, the man's DNA has been found at the scene of the crime, and so on. When he appears in court, however, the suspect maintains that he is innocent. He claims that a perfect doppelganger of him has beamed down from an alien spaceship that is buried on the dark side of the moon. It is this doppelganger who committed the crime. How would the court decide whether the suspect's claim is true or false given that there is no easy way to ascertain whether or not the spaceship exists?

Imagine this actual situation from the 1940s. Scientists are trying to understand whether cigarettes are harmful or not. A number of very large corporations in the United States—corporations with a great deal of money and power, armed with large teams of lawyers and massive advertising campaigns—are claiming that cigarettes are safe. The United States military has supplied millions of soldiers during World War II with free cigarettes packed into their C-rations. Tens of millions of Americans, representing nearly half of the adult population, are smoking happily with no overt signs of distress. How would scientists decide whether the manufacturers' safety claims are true or false?

The dictionary defines *truth* in the following way: "The true or actual state of a matter; conformity with fact or reality." Given this definition, how does anyone decide if something is true or not?

Now examine the following situation. There are billions of people on our planet today who believe in a supernatural being. Muslims believe in Allah, Christians believe in God and Jesus, and so on. They believe that God is real. They believe that God answers their prayers. Many of them claim to have a personal relationship with God, as in they communicate with God and God responds directly to them. They cite numerous pieces of evidence from their own lives and from the lives of others demonstrating that their God exists. They have built millions of churches and mosques around the world as physical and tangible expressions of their belief. In the United States alone there are approximately 350,000 churches. To put that into perspective, there are about three times as many churches in the United States as there are gas stations.

Statistically speaking, if you live in the United States, there is a 75 percent chance that you are a Christian believer. Seventy-five percent of adults living in the United States today—an overwhelming majority—claim to be Christian and to believe in God and Jesus Christ. To put this into perspective, the United States president with the largest percentage of the popular vote on record is Lyndon B. Johnson in 1964 with 61 percent of the vote. He was swept into office after John F. Kennedy's assassination and he faced a weak opponent in Barry Goldwater. Yet that 61 percent landslide doesn't come close to the majority that

Christianity holds in the minds of the American public. A 75 percent majority represents an unprecedented level of agreement and approval.

Given all of this momentum, it seems obvious that God must be real, doesn't it? How could this many people be wrong?

But then there is the situation in Banda Aceh, and hundreds of other occurrences like it. To a thoughtful person, these catastrophes raise an inevitable question: Is it true that God is real? And if God is real, where is He? A thoughtful person is not really interested in an appeal to popularity or an impressive-seeming collection of evidence that might turn out to be false if we examine it closely. A thoughtful person wants to know the truth, and wants to base his or her life on reality and fact.

OUR JOURNEY TOGETHER

We are about to embark on a fascinating journey together. We are going to explore the question of God's reality in an honest way. We will ask and honestly answer the question: Is God real or imaginary? In the process, we will understand how God works. Our goal is to probe into the truth of the matter, while at the same time utilizing the techniques that people use to understand and discover the truth. This is a book about God, yes, but it is also a book about how things work in the world we live in today. Our goal is to separate the real from the imaginary and to understand how people can do this reliably in the different parts of their lives.

No matter what else happens in this book, there is one core question we will have to deal with. Let's hypothesize for a moment that God is imaginary. If that is the case, then how is it possible that so many billions of people believe in various gods? That's billions, with a "B." More than half of the people on this planet believe in a god of some sort. There are approximately 2 billion Christians who believe in God and Jesus Christ. There are nearly the same number of Muslims who believe in Allah. Approximately another billion people follow the Hindu faith. And so on. If these gods are all imaginary, how can so many people believe in them? What process could possibly lead such an immense number of people to this conclusion? With this many people believing in one god or another, how could anyone suppose that God could be imaginary?

In this book I will assume that you are a believer in a higher power. These same questions apply to Christians, Muslims, Hindus, and other theistic religions, although each religion has a unique relationship to faith and belief in a higher power. I often use Christians and Christianity as an example when discussing faith in God for three reasons. First, Christianity is the largest religion on the planet today. Second, in order to investigate God as a concept, we need to refer to a particular source in order to define his attributes. In the case studies in this book, we largely refer to the Bible in order to do so. Third, I live in the United States and I am therefore immersed in Christianity every day. Statistically, 75 percent of the people around me are Christian believers. Since I live in the southern United States, the percentage is even higher. However, please note that we are investigating God as a higher power, not specifically God as defined by Christianity.

Your level of belief is important to this investigation, so let's discuss it briefly. Its importance stems from the fact that it controls your religiosity, your worldview, your acceptance or rejection of new ideas, and many other aspects of your day-to-day life. We might broadly divide the collection of people who call themselves believers into four different categories. Where do you fit?

Let's take Christianity for an example. You may be a Christian who was born and raised in a devoted Christian family. If so, you have been hearing about God and Jesus since you were an infant. You probably went to Sunday school every Sunday as a child, and it's quite likely that you go to church every Sunday as an adult as well. God may be integrated into your entire life. For example, you might pray to God several times a day. You most likely have a personal relationship with God and He answers your prayers on a regular basis. You may even keep a prayer journal. You donate generously to your church and might tithe the full 10 percent recommended by the Old Testament. You may subscribe to one or more Christian magazines or organizations outside your church. You might also be "born again," either as a teenager or an adult.

If you are a devoted Christian like this, it may have never occurred to you to ask whether God might be imaginary. It might seem, on initial examination, to be an impossible proposition, because God and

Jesus have been a part of your life for as long as you can remember. You *know* that God is real through direct experience. Even so, disasters like earthquakes and tsunamis might get your attention and cause you to wonder about God. Why does God behave this way if He is all-loving and all-knowing? If you have ever stopped to think about a question like this, you may find yourself engrossed in this book.

On the other hand, you may have been raised as a more casual Christian. You don't go to church every single Sunday, but you do go with some regularity, and especially on a big occasion like Christmas. You definitely do believe in God, but you may not think about Him every single day. You also believe in heaven and hell, and you would surely prefer the former over the latter. You might not pray daily, but you do pray frequently. You may have heard the idea that God might be imaginary, although you may have never really given it any serious thought. However, you might have increased interest in the idea because of media coverage. By reading this book, you will have the opportunity to discover for yourself whether God is real or imaginary.

Or you might actually have given God a *lot* of thought. You may have looked into the idea of God and the Bible quite intensely and you have come to the conclusion that the Bible is literally true and God's existence is indisputable. You may have read the Bible extensively. In your opinion, God wrote the Bible and God is omniscient. Therefore, everything in the Bible is God's word and it must be truthful no matter what. Depending on where you live, you may find yourself to be in very good company. In some parts of the United States, up to 70 percent of adults share your belief that the Bible is literally true. You might call yourself an evangelical Christian, or a fundamentalist. For you, the idea that God is imaginary may seem utterly ridiculous and unworthy of consideration. However, a book like this might be interesting to you as a way of gathering ammunition and strengthening your faith.

At the other end of the spectrum, you might be a Christian who doesn't really practice Christianity in your daily life in any tangible way. If someone were to ask you if you believe in God, or if you are a Christian, your answer would be yes. But if the questioning were to get very deep, you know there's not much there. For example, you don't attend church at all. In an emergency or for something important you might pray to God, but God is not a significant part of your life otherwise. You have never read the Bible and don't see the need. You don't ever talk about religion. God, Jesus, and heaven are rather vague concepts. In your case, you might be quite open to the exploration of God's reality. If God could be proven real, it might give you a reason to pay more attention to religion. On the other hand, if God were to be imaginary, you could forget about religion entirely and get rid of that small nagging voice in your head that occasionally pesters you about going to church.

Where do you stand on the Christianity spectrum? Do you consider yourself to be an evangelical Christian, a devoted Christian, a casual Christian, or an occasional Christian? How important is God and Christianity in your life today? From that position, are you interested in exploring the question of whether God is real or imaginary? Would you enjoy learning about the techniques that people use to discern whether something really is true or false?

Regardless of your position on the spectrum of belief, we truly will be embarking on a fascinating journey together. We will discover how people arrive at an understanding of truth, and in the process, we will get at the truth about God. We will see how thoughtful, curious, open-minded people come to understand the truth about anything.

This is a book about truth, and how human beings arrive at it. Let us begin our journey with a rather unusual starting point . . .

2:

CAN WE PROVE THAT
SOMETHING IS IMAGINARY?

IMAGINE THAT YOU AND I WERE TO TRAVEL TO CHINA FOR THE FIRST TIME. Having never been there before, many sights, smells, and sounds would strike us as unusual and interesting. You can get the same kind of feeling, albeit on a much smaller scale, in the Chinatown district of a major city like New York City or San Francisco. But being in China itself is something like being transported to a different planet. The language is very different in both its written and spoken forms. The foods are unique and distinct. The customs, festivals, and decorations have a special feeling to them unique to China. Even the air in Chinese cities is different. And you are completely engulfed by it. In New York City's Chinatown, you can walk two blocks and return to America. When in China itself, you are in a nation with approximately the same landmass as the continental United States, with a dense population four times that of the United States. It truly is a different world.

One thing that we would definitely take note of as we got to know the Chinese people better is the pervasiveness of something called Traditional Chinese Medicine. It is an important and deep-seated part of Chinese culture that stretches back for many centuries. In practice, Traditional Chinese Medicine involves the use of many natural substances, often mixed together in different proportions, to treat diseases and maladies common to human beings. The substances used can range from common spices found in any kitchen—for example, dried ginger root—to quite exotic things like bug shells. In most cases, a mixture of dried leaves, roots, bugs, etc. is prepared by a practitioner of

Traditional Chinese Medicine. This mixture is then placed in boiling water to prepare an herbal tea. The patient then drinks the tea each day for a period of time to effect a cure.

One substance that happens to be part of Traditional Chinese Medicine is rhinoceros horn. The horn is cut off of a rhinoceros, which usually results in the death of the animal. The horn is then ground into a powder and prepared as a tea to treat a variety of ailments including fever and gout.

One question that any thoughtful person would ask about the use of rhinoceros horn is this: Is rhinoceros horn effective in the treatment of things like fever and gout? Or, is the claimed efficacy of rhinoceros horn for these conditions imaginary? It turns out that this is an incredibly important question. For one thing, it is important for consumers to know whether the horn is an effective treatment because the horn is extremely expensive. If its effects are imaginary, then the use of rhinoceros horn represents a huge waste of money.

But there is a far more important reason for understanding whether the effectiveness of rhinoceros horn is real or imaginary. Illegal rhinoceros poaching, which is the only way to obtain rhinoceros horn, is rapidly driving all species of rhinoceros toward extinction. Demand for rhinoceros horn in China has increased dramatically in recent years and the price of rhinoceros horn has skyrocketed. Large sums of money can be earned by killing rhinoceros and harvesting their horns. This money provides the primary incentive for poaching. In other words, the belief in the effectiveness of rhinoceros horn by a large group of Chinese people is causing the extinction of an important and well-known animal species in the wild. If scientists can prove that the effectiveness of rhinoceros horn is imaginary and educate people so they stop using rhinoceros horn, then demand should decrease and rhinoceros would have a better chance of surviving in the wild.

Therefore we are led to this question: Is it possible to determine whether the claimed healing effects of rhinoceros horn are real or imaginary? You may have heard things that might make you believe that it is impossible to prove that something does not exist. For example, you might have heard the expression, "You cannot prove a negative." Or you might have heard, "The absence of evidence is not evidence of absence."

But the fact is that scientists prove that things are imaginary all of the time. One of the best places to see that process is to look at the difference between **evidence-based medicine** and what is known as **alternative medicine**. In simple terms, evidence-based medicine, also known as modern medical science, is the kind of medicine you find in a hospital or in the office of a licensed doctor in a developed country like the United States. Evidence-based medicine consists of drugs and procedures that have been proven to provide a benefit to patients. The evidence comes from scientific experiments, and the evidence provides proof of efficacy. Alternative medicine, on the other hand, consists of substances and procedures for which there is no compelling evidence of effectiveness. When tested scientifically, the compounds and procedures of alternative medicine have no discernible benefit for the patients who use them. Even more interesting is this fact: If something from the world of alternative medicine were to show compelling evidence that it is effective, it stops being categorized as alternative medicine and becomes evidence-based, scientifically proven medicine.

So let's imagine that scientists pose this question: Does rhinoceros horn act as an effective treatment for fever? This is the kind of question that medical scientists ask and answer every day. However, it is noteworthy that the process used to answer the question in the medical realm is not trivial. The tool that science must use to approach this question and get an accurate answer is called a **double-blind test.** The fact that scientists have to go to the trouble of double-blind testing is quite interesting because it teaches us several things about how human beings work.

Why do we need double-blind testing? Why can't we just take a person with a fever, give him some rhinoceros horn, and see if he starts feeling better? Because, from a scientific standpoint, this doesn't tell us anything. It is not a valid experiment. After all, there is some chance that our patient would start feeling better on his own, regardless of whether we give him rhinoceros horn or not. People have immune systems, and the human immune system can cure most fevers on its own, given sufficient time. If the patient is going to start feeling better anyway, any effect that seems to be a result of the rhinoceros horn could simply be a coincidence.

We need a better test if we are going to rule out coincidence and gather any valid scientific evidence. We really need to do a side-by-side comparison of test subjects—with some taking rhinoceros horn and some not taking it, to eliminate the coincidence factor. Scientists call this second group of people a **control group**, defined in the dictionary as:

> A group of subjects closely resembling the treatment group in many demographic variables but not receiving the active medication or factor under study and thereby serving as a comparison group when treatment results are evaluated.

We take one group of people who have fevers and give them rhinoceros horn. We can call these people Group A. Then we take another group of people and give them nothing. Call these people Group B, and they will act as our control group because they did not receive any treatment at all. If the members of Group A report fewer fever symptoms after taking the rhinoceros horn—for example, as measured by reports from the patients about how they feel—than the members of Group B, can we decide that rhinoceros horn is effective? The answer is no, and the reason is both unexpected and fascinating. A phenomenon known as the **placebo effect** gets in our way, and we need to take it into account if we hope to get valid results. The placebo effect is defined in the dictionary like this:

> A beneficial effect in a patient following a particular treatment that arises from the patient's expectations concerning the treatment rather than from the treatment itself.

For reasons that are not completely clear yet, human beings sometimes report feeling better simply through the effects of having someone care for them. In other words, we might see the same effect in Group A if we give the patients a sugar pill (a placebo) instead of tea made from rhinoceros horn. We know that the sugar pill is not doing anything—it is the act of having a doctor administer the sugar pill, and the acts of professionalism and caring surrounding that administration, that sometimes helps people report that they feel better after receiving a placebo.

Some of the outcomes that surround the placebo effect can be surprising. For example, if a teenager in jeans and a t-shirt administers the placebo in a clinical trial, the placebo effect might be much weaker than if an older gentleman dressed in a white lab coat administers it. From the patient's perspective, the teenager may lack things like authority, credibility, or gravitas. These missing features can diminish the placebo effect. And the bizarre nature of the placebo effect goes further than that: If a doctor injects sugar water into a patient with a syringe, the placebo effect is often stronger than with a sugar pill taken by mouth. It appears that the injection is perceived to be more "powerful" and "medical" in the mind of the patient, so the placebo effect of an injection can be different from the placebo effect of a pill. Even things like the color and shape of a pill can influence the placebo effect.

Because of the placebo effect, we cannot do a valid clinical trial on the effectiveness of rhinoceros horn if one group receives something that seems like treatment while the other group receives nothing. The group receiving the treatment will be affected by the placebo effect while the other will not, invalidating the results of the trial. We have to design the test to eliminate the problem created by the placebo effect.

Therefore, we might next try a protocol called **single-blind testing**, which the dictionary defines as:

> Of or pertaining to an experiment or clinical trial in which the researchers but not the subjects know which subjects are receiving the active medication or treatment and which are not: a technique for eliminating subjective bias, as the placebo effect, from the test results.

In this protocol, the members of Group A and Group B both receive what appears to them to be the same kind of treatment. The doctor in charge of the test prepares the medicine and gives it to the patients.

However, unknown to the patients in the two groups, one group is receiving actual rhinoceros horn tea while the other is receiving an indistinguishable decoy—a placebo. The trial must be designed so that the patients have no way to know whether they get the real thing or the decoy—this is called **blinding**. For example, if rhinoceros horn tea tastes disgusting, both groups will receive a tea that tastes similarly disgusting, even if one tea is made from some sort of benign, awful-tasting seaweed extract while the other is actual rhinoceros horn. In addition, the patients in the two groups must also be treated in the same type of setting by the same kind of doctor, so the amount and type of care they are receiving is identical.

Having gone to all of this trouble, making sure that both groups A and B are being treated identically, we might expect that the results of such a test would be valid. But we would be wrong again. Single-blind testing with human beings involved generally does not provide valid results. Why not?

Unfortunately, it turns out that if the doctor knows which patients are receiving the rhinoceros horn and which ones are receiving the decoy, this knowledge can invalidate the test. It has been discovered, over the course of conducting thousands of clinical trials over many decades, that the doctor administering the trial can spoil the results of a single-blind test. Tiny changes in behavior can tip off the members of Group A and Group B, in some cases without them even realizing it, and pollute the results of the test.

Thus the need for **double-blind testing**, defined as:

> Of or pertaining to an experiment or clinical trial in which neither the subjects nor the researchers know which subjects are receiving the active medication, treatment, etc., and which are not: a technique for eliminating subjective bias from the test results.

In the case of double-blind testing, the members of Group A and Group B both receive treatment that looks identical. In reality, one group gets the rhinoceros horn while the other gets a placebo. This is no different from the protocol used for single-blind testing.

But in double-blind testing, the crucial difference is that the person who administers the test has no idea whether Group A or Group B is receiving the actual rhinoceros horn. The sample medicines—either real or decoy—are prepared in such a way that neither the patients nor the administering doctor can tell the difference. Now the doctor has no bias either way and therefore cannot telegraph any subtle messages to the members of Group A or B.

What is going on here? Why is double-blinding necessary? It seems quite odd if you think about it—what could an honest doctor do to spoil a single-blind test? There is a well-known ability for doctors, often unintentionally, to telegraph that information with subtle cues. The doctor might use a different vocabulary with the two groups, or different body language, or might smile and laugh more with one group or the other. These cues can influence the results of the test because the two groups are not being treated identically. Double-blinding eliminates the doctor's knowledge of which group gets what, thus eliminating any difference in treatment.

Is the double-blind test now valid? Not yet. There are at least two more things to consider. First, we must ensure that the members of Group A and Group B are truly **randomized**. Randomized is defined by *The Random House Dictionary* as:

> To order or select in a random manner, as in a sample or experiment, especially in order to reduce bias and interference caused by irrelevant variables.

The doctors doing the test can have no interaction with, and no control over, the members of Groups A and B. If the doctors doing the test have the ability to select who goes into groups A and B, they will sometimes either consciously or unconsciously sort the people. To avoid this, members of Groups A and B must be completely random, ideally chosen by a computer program's random number generator or some other totally impartial mechanism.

We also need to consider the size of groups A and B. Why is **group size** important? Size matters because people are different. Let's imagine that Groups A and B each have only one member. In Group A we have Suzy, and in Group B we have Jane. Jane might be much more susceptible to the placebo effect than Suzy is. Therefore, if Group A receives the real rhinoceros horn and then we look at the results, we might falsely conclude that rhinoceros horn is ineffective. However, what we are actually seeing is the increased response in Jane to the placebo effect, not the effectiveness of the rhinoceros horn. In other words, the differences in human behavior can create noise in the data produced by an experiment. In this case, differences between Jane's and Suzy's responses to the placebo effect can skew the results.

To solve this problem, the size of the groups has to be large enough to eliminate these random human behavioral differences as much as possible. For example, if Groups A and B each have ten people in them, some of this problem, but not all, washes out. Group A might have a few more people who respond strongly to the placebo effect than Group B, and these differences can skew the results. If we increase the size of Groups A and B to one hundred or one thousand members, the effect of random variation is reduced significantly.

The effect of group size on the results of a double-blind test is described as the **statistical significance** of the results. Statistical significance is described by *The American Heritage® New Dictionary of Cultural Literacy* as:

> In statistics, a number that expresses the probability that the result of a given experiment or study could have occurred purely by chance. This number can be a margin of error ("The results of this public opinion poll are accurate to 5 percent"), or it can indicate a confidence level ("If this experiment were repeated, there is a probability of 95 percent that our conclusions would be substantiated").

Scientists can calculate, statistically, how much noise is possible in the data based on group size. The results of the test have to be greater than that noise value in order to be valid.

Now, if we take all of these things into account—the patients in Group A and Group B are blinded, the patients in Group A and Group

B are treated identically in every way, the researchers administering the test are blinded, the people in groups A and B are truly randomized without influence by the researchers, and the group size is adequate—we can find out whether the medical effects of rhinoceros horn are real or imaginary. If all of these conditions hold true, the results of a double-blind test truly tell us something.

It seems like an awful lot of trouble to go to, doesn't it? However, because of the way human beings work, this amount of trouble is absolutely necessary if researchers hope to gather accurate results from a test of rhinoceros horn's effectiveness. Scientists can look at the results of a properly conducted double-blind test with confidence. If rhinoceros horn is effective against fever, that effectiveness will show up in the test results in a significant way. If the effectiveness of rhinoceros horn is imaginary, no statistically significant differences will be seen in the results from the two groups. In other words, the placebo effect will be the same in the two groups, so there will be no difference between the results of the two groups.

Now that you have this information, imagine that David has psoriasis and his friend Cindy finds out. Cindy says, "My mother told me to use a banana paste for my psoriasis, so I did. I mashed up some bananas and massaged the paste into my skin three times a day. Two weeks later my psoriasis was gone. You should try it!" Based on this conversation, can we conclude that a paste made of mashed-up bananas is effective against psoriasis? You should now be able to understand that without a properly administered double-blind test, we really have no idea whether banana paste is effective or not. An anecdotal story about the experiences of one friend is absolutely meaningless.

EXAMINING THE RESULTS

Let's see how double-blind testing works in a successful case. Imagine the following scenario: We create two groups of patients who are complaining of arthritis pain. We put a thousand patients in each group. Now we prepare two sets of pills that look, feel, and taste identical. One set of pills acts as placebos—simple sugar pills with a gel coating—while the other set consists of tablets containing a new, experimental painkiller. We administer the pills in an identical double-blind way to the members of Groups A and B, two groups that are fully randomized and large enough to yield easily measured results. In other words, we have taken all of the steps necessary to create a valid clinical trial for this experimental painkiller.

After administering the pills to the two groups and waiting an hour, we ask the patients how they feel. Eight hundred of the people in Group A—the group that received the real painkiller—report feeling significantly less pain an hour after taking their pills. In Group B, only fifty people report significantly less pain (because of the placebo effect). This difference (eight hundred people vs. fifty people) represents a statistically significant result, so we would report that the new painkiller is effective. Using a valid double-blind clinical trial, the new painkiller's effect has been proven to be real. Assuming that other experiments do not discover severe side effects from the painkiller, drug interactions, or long-term complications, etc., people with arthritis could start taking this new painkiller and feel real results. The painkiller has been scientifically proven to work, and therefore when people take it, it actually does work at a level much greater than placebo.

What does it mean if we create a clinical trial for a drug and the results for Group A and Group B are identical or nearly so? It means the drug does not work any better than a placebo would. In that case, the claimed effects made for the drug have been proven to be imaginary.

The question that opened this chapter was, "Is it possible to prove that something is imaginary?" As you can see, the answer is yes and scientists do it all the time. Through the scientific methodology known as double-blind testing, we can prove conclusively whether the claims made for a drug or procedure are real or imaginary.

Now imagine that we do an actual double-blind test on the effectiveness of rhinoceros horn. One of several things might happen:

1. Rhinoceros horn might be shown to have a real effect on fever—just as powerful, for example, as other popular fever drugs.
2. Rhinoceros horn might be shown to have no effect at all above the level of placebo. In that case, the purported

effectiveness of rhinoceros horn is imaginary. We could then educate practitioners and followers of Traditional Chinese Medicine about these results and they would stop wasting money on rhinoceros horn.

3. Rhinoceros horn might be shown to have no effect at all above the level of placebo—the purported effectiveness of rhinoceros horn is imaginary. However, people continue using it all the same. Practitioners of Traditional Chinese Medicine continue using rhinoceros horn as though it works, even though it has no more effect than any placebo would.

Option #3 would be tragic, wouldn't it? Yet it happens all the time, as we will see in the next chapter. And the results can be devastating. It is quite possible that, because of rhinoceros poaching that is driven by the demand for rhinoceros horn, rhinoceros will soon become extinct in the wild.

That might sound impossible to you. How can it be that the effectiveness of a substance is proven to be imaginary, yet people continue using it? How can people—especially huge groups of people at a nationwide level—act in such an illogical, irrational way? How can they do it when they are simultaneously wasting money and driving a magnificent wild animal to the brink of extinction?

It turns out that the answer to these questions is both fascinating and disturbing. It has to do with a failure in critical thinking. This failure affects billions of human beings all over the planet. Statistically speaking, there is a good chance that you yourself are affected by failures in critical thinking on a daily basis. You may have no idea that it's happening.

The good news is that this is a solvable problem. It's a problem that can be cured through education. The next chapter will help you begin to understand what's going on and why failures in critical thinking are so common.

3:

WHY DO PEOPLE BELIEVE
IN IMAGINARY THINGS?

AFTER READING THE PREVIOUS CHAPTER, YOU MAY HAVE NOTICED THREE THINGS ABOUT HUMAN BEINGS.

The first thing you might have noticed is that scientists have to go to a tremendous amount of trouble to conduct a valid clinical trial that involves human patients and human researchers. A scientist cannot give a drug to a couple of people to decide if it works. Instead, scientists have to carefully design and conduct valid double-blind trials to get accurate results. Scientists have to make sure that patients are blinded to account for the placebo effect. They have to make sure the people conducting the trial are blinded to avoid their biases creeping into the results. They have to make sure that the test patients are truly randomized when divided into groups, again to avoid bias. And they must ensure that the groups are large enough to take into account variations in human responses to placebos and drugs. All of these activities combine together to create a valid clinical trial. But none of them are easy or implicit—real effort must be expended to get clean, accurate results from a clinical trial.

The second thing you probably noticed is that, if you go to all of this trouble, it is easy for human beings to gather the evidence needed to prove whether a drug's (or a procedure's) effect is real or imaginary. Scientists do this all the time. A drug company makes claims about a new drug's effects, and a clinical trial tests those claims. If a drug really does what it says it will do, then statistically significant evidence will result from well-designed experiments. If the drug's effect is imaginary, the drug will perform in the same way that a normal placebo does.

The third thing that you probably noticed in the last chapter is that people often behave in ways that are illogical and difficult to understand when they see the results of a clinical trial. In the case of Traditional Chinese Medicine and in the cases of many other forms of alternative medicine, millions of people use these treatments even though there is no scientific evidence indicating that they work, and in some cases, plenty of scientific evidence indicating that they do not. Often these treatments are expensive and the money spent is completely wasted. It makes no logical sense, but millions of people do this all the time.

Even rich, famous, otherwise intelligent people can fall prey to these tendencies. Even Steve Jobs, the extremely wealthy and famous co-founder of Apple, was for a time seduced by the siren song of alternative medicine. In a post-mortem report published in *Scientific American* magazine, it is noted that Steve Jobs tried alternative techniques, including a juice fast. The most obvious problem that this approach created is that his detour into alternative medicine delayed evidence-based treatment.

Why would a person use something—in many cases paying money for it in the process—if its effect has been shown to be imaginary? In almost all cases, this problem is caused by a failure in critical thinking. To understand why this happens, let's do a little exploration.

CRITICAL THINKING

What is critical thinking and why do we need it? **Critical thinking** is a response to a rather bizarre and unexpected fact about the way human beings naturally think. It turns out that typical human beings, left to their own untrained devices, are not very good thinkers at all. In fact, the average human being who is not provided with any training in critical thinking skills may, potentially, be terrible at logical, precise thinking. Human beings are subject to a wide variety of errors and problems in their thinking, some well known and some more esoteric. The combined effect of all of these different errors can lead people very far away from the truth.

The dictionary defines critical thinking as:

> Disciplined thinking that is clear, rational, open-minded, and informed by evidence.

Critical thinking is logical thinking that is free from biases, fallacies, misinterpretations, fears, and superstitions. As such, critical thinking leads people toward the truth when answering any particular question or when understanding the way the world really works. Double-blind testing is one tool in the critical thinking toolbox. By its design, double-blind testing removes biases and sources of error from a trial. Double-blind testing produces valid results that can be used to discover the truth and make accurate decisions.

What is an example of uncritical or erroneous thinking? It is likely that you have heard of a **superstition**, defined in the dictionary as:

> A belief or practice resulting from ignorance, fear of the unknown, trust in magic or chance, or a false conception of causation.

That last part—the "false conception of causation"—is particularly important. Superstitious people frequently notice patterns of causation that they believe to be real but which are, in fact, completely imaginary. A simple example: Imagine that one day John finds a $5 bill on the sidewalk while wearing his red socks. He notices the socks when he bends down to pick up the bill. The next week he wins a raffle at work and notices he is wearing his red socks again. John's red socks become his "lucky socks" and he starts wearing them to important events. This is certainly a superstition. The fact is that a pair of "lucky red socks" has no control over the outcome of events in the real world. If necessary, this fact can be easily proven with double-blind testing.

Another example: Sally goes to a restaurant and orders beef liver and onions. She has never had beef liver before, and it sounds gross, but she has just read an article about improving her life by trying new things. So she decides to give beef liver a try. She is surprised to find that she enjoys the meal, but an hour later she is quite ill. She decides that she will never eat beef liver again. This is also a superstition—it would take quite a bit of experimentation to know whether beef liver was the cause of the illness or not. The illness could be a complete coincidence. It could have been caused by something other than beef liver in the meal, it could have been caused by a completely different meal earlier in the day, it could have been caused by insecticides used in her house, and so on. Ascribing the cause of the illness to beef liver without any evidence is an example of superstitious thinking.

The average human brain appears to have a natural affinity for superstitions unless it is trained to recognize, understand, and disregard them. Take, for example, the fear of the number thirteen. It is one popular superstition that is widespread in many countries, including the United States. This superstition is so common that it has a name: triskaidekaphobia. In some parts of the world, there are hotels and apartment buildings that do not have a thirteenth floor—so many people have so much faith in this superstition that they will shun the thirteenth floor. In other words, the thirteenth floor becomes difficult to rent because of a widespread superstition that has no basis in fact. The number thirteen is no different than any other number.

One of the world's more bizarre superstitions can be found in South Korea. This superstition is called fan death—the belief that if a person falls asleep in a closed room with a running fan, the person will die in his sleep. This superstition is so prevalent in Korea that most household fans sold in the country have timers on them to prevent fan death.

Other superstitions center around objects or actions. In many parts of the United States, for example, "bad luck" is associated with breaking a mirror, walking under a ladder, or seeing a black cat. "Good luck" is associated with crossing your fingers, finding a penny, or carrying a rabbit's foot. Other common superstitions involve knocking on wood, throwing coins in fountains, wishing on falling stars, blowing out birthday candles, or breaking a wishbone.

Where does a superstition like the fear of the number thirteen come from, and how can these superstitions be so widespread?

One source is **anecdotal evidence**, defined in the dictionary as:

> Based on personal observation, case study reports, or random investigations rather than systematic scientific evaluation.

People tend to put a great deal of faith in stories that are personally told to them by people they trust. So if Bob's trusted friend Jessica comes up to him and tells him about the problems she has had with the number thirteen—for example, on Friday the thirteenth, or on the thirteenth floor of a hotel—Bob will tend to believe her. This is how anecdotal evidence works—this trust of people and their personal experiences seems to be wired into the human brain. A story in *The Economist* puts it this way:

> The problem is that anecdotal evidence often seems much more compelling than dry statistics. Man seems to have a tendency to impart information in the form of a story. This is often known as the availability heuristic and leads to arguments like "Smoking's not dangerous. My mother smoked 40 cigarettes a day and lived to 90."

For many people who are prone to accepting anecdotal evidence, it doesn't really matter if a friend has done a double-blind test on, for example, the health consequences of cigarette smoking. Her personal story, coming from her own personal (and usually one-time) experience, based on no broader evidence or experimentation whatsoever, is good enough to convince many uncritical thinkers that smoking is okay.

Once superstitious people have been presented with the idea that thirteen is a problem, many of them are likely to start avoiding the number thirteen. If the number thirteen *could* mean trouble because a trusted friend has suggested the possibility, and if there really isn't any cost or work involved in avoiding the number thirteen, why not avoid it? Suddenly people begin shunning the thirteenth floor and being careful on Friday the thirteenth. This avoidance is a direct side effect of uncritical thinking and the power of anecdotal evidence, and it can create many problems and imbalances in any human system that is not vigilant against superstitions.

For example, imagine that black cats get a bad reputation because of a superstition linking black cats to bad luck. Now black cats are more likely to be killed or mutilated by suspicious people who see them. In the United States, superstitions around black cats are strong enough that many animal shelters will not allow the adoption of black cats around Halloween. These shelters fear for the safety of the animals.

If enough superstitious people characterize people of a certain skin color as lazy, and if these characterizations are repeated often enough, then a bias builds up against this skin color that can make it difficult for people of certain races to live their lives in certain societies. The charge of laziness is completely unfounded. There may actually be scientific evidence to refute the charge absolutely. But in a society prone to superstition and anecdotal evidence, the idea may persist for many decades.

Why are some superstitions—even ones that appear to be completely nonsensical—so persistent? Superstitions may persist because of repetition, inertia, common knowledge, a lack of testing, and simple lazy and uncritical thinking on the part of people in a society. This is how the superstition around the number thirteen has persisted for so long. But another form of illogical thinking is particularly effective at keeping many superstitions alive. This type of thinking is called **confirmation bias**, defined as:

> A type of selective thinking whereby one tends to notice and to look for what confirms one's beliefs, and to ignore, not look for, or undervalue the relevance of what contradicts one's beliefs.

Imagine that Tom tells Linda that Friday the thirteenth is unlucky. The next time Friday the thirteenth rolls around, Tom reminds Linda to watch for all of the unlucky things that happen to her on this particular day. Now, as Linda goes through the day on Friday the thirteenth, she will notice every bad thing that happens and pay attention to it (similar to the Baader-Meinhof Phenomenon). At the end of the day, Linda might have a whole list of bad things that happened. All of the data in Linda's list confirms to her that Friday the thirteenth is bad news. In fact, it makes Friday the thirteenth look awful. Linda might think to herself, "This is no superstition—this is real! Look at all of these real data points I collected!"

The problem is that the process Linda used to collect her data is fundamentally flawed. Without a background in critical thinking, Linda has gathered her data incorrectly. If Linda were unbiased and scientific in her data gathering—that is, if Linda is skilled in critical thinking—she would have made note of every event on Friday the thirteenth. She would have then characterized each of those events as good or bad. Then she would do the same data gathering on Thursday the twelfth, Monday the sixteenth, Friday the twentieth, and a number of other days. Then she would compare her lists from the different days—enough days to avoid statistical bias. Using a balanced and unbiased protocol like this to gather her data, Linda would see that Friday the thirteenth is just the same as any other day. Good and bad things happen every day, and the day of the week or the day of the month has no effect on that. That is reality. But the confirmation bias brought on by the superstition skews the data. By only counting the bad things that happen on Friday the thirteenth and ignoring the good, the data seems to confirm the superstition. In the process, confirmation bias causes a superstitious person to completely misunderstand reality and the truth.

The term cherry-picking describes the same kind of thing. When someone is cherry-picking, the person is selecting only data and examples that match her expectations, while ignoring the data or examples that conflict with them. For example, a person making a case for widespread gun ownership might cherry-pick stories about people who are able to use guns successfully for self-defense, while ignoring all of the accidents and suicides that result from gun ownership. By looking exclusively at the data that supports a foregone conclusion, the cherry-picker forms a skewed view of reality.

Billions of human beings let these forms of faulty thinking—things like anecdotal evidence, confirmation bias, cherry-picking, and superstition—lead them to false conclusions every day. Many groups, and even entire societies, can actually promote these faulty thinking patterns rather than valid critical thinking methods.

You might think that people in modern societies would be immune to this kind of behavior. But if you watch television ads, you will see that things like anecdotal evidence and confirmation bias are common. For example, you see an ad for the XYZ weight-loss program on television. Cheryl M., a famous singer, comes on to breathlessly tell you how she lost fifty pounds in just eight weeks using the XYZ system. The fact is that Cheryl M.'s testimony represents nothing more than anecdotal evidence, but that fact is lost on millions of people watching the ad.

The fact that this sort of ad works is a rather sad testimony to just how bad the critical thinking skills of the average consumer can be. It is also a sad testimony to the lack of oversight on deceitful advertising. But this kind of ad is allowed, and for consumers who lack critical thinking skills, it works. All that the XYZ company has to do is run some number of people through the XYZ program, find that it works well for any one person, and then let that one person tell her anecdote in a television commercial. All of the people who failed on the XYZ diet program never get to tell their stories.

Even more deceitful is the celebrity spokesperson. The XYZ company can hire one celebrity, coach that person intensely for eight weeks while providing a huge financial incentive to lose weight (in the form of a lucrative spokesperson contract), and then run an ad where the celebrity touts her success. For this reason, no critical thinker should believe an ad featuring a celebrity spokesperson. But because there are billions of uncritical thinkers in this world, ads containing celebrity spokespeople are effective.

Consider all of the negative effects that occur in a society filled with people who are unable to think critically. These uncritical thinkers are able to vote, yet they are subject to believing erroneous statements and unsupported stories from candidates. They enter the workplace, yet they are poor decision makers who do not rely on valid evidence. They may group together into bigoted blocks of people who openly discriminate and harass other members of the society, leading to things like racism, sexism, and homophobia. Much of the evil we find in many human societies traces its roots to the lack of critical thinking skills in the populace.

HOMEOPATHY

You might think that, in a modern, technological society, human beings would move past superstitions, confirmation bias, and anecdotal evidence. But these tendencies appear to be wired into the human brain. Regardless of how advanced a society becomes, this hard wiring seems to take over unless people are specifically educated in critical thinking.

One place in modern Western society where the effects of superstition, anecdotal evidence, and confirmation bias are notably exemplified is in an alternative medical practice known as **homeopathy**. Like Traditional Chinese Medicine, the followers of homeopathy number in the millions, despite a lack of evidence indicating that homeopathy works. In reality, the effects of homeopathy are completely, provably imaginary. Nonetheless, homeopathy represents a multibillion-dollar industry around the world.

Homeopathy is defined by *The American Heritage Dictionary* as:

> The method of treating diseases by drugs, given in minute doses, that would produce in a healthy person symptoms similar to those of the disease.

What this means in practice is the following: Imagine that you find a substance like the root of a tree, and it causes some kind of reaction. For example, when a healthy person eats this root, he gets a runny nose. According to the principles of homeopathy, this substance has the ability to cure a runny nose in a sick person if the sick person receives an extremely small dose of the root.

How does a practitioner of homeopathy (also known as a homeopath) produce a minute dose? The minute dose of a "homeopathic medicine" is created through a process of successive dilution. A bit of crushed root is dissolved in a container of water. The water in the container is shaken well. Then a tiny bit of this root-laced water is mixed into another container of pure water and shaken. Perhaps one drop of root-laced water is mixed into a new container that holds one hundred drops of pure water, and then the new container is shaken. This process of dilution is repeated successively, perhaps thirty times. At each step, the original solution is diluted by a factor of one hundred. By doing it thirty times, the homeopath creates an unbelievably dilute mixture—a minute dose.

If you take the time to carry out the mathematical calculations, you realize that the final mixture might have just one molecule (but more likely zero molecules) of the original root compound of the original root compound in a homeopathic dose. In other words, anyone who takes a homeopathic "medicine" is actually drinking what is essentially pure water.

At the end of the process, this extremely dilute mixture—so dilute that it is pure water—is given to someone suffering from a runny nose. According to believers in homeopathy, this "homeopathic medicine" will effect a cure. There are homeopathic "cures" designed to provide relief for nearly every ailment experienced by human beings.

It turns out that there are millions of believers in homeopathy. These believers tend to be educated people living in modern Western democracies, especially in Europe. For example, as many as 40 percent of people in France rely on homeopathic cures.

A critical thinker might have one important question after hearing about homeopathy: Is there any evidence that homeopathy works? The answer is no. When double-blind clinical trials are performed, there is no indication of effectiveness whatsoever.

So why do millions of people believe in homeopathy? And what might we call this belief in the curative power of pure water? The common English word for this process is **delusion**, defined by the dictionary as:

> A fixed false belief that is resistant to reason or confrontation with actual fact.

Where does the delusional belief in homeopathy come from? Why would anyone believe that homeopathy works when it is quite clear, through valid scientific experiments, it does not? One reason is anecdotal evidence and its power over the human mind. Another is confirmation bias, as discussed previously—if you believe that homeopathy works and you look only for the successes, homeopathy appears to work. And a third reason is the placebo effect.

If Simon is not a critical thinker, and if Simon's friend excitedly tells him that she was cured of her fatigue with a homeopathic treatment, Simon might try homeopathy himself. Since Simon is not a critical thinker, he will not ask for evidence. He ignores the fact that his friend arrived at her conclusion because of a bout of confirmation bias brought on by the placebo effect after visiting a homeopath. Simon simply listens to her story of success and believes it.

Homeopathy, being a form of alternative medicine, benefits from several other lapses that occur in the critical thinking process when it comes to medical treatments. There is a fascinating fact about the human disease process that many people neglect to account for in their thinking: In the vast majority of cases, the human body heals itself. If an alternative therapy—whether it be homeopathy, Traditional Chinese Medicine, or voodoo incantations—does no damage, there is a significant probability that the patient will get better simply through the natural activities of the human immune system and other human healing processes. This is also true if you administer a placebo, or in fact if you do nothing at all—but this fact is lost on uncritical thinkers.

Imagine the simplest possible example: Laura gets a common cold. If Laura does absolutely nothing, Laura has a very high probability of getting better. It takes the human immune system approximately a week to rid the body of the virus that causes cold symptoms in nearly all cases. That is a fact. But let's say Laura is miserable with her runny nose and her scratchy throat, so she goes to see a homeopath and explains her problem. The homeopath will listen to Laura attentively, nod sagely, perhaps look something up in a big impressive-looking book. He gives Laura a vial of "homeopathic medicine," otherwise known as water, tells her all about how effective this vial will be with a long soliloquy of scientific-sounding words, and then charges Laura $50 for his trouble.

Why does the homeopath sound so convincing? Because this is his livelihood and he has done this spiel a thousand times. Also note the financial incentive—he just made $50 from Laura for a vial of water and a bit of his time. Laura goes home, takes the water as prescribed over the course of a week, and lo and behold, Laura's cold is cured. Laura becomes a believer in homeopathy if she is not a critical thinker.

If you are a critical thinker, you realize that Laura would have gotten better without the $50 expenditure or the time lost in visiting the homeopath. You realize, by looking critically at clinical trial evidence gathered on homeopathy for many decades, that homeopathy is a scam. A vial of water does not do anything, despite what the homeopath says, his impressive book, and his scientific-sounding vocabulary.

HEALING POWER

While we understand that the human body does heal the common cold, it turns out the human body heals a great many things if left to its own devices. One surprising area where this is true is lower back pain. One study reported in *The Lancet* involved a group of 240 lower back pain sufferers. The goal of the study was to look at the efficacy of a back pain drug as well as chiropractic care. The 240 patients were randomized, split up, and placed in one of four treatment groups for a double-blind clinical trial.

- The first group received a "real" drug believed to be effective against back pain and "real" care from a chiropractor.
- The second group received a placebo drug and "real" care from a chiropractor.
- The third group received a "real" drug and fake care from a chiropractor.
- The fourth group received a fake drug and fake care from a chiropractor.

What the study found was that there were no significant differences in the recovery speed among any of the patients in any of the groups. In other words, neither the "real" drug nor the "real" chiropractic care had any effect whatsoever on the outcome.

In addition, this study provided an amazing result—after twelve weeks, 237 out of 240 patients had recovered from their lower back pain. Think about that—the drug and the chiropractic care did nothing—they were expensive placebos. And almost everyone got better. All that was needed was time.

The natural healing process of the human body makes it look like homeopathy, Traditional Chinese Medicine, and chiropractors are effective. But in reality these treatments are not. All that a practitioner has to do is give a fake treatment that is harmless, and then let the human immune system do its thing, just like it naturally would. The fact is that these remedies don't do anything—the body heals itself. Since the practitioners make money for what they do, they have a great incentive to promote their placebos. And because of the lack of critical thinking skills in the general population, the patients generally believe what they hear from the practitioners. But the money they spend is wasted.

Why do people believe in alternative medicine? Even "smart" people, even "college educated" people, even people with a lot of "common sense." It's because of a lack of critical thinking skill and a failure to understand, or even look at, the contrary evidence demonstrating that alternative medicines are scams. And you can understand why these placebos and superstitions persist—as a general rule, patients who lack training or interest in critical thinking skills believe the pontifications of homeopaths, chiropractors, and practitioners of Traditional Chinese Medicine. When people have a pain or an illness, they are suffering. The tendency is to want to "do something." Alternative medicine tends to do no harm while allowing the human body to heal itself.

There is one other thing to note about alternative medical practices. In most cases, there is a practitioner who spends time with the patient. A chiropractor will spend time talking to a patient and then rubbing her back. A homeopath will spend time talking with the patient, then consult a large, official-looking book called a repertory before prescribing a vial of water. A practitioner of Traditional Chinese Medicine will do the same kind of thing before prescribing a collection of dried roots, flowers, and bug shells that are boiled into a tea. Many human beings enjoy this type of personal attention, in the same way that many human beings enjoy eating in restaurants. Many people seem to enjoy the "experience" that they get from a practitioner of alternative medicine, even if the experience is nothing more than an expensive way of delivering a placebo that, in reality, does nothing.

There is one other thing to note as well. Let's say that we find a person who believes in homeopathy. We show her all the evidence that homeopathy is ineffective. We carefully explain that she is wasting her money. We offer her a semester-long college course in critical thinking. She may *still* go back to her homeopath and pay money for the placebo he offers. How is this possible? How can she waste her money like this and participate in a process that is clearly ineffective? There are a number of possible reasons:

- She might truly enjoy the experience of visiting the homeopath. She likes the traditions, the ceremony, and the attention that surrounds her visit.
- She may like her homeopath very much, and trust him as a personal friend, because she has frequently visited him for fifteen years. There is a strong human relationship in place that feels warm and comfortable.
- Her homeopath may wear a flowing robe and an unusual hat, while carrying himself with a certain deportment and gravitas. He might also have a high standing in the community. In the same way that she would be honored to talk to the star of a Broadway play, she feels honored when she talks to him.
- She may feel comfortable with her homeopath in a way that she might never be comfortable in a sterile doctor's office, or with a doctor's perfunctory, impersonal three-minute diagnosis based strictly on lab results.
- She might have been raised in a homeopathic household. She may have heard about homeopathy and taken homeopathic medicines since infancy, and in her experience they always "worked." This long history through childhood into adulthood may cause her to discount all scientific evidence to the contrary, despite the fact that all of the scientific evidence is correct.

- She might be able to compartmentalize homeopathy in her mind. So, while she appears to be quite logical and rational in other aspects of her life, when it comes to homeopathy, the principles of critical thinking are never applied and she truly is delusional on this topic. Perhaps this compartmentalization process is enhanced by the reasons mentioned above.

And so on. The point is that human beings can be irrational for a wide variety of reasons. Their decisions make no sense in the context of logic and critical thinking. Yet these people may "feel better" with their irrational behaviors. So they do things that do not make sense from an intellectual perspective. The problem is that these feelings do not change reality. Homeopathy has no effect beyond a placebo effect.

Does it matter? What difference does it make if millions of people choose to use homeopathy and other alternative therapies even though these therapies are known to be ineffective? Isn't this something that boils down to harmless fun? When dealing with medical treatments, there actually can be consequences and the consequences can be deadly. The problem with alternative medicine is that it can delay the use of real treatment. The tragic case of Steve Jobs, who delayed scientific treatment for many months while trying alternative medicine, is one high-profile example. This is not uncommon. The effects are especially troubling when parents apply alternative medicine in lieu of scientific medicine to their children and their children end up needlessly suffering or dying. Alternative medicines can actually have severe repercussions, all because of a lack of critical thinking skills.

This is a book about God. You might be wondering what all of this discussion about critical thinking, clinical trials, double-blind testing, anecdotal evidence, confirmation bias, cherry-picking, and alternative medicine has to do with God. It turns out that the lack of critical thinking skills that prop up the multibillion-dollar alternative medicine industry is simply the tip of the iceberg. Many other parts of human culture are impacted by this societal tendency to avoid clear and critical thinking. Let's start taking a look at how God works.

4:

WHO IS GOD?

IN THE PRIOR TWO CHAPTERS, WE HAVE DEMONSTRATED THE SCIENTIFIC ABILITY TO PROVE OR DISPROVE A CLAIMED EFFECT. It's a straightforward process. We can use a double-blind clinical trial to decide whether the claimed effect for a medicine is real or imaginary.

We have also discussed why people who are not thinking critically are inclined to believe in things that are imaginary. Mental detours like superstitions, anecdotal evidence, confirmation bias, and the placebo effect get in the way of clear, precise thinking. It's very easy to scientifically prove that things like homeopathy have no real efficacy beyond the placebo effect, simply by performing carefully designed and executed double-blind scientific experiments. Yet millions of uninformed people and people who are not thinking critically use alternative therapies every day. Alternative medicine is a multibillion-dollar industry, often in spite of scientific evidence demonstrating its ineffectiveness. We also discussed a problem created by alternative medicine: People can endanger their lives, and parents can endanger the lives of their children, by wasting time on ineffective treatments.

So how would we apply these same critical thinking principles to God? How would we approach the question of whether God is real or imaginary? One way to do it is to take positive claims made for God and test them. We can look at the definitions and attributes of God—and the claims that people make about God—and determine whether the claims are real or imaginary. For example, if the Bible and Christian leaders clearly state that God does X, then we can test that claim to see whether it is true or false.

One problem that can arise when trying to do these tests is that many people have many different definitions for God. In fact, Christianity alone spans a wide spectrum of beliefs, some of them mutually exclusive. Some Christians, for example, believe that God hates homosexuals and wants them all killed. They derive this pattern of thinking from Bible verses like Leviticus 20:13. Other Christians believe that God loves homosexuals and wants homosexuals to have all the same rights as heterosexuals, referring to verses like Mark 12:30–31 to support this idea. And many other Christians stand somewhere in the middle of the spectrum. This same sort of variation among Christian believers (in fact, among the believers in any religion) can be seen on dozens of different topics: child rearing, capital punishment, abortion, contraception, health care, welfare, charity, gun control, environmental pollution, alcohol consumption, forbidden foods, patriotism, premarital sex, marital sex, polygamy, divorce, adultery, women's rights, and innumerable other issues. In the Christian faith, all of this variation is expressed through the existence of thousands of different denominations. When we look at Christianity in its many forms—Catholics, Lutherans, Methodists, Baptists, Presbyterians, Anglicans, Pentecostals, Seventh-Day Adventists, Unitarians, and so on—we know that Christianity is fragmented on many aspects of God. Given this level of fragmentation, is it even possible to develop a definition for God that most Christians can agree on, let alone members of other faiths who believe in God?

It turns out that it is possible to find a good bit of common ground when defining God and his attributes. Here are several definitions of **God** that can be found in different dictionaries, and most Christians seem easily able to agree with them:

- The one Supreme Being, the creator and ruler of the universe.
- The sole Supreme Being, eternal, spiritual, and transcendent, who is the Creator and ruler of all and is

infinite in all attributes; the object of worship in monotheistic religions.

- A being conceived as the perfect, omnipotent, omniscient originator and ruler of the universe, the principal
object of faith and worship in monotheistic religions.
- The perfect and all-powerful spirit or being that is worshipped especially by Christians, Jews, and Muslims as
the one who created and rules the universe.
- God is often conceived as the Supreme Being and principal object of faith. The concept of God as described by
theologians commonly includes the attributes of omniscience (infinite knowledge), omnipotence (unlimited
power), omnipresence (present everywhere), omnibe-
nevolence (perfect goodness), divine simplicity, and
eternal and necessary existence. In theism, God is the
creator and sustainer of the universe, while in deism,
God is the creator (but not the sustainer) of the universe. Monotheism is the belief in the existence of one
God or in the oneness of God.

The Southern Baptist denomination is the largest Protestant
denomination of Christianity in the United States, with more than 15
million members. Here is how the Southern Baptist Convention (SBC)
defines God:

> There is one and only one living and true God. He is an
> intelligent, spiritual, and personal Being, the Creator, Redeemer,
> Preserver, and Ruler of the universe. God is infinite in holiness
> and all other perfections. God is all-powerful and all-knowing;
> and His perfect knowledge extends to all things, past, present,
> and future, including the future decisions of His free creatures.
> To Him we owe the highest love, reverence, and obedience. The
> eternal triune God reveals Himself to us as Father, Son, and Holy
> Spirit, with distinct personal attributes, but without division of
> nature, essence, or being.

There are also creeds, like the Apostles' Creed, which capture the high points of agreement and provide useful summaries of the attributes of God:

The Apostles' Creed

I believe in God the Father Almighty,

Maker of heaven and earth:

And in Jesus Christ his only Son our Lord,

Who was conceived by the Holy Ghost,

Born of the Virgin Mary,

Suffered under Pontius Pilate,

Was crucified, dead, and buried:

He descended into hell;

The third day he rose again from the dead;

He ascended into heaven,

And sitteth on the right hand of God the Father Almighty;

From thence he shall come to judge the quick and the dead.

I believe in the Holy Ghost;

The holy Catholick Church;

The Communion of Saints;

The Forgiveness of sins;

The Resurrection of the body,

And the Life everlasting.

Amen.

Millions and millions of Christians recite the Apostles' Creed or a close facsimile every Sunday, and they believe what the creed says.

Many Christian organizations have Statements of Faith. The Statement of Faith used by Patrick Henry College in Virginia is concise and representative, and available on the Internet. It mirrors the beliefs of the SBC and many other Christian sects in the United States. It has ten points. The first describes God as a trinity. The second describes God as spirit. The third describes Jesus Christ as the product of a virgin birth and the corporal version of God. The fourth describes the Bible as the inspired, inerrant Word of God. It is infallible and sufficient as a guide for Christians. The fifth describes man as sinful by nature, thus needing salvation, with Jesus Christ being the sole source of salvation. The sixth explains that the death of Jesus Christ is able to provide "substitutionary atonement for our sins." The seventh describes the source of salvation. The eighth describes the nature of Christ's resurrection. The ninth describes Christ's eventual return in the second coming. The tenth describes Satan and Hell, and the fact that nonbelievers will end up in Hell for eternity, where they will consciously suffer torment.

If we look at these definitions, creeds, and statements, as well as the language used to refer to God by millions of Christians, we can create a list of facts about God that should be agreeable to just about every Christian:

- God is the almighty creator and ruler of the universe. He is omnipotent, omniscient, omnibenevolent, omnipresent, eternal, timeless, and perfect. Genesis 1:1 states that God is the creator. Matthew 19:26 states God's omnipotence by saying, "With God all things are possible." Omniscience is clarified in Acts 15:18 when it says, "Known unto God are all his works from the beginning of the world," and Luke 12:7 says, "But even the very hairs of your head are all numbered." And so on. It's easy to find Biblical backing, as well as public testimony from a wide variety of Christian leaders, for these points.
- God is the creator of everything. He created the universe, the earth, life on earth, and human beings. The majority of Christians believe that God literally created the first man (Adam) and woman (Eve) in his own image, and that we are all Adam and Eve's descendants. Others take a less-than-literal position and believe that God created man through some sort of guided evolution or other form of intervention. The Bible's book of Genesis expresses the creation story.
- God instills in each of us a unique and everlasting soul. Matthew 10:28 says, "And fear not them which kill the

body, but are not able to kill the soul: but rather fear him which is able to destroy both soul and body in hell," while Ecclesiastes 12:7 says, "Then shall the dust return to the earth as it was: and the spirit shall return unto God who gave it."

- God gives us eternal life after death. When we die, our souls return to God in Heaven for eternity if we have accepted Jesus as our savior. Otherwise, our souls are tortured in Hell for eternity. John 3:16 says, "For God so loved the world, that he gave his only begotten Son, that whosoever believeth in him should not perish, but have everlasting life." Many Baptist congregations describe Hell in this way: "Everlasting conscious suffering in the lake of fire."

- God wrote the Bible. The Bible is God's word. There is a sentence that summarizes the Bible for many people: The Bible is infallible, inspired, and inerrant. 2 Timothy 3:16 says, "All scripture is given by inspiration of God, and is profitable for doctrine, for reproof, for correction, for instruction in righteousness: That the man of God may be perfect, thoroughly furnished unto all good works." According to polls, more than 50 percent of adults in the United States believe that the Bible is literally true. The number rises as high as 75 percent in some southern states.

- God sent his son Jesus to Earth as God incarnate. Jesus performed many miracles while He was alive, and after his death Jesus was resurrected, appeared to hundreds of people, and then ascended into heaven, proving that He is God. The four Gospel books of the Bible tell the story of Jesus' time on Earth, and are, in fact, the only detailed record of it that exists today.

- God is a benevolent and loving ruler. God is good and God is love. 1 John 4:8 says, "He that loveth not knoweth not God; for God is love." 1 John 4:16 says, "And we have known and believed the love that God hath to us. God is love; and he that dwelleth in love dwelleth in God, and God in him." Matthew 7:11 says, "If ye then, being evil, know how to give good gifts unto your children, how much more shall your Father which is in heaven give good things to them that ask him?" 2 Corinthians 9:8 says, "And God is able to make all grace abound toward you; that ye, always having all sufficiency in all things, may abound to every good work."

- God is a living being who knows and loves each one of us. Each of us can speak to God and have a personal relationship with God. The way that we speak to God is through prayer. James 4:8 says, "Draw nigh to God, and he will draw nigh to you."

- God hears and answers prayers. In Matthew 7:7, Jesus says, "Ask, and it shall be given you; seek, and ye shall find; knock, and it shall be opened unto you: For every one that asketh receiveth; and he that seeketh findeth; and to him that knocketh it shall be opened. Or what man is there of you, whom if his son ask bread, will he give him a stone? Or if he ask a fish, will he give him a serpent? If ye then, being evil, know how to give good gifts unto your children, how much more shall your Father which is in heaven give good things to them that ask him?" In Chapter 5 we discuss prayer in detail.

- God has a plan for each of us. We each have a distinct and unique purpose in God's universe. Proverbs 3:5-6 says, "Trust in the Lord with all thine heart; and lean not unto thine own understanding. In all thy ways acknowledge him, and he shall direct thy paths." Jeremiah 29:11 says, "For I know the thoughts that I think toward you, saith the Lord, thoughts of peace, and not of evil, to give you an expected end." Psalm 139:16 says, "Thine eyes did see my substance, yet being unperfect;

and in thy book all my members were written, which in continuance were fashioned, when as yet there was none of them."
- God is truthful. Titus 1:2 says, "God, that cannot lie."

From this list we can derive a shorthand version—what we might call the twelve attributes of God or the twelve pillars of God. These are positive claims that the majority of Christians make about God:

1. God is omniscient.
2. God is omnipotent.
3. God is perfect.
4. God does not lie.
5. God answers prayers.
6. God is all-loving and good.
7. God is perfectly moral and is the moral standard by which humans are judged.
8. God wrote or inspired the Bible.
9. God is the creator of the universe and life on Earth.
10. God incarnated himself as Jesus.
11. God enters into personal relationships with his followers on Earth.
12. God gives people eternal souls that go to heaven or hell upon death.

In other words, God is an amazing being as summarized in these twelve attributes. This is obvious from the common definitions of God, the Apostles' Creed, and the many descriptions of God that we hear in public. Billions of people here on Earth believe in this, or a similar, picture of God. More than three quarters of the people in the United States believe the Christian message: God exists, He incarnated Himself in Jesus, and God will judge all people when they die. More than half of adults in America believe that the Bible is literally true (see also Chapter 13 on page 165).

The large majority of Christians in the United States would agree with all twelve of the attributes described above. A minority might quibble with one or two of them. And then a smaller minority has a much looser and divergent definition of God. They have invented their own unique versions of God that lie well outside the attributes described by the Bible and mainstream thought. These definitions may change fluidly depending on a variety of factors. Dutch philosopher Baruch Spinoza represents one extreme end of the spectrum. Frank Thilly writes in *A History of Philosophy*:

> Spinoza expressly denies personality and consciousness to God; he has neither intelligence, feeling, nor will; he does not act according to purpose, but everything follows necessarily from his nature, according to law.

Definitions like these, while interesting, lie so far outside the boundaries of mainstream Christian thought that they are irrelevant to the discussion here.

As mentioned in Chapter 1, billions of people believe in various versions of God through multiple theistic religions, including Judaism and Islam. Each religion, even some denominations, can have different views. In this book, we are interested in a specific definition of God as defined by a large number of people, and given that Christians make up the majority—roughly one third of the world's population—we will use the Christian God here as an example. The twelve pillars listed on the opposite page describe the mainstream, Christian, Biblical God held to be true by the large majority of Christians in the United States.

Now that we have defined God, the question that any critical thinker would ask is very simple: Is this being called God, who is described by these attributes, real or imaginary? How can we decide one way or the other? The reason why a critical thinker starts down this path and asks these questions is because, for such an amazing being, there are certain holes in the story. For example, God is invisible. And God is publicly silent. When we ask God to appear, nothing happens. Immense tragedies unfold, as we saw in Chapter 1, with no intervention from God. Christians claim that there is no scientific technique that can detect God. Although God is quite active in the

Bible in terms of speaking and appearing, we never see Him doing anything verifiable in today's modern world. And so on. In other words, to a critical thinker, God has all the normal hallmarks of an imaginary being. These holes are obvious to any observer, so the question is a valid one: Is God real, as Christians believe, or is He imaginary, as evidence like this suggests?

How would we come to the conclusion, with certainty, that God is imaginary? One way to decide this question is to look at the twelve pillars listed on page 56. What if we can knock down all twelve pillars and prove their positive claims as untrue? This would be a useful approach, because if all twelve of these attributes are false, there really is nothing left. We, as critical thinkers, can understand that God is imaginary.

How would we knock down a pillar? We would use the same kind of approach that critical thinkers use to decide if a drug or medical procedure's effects are real or imaginary. We pick a claimed property or attribute that is ascribed to God, and then we use scientific principles and the scientific method to test the claim and decide whether it's real or imaginary. We can also look for things like contradictions and disagreements with reality. If one claimed attribute about God contradicts another, or if a claimed attribute contradicts reality, then that attribute is clearly imaginary. The available evidence can show whether an attribute is true or false. If a particular claim about God is proven imaginary, then there is a problem. If all of the claims about God are proven imaginary, then it's easy to see that God is, in fact, imaginary.

Then there is a second challenge that we must address. Let's imagine that we can knock down all twelve pillars and nothing is left of God. If this is the case, then how can so many billions of people on planet Earth claim to believe in this imaginary God or other gods? What errors and faults in their thinking would allow such a large mass illusion to exist, and how might those faults be repaired so that all of these people can see and accept reality? How can we make the world a better place by replacing mass illusion with truth?

Let's start this exploration into God and His true nature by taking a look at prayer.

5:

DOES GOD ANSWER PRAYERS?

GIVEN WHAT WE HAVE LEARNED ABOUT ALTERNATIVE MEDICINES AND THE SCIENTIFIC UNDERSTANDING OF THEIR EFFICACY IN CHAPTER 3, WHAT CAN WE SAY ABOUT PEOPLE WHO USE ALTERNATIVE REMEDIES LIKE HOMEOPATHY? We can say this: A person who believes in homeopathy must ignore, either consciously or unconsciously, the ample evidence proving that homeopathy's claimed effects are imaginary. In either case, by definition, a person who believes in homeopathy is said to be delusional.

> Delusion: A fixed false belief that is resistant to reason or confrontation with actual fact.

In other words, the believer in homeopathy sees all of the evidence that homeopathy is ineffective and decides, for whatever reason, to ignore that evidence. Or she never questions what she believes about homeopathy by seeking out any evidence. She decides to believe in something imaginary. The word that describes such behavior is "delusion." One possibility is that the believer in homeopathy has never chosen to learn about the principles of critical thinking that allow people to process evidence correctly, avoid logical errors, and eliminate logical fallacies from their thinking. The other possibility is that a person who believes in homeopathy has learned these things, but has willfully chosen to ignore the principles of critical thinking when it comes to homeopathy.

This type of active ignorance is unfortunate, but it happens quite frequently in human beings. For example, it's fairly common for a person who knows the difference between right and wrong to choose to do what he knows to be wrong. Catholic priests have certainly been trained so that they understand morality, ethics, and the difference between right and wrong. Nonetheless, pedophile priests have been shown to willfully participate in activities that are in direct contradiction with those teachings. It seems impossible to believe that priests would sexually molest young boys, yet they have been shown to do so in massive numbers—more than 6,000 priests have participated in this form of pedophilia according to one count.

In the same way, it seems impossible for anyone to participate in homeopathy, because homeopathy is expensive and has been proven to be ineffective. Yet millions seek out homeopathic care, either through ignorance or irrationality.

Now imagine that you go to church one Sunday. The minister rises and walks to the pulpit. And then he states what is, to him and the congregation, a fact: "God answers prayers." Or he asks the congregation to join in the act of prayer by saying, "Let us pray." You have probably witnessed this kind of scene hundreds of times because we see prayer all around us: at weddings, funerals, ball games, graduation ceremonies, church services, hospitals, nursing homes, as well as in films, television shows, books, and poems.

Why do we see prayer all around us? It's because prayer is such a big part of the Gospels in the New Testament, and of most other religious traditions. In the Christian faith, God and Jesus answer prayers—this is a consistent message. There are many places in the Bible where Jesus/God claims to answer prayers. And people believe these claims. If you go to a search engine and type in "prayer" as your search term, there are tens of millions of results. As of this writing, Amazon shows tens of thousands of books on prayer. YouTube has millions of videos on the topic. Prayer is everywhere, and Christians overwhelmingly believe in the power of prayer.

But what if these billions of Christians are wrong, in the same way that believers in homeopathy have been shown to be wrong? What if the effectiveness of prayer is imaginary? As critical thinkers, we are able to examine the claims for prayer and honestly ask: Is the effectiveness of prayer real or imaginary? Having asked that question, what if we can prove conclusively that the belief in prayer is nothing more than a superstition? In that case, it would nullify several of God's attributes discussed in the previous chapter. Several of the pillars supporting the belief in God would be gone.

So let's start at the beginning: What, exactly, is prayer and what does the Bible have to say about prayer? The dictionary defines praying as:

> To speak to God especially in order to give thanks or to ask for something.

That seems simple enough, and we all understand it to be true. We have all seen thousands of examples of prayer, and if you yourself are a religious person, it may be the case that you pray every day. But there is quite a bit more to it. It's actually quite amazing what prayer can do according to the Bible. For example, in Matthew 7:7, Jesus says:

> Ask, and it shall be given you; seek, and ye shall find; knock, and it shall be opened unto you: For every one that asketh receiveth; and he that seeketh findeth; and to him that knocketh it shall be opened. Or what man is there of you, whom if his son ask bread, will he give him a stone? Or if he ask a fish, will he give him a serpent? If ye then, being evil, know how to give good gifts unto your children, how much more shall your Father which is in heaven give good things to them that ask him?

In Matthew 17:20, Jesus says:

> And Jesus said unto them, Because of your unbelief: for verily I say unto you, If ye have faith as a grain of mustard seed, ye shall say unto this mountain, Remove hence to yonder place; and it shall remove; and nothing shall be impossible unto you.

In Matthew 21:21, Jesus says:

Jesus answered and said unto them, Verily I say unto you, If ye have faith, and doubt not, ye shall not only do this which is done to the fig tree, but also if ye shall say unto this mountain, Be thou removed, and be thou cast into the sea; it shall be done.

The message is reiterated in Mark 11:24:

Therefore I say unto you, What things soever ye desire, when ye pray, believe that ye receive them, and ye shall have them.

In John 14:12–14, Jesus says:

Verily, verily, I say unto you, He that believeth on me, the works that I do shall he do also; and greater works than these shall he do; because I go unto my Father. And whatsoever ye shall ask in my name, that will I do, that the Father may be glorified in the Son. If ye shall ask any thing in my name, I will do it.

In Matthew 18:19, Jesus says:

Again I say unto you, That if two of you shall agree on earth as touching any thing that they shall ask, it shall be done for them of my Father which is in heaven.

James 5:15–16 says:

And the prayer of faith shall save the sick, and the Lord shall raise him up; and if he have committed sins, they shall be forgiven him. Confess your faults one to another, and pray one for another, that ye may be healed. The effectual fervent prayer of a righteous man availeth much.

In Mark 9:23:

> Jesus said unto him, If thou canst believe, all things are possible to him that believeth.

In Luke 1:37:

> For with God nothing shall be impossible.

These statements are clear and straightforward. They are not vague, ambiguous, or wishy-washy. The Bible dictates that Christians believe in a perfect God, who never lies, and this God speaks through Jesus, his perfect son, when he says that, "You may ask me for anything in my name, and I will do it." He says, "For with God nothing will be impossible." There is no ambiguity. There is no allegory. We have not taken these clear statements out of context. These are positive claims of effectiveness.

There is no difference between these positive claims for prayer and the positive claims of effectiveness that a drug manufacturer would make for a new drug. Therefore, we can test these claims for the effectiveness of prayer just like we test a manufacturer's claims for the effectiveness of a drug.

In previous chapters we have seen that it is possible to test positive claims and decide whether the claimed effectiveness is real or imaginary. Any critical thinker therefore asks: Are the claims that God makes about prayer true or false? The way to find out is to do some experiments.

A SIMPLE EXPERIMENT

Imagine that you go to a casino and you are playing craps. However, as you are playing, something does not seem right. The dice just are not rolling the way they should be rolling. It feels like one certain number is coming up more than it should. This would be unlikely in a reputable establishment, but the place you are playing is not one of the most reputable, and thus it is not impossible to imagine that something is amiss. In fact, you believe that the dice may be loaded.

There are a dozen ways to create loaded dice. The most common way to load a die is to weight one of its faces. Because of the extra weight, the opposite face will tend to come up more often than it should.

Weighted dice were once a huge problem in gambling establishments. It was so common that any reputable casino today uses transparent dice as a way of demonstrating that the dice are straight. But it is still possible to add weight. For example, if the dots on a die are dimpled, it is possible to add a tiny amount of lead to a dot and then paint over it. This certainly will not guarantee that the opposite face always comes up, but it changes the odds slightly in favor of the opposite face.

How could you know if you are dealing with weighted dice? You can perform an experiment. If you roll a die six hundred times, the number of times each face comes up should be approximately equal. If you tabulate the results of six hundred throws and look at the result, each face should come up about one hundred times. If one of the faces consistently comes up more often than the other faces (and the opposite face the reverse), it is certain that something is fishy about the die. It is also possible to drop the die into water, where any weighting will have a more pronounced effect.

Let's imagine that the same kind of weighting could be done with a coin to make one side come up more often than the other. The scientific process to determine if a coin is weighted would be just as straightforward—the laws of probability dictate that a fair coin will land heads and tails in approximately equal proportion over the course of time. To test for a loaded coin, simply flip a coin a thousand times, do the appropriate statistical analysis, and see if the coin is fair. A simple statistical test with a die or a coin does not require a double-blind setup to perform a valid experiment. You can simply flip the coin or roll the die and honestly record the results. There is no possibility of the placebo effect or bias entering into the experimental results of a coin toss like there is during a drug trial. You simply flip the coin or roll the die enough times to have statistical confidence in the results.

Given what we now know about the Bible's claims for prayer, what would we expect prayer to do during a coin toss or the roll of the dice? We would reasonably expect that prayer would skew the results. According to the claims in the Bible, prayer should have an obvious, measurable effect on a coin toss—Jesus is quite clear about this. And keep in mind the attributes of God from the previous chapter, such as: God is perfect, God never lies, Jesus is God's perfect son, the Bible is God's word, and so on. Either these attributes are true or false.

So, let's imagine that you are a Christian who believes in the power of prayer. Here is a simple experiment that will show you something very interesting about your faith in prayer's effectiveness.

Take an ordinary, fair coin out of your pocket. Now pray to Jesus Christ. Pray sincerely to Jesus, like this:

> Dear Jesus, I have great faith that you hear and answer prayers as you promise in Bible verses like John 14:12–14. I am going to flip this ordinary coin fifty times, and I am asking you to cause it to land tails-side up all fifty times. In your name I pray, Amen.

Now start flipping the coin. There is a 50 percent chance that it will land tails on the first flip. There is a 25 percent chance that it will land tails again on the second flip. There is a 12.5 percent chance that it will land tails again on the third flip. After the fifth or sixth flip, the coin will have probably landed heads at least once and ended your run of tails. You certainly will not get a run of fifty tails in a row with a fair coin. It is possible, yes. But the chances of it happening are exceedingly small—the chances are approximately one in one quadrillion that you'll get fifty tails in a row with a fair coin. This chance is so low that if it were to happen, we would suspect that the coin is rigged and has tails on both sides.

But if Jesus and God answer prayers as claimed in the Bible, we should be able to pray and have a fifty-tails run happen whenever we wish. After all, Jesus says:

In Mark 9:23:

> Jesus said unto him, If thou canst believe, all things are possible to him that believeth.

In Luke 1:37:

> For with God nothing shall be impossible.

In John 14:14:

> If ye shall ask any thing in my name, I will do it.

If prayer is effective, as promised by Jesus in the Bible, and if the attributes of God are true, then prayer should affect a coin toss in obvious, measurable ways. We should be able to see clear statistical patterns emerge when we pray about a coin toss, just like we would see with a loaded die.

Here is another experiment to try: Flip the coin a thousand times, praying to Jesus on each flip for it to land tails. Record the way the coin lands each time. What would we expect to happen if what Jesus says about prayer in the Bible is true? If the Bible's claims about the efficacy of prayer are true, we would expect the coin to land tails every time we flip it and pray. If we flip it and don't pray, we would expect the coin to follow the regular laws of probability.

Perform the experiment yourself. Regardless of how you pray or how much you pray, you will find that the coin lands heads or tails in exact correlation with the normal laws of probability. Our prayers to Jesus have absolutely no effect on the coin no matter how much we pray. Even if we find hundreds of Jesus' most faithful believers and have them all pray together for the coin to land tails, these prayers are ignored. The normal rules of probability always prevail. All that you need are a piece of paper and a pencil to tabulate the results and you can prove it to yourself.

How would an unbiased critical thinker look at this situation? A critical thinker would read the Bible and see what it has to say about prayer. This is like reading and following the directions on a bottle of medicine. A critical thinker would then do an experiment—for example, flipping a coin or rolling some dice—and tabulate the results of the experiment. And then the critical thinker would examine the results—the evidence—in a clear, rational, open-minded way.

This is such a simple experiment that it is easy to see and understand what has happened. If you are a critical thinker, the results are transparently clear. Prayer simply does not work the way Jesus says it does in the Bible. With these simple, easily reproducible experiments, we have proven it conclusively. And if you extrapolate just a bit, that clarity extends worldwide. It's not like there are two laws of probability—one for religious people who pray and the other for people who are not praying. There's only one law of probability and it works the same way for everyone, everywhere, all the time, regardless of how much prayer is involved. Prayer never influences the laws of probability.

What are we to make of this? Based on the experiments performed so far, and the lack of any statistical evidence over the centuries to indicate that prayer has any effect, a critical thinker would conclude that prayers are ineffective in the real world. The claims for the effectiveness of prayer in the Bible contradict the reality that we see in the real world here on Earth. Therefore, the claims are false.

Note the parallel here. If a drug manufacturer makes claims about the effectiveness of a drug, we can test the drug scientifically as described in Chapter 2 to decide whether those claims are true or not, real or imaginary. In the same way, the Bible makes claims about the effectiveness of prayer. The same type of scientific tests can determine whether the claims of the Bible are true or not. With our coin experiments, we have proven scientifically that the claims made in the Bible about prayer are false.

If you are a person who is able to think critically, you can see what has happened here. When flipping coins, tossing dice, playing cards, rolling balls on roulette wheels, or playing slot machines, prayer is ineffective. Even if prayer worked just a tiny bit, the effect would show up statistically and statisticians would be required to account for it. Instead, we know with certainty that there is no effect. You can repeat the experiment in your kitchen right now if you'd like. The Bible says, "You may ask me for anything in my name, and I will do it." Here we are asking, but nothing happens. Why might that be?

RATIONALIZATIONS

If you believe in God and the Bible's promises about the power of prayer, something may be happening inside your head as you are reading this chapter. You may be unable to accept the reality that's right in front of you. Instead, in your mind, you are probably coming up with one or more rationalizations to explain why God did not respond to any of the previously mentioned prayers:

- It's not His will
- He doesn't have time
- I didn't pray the right way
- I'm not worthy
- I don't have enough faith
- I can't test the Lord like this
- It's not part of His plan for me
- Those verses in the Bible do not apply to coin tosses
- One must read the entire Bible and synthesize its true meaning
- And on and on and on.

How might a critical thinker interpret rationalizations like these? A critical thinker might note that the dictionary defines **rationalization** as:

> The most commonly used defense mechanism, in which an individual justifies ideas, actions, or feelings with seemingly acceptable reasons or explanations. It is often used to preserve self-respect, reduce guilt feelings, or obtain social approval or acceptance.

Also, **rationalize**:

> To ascribe (one's acts, opinions, etc.) to causes that superficially seem reasonable and valid but that actually are unrelated to the true, possibly unconscious and often less creditable or agreeable causes.

Contrast the rationalization process with the definition of **critical thinking**:

> Disciplined thinking that is clear, rational, open-minded, and informed by evidence.

A critical thinker simply looks at the evidence and understands what it indicates. In this case, all evidence consistently indicates that prayer has no effect in the real world when we look at the statistical outcomes of coin tosses, dice rolls, and so on. The use of rationalizations to try to explain away the clear evidence in this case does not change the evidence.

If you're a Christian, one rationalization that you may find yourself developing is particularly interesting. You may say to yourself something like this: "Well, of course Jesus doesn't answer me when I pray about a coin toss, because it would be too obvious."

Where does this rationalization come from? If a Christian prays for a cure for her cancer, and the tumor disappears, that is completely obvious. In fact, any time a Christian claims an answered prayer, the result is usually obvious—otherwise, the claim could not be made. Christian inspirational literature is full of stories of answered prayers, most of them "obvious." To claim that a coin toss is "too obvious" is simply a rationalization as defined above.

In addition, if you read what Jesus says about prayer in the Bible, Jesus does not ever say, "do not pray to me about coin tosses" or "do not pray about obvious things." Jesus clearly says he will answer your prayers, and he puts no boundaries on what you may pray about. There is nothing confusing about "You may ask me for anything in my name, and I will do it." Coin tosses certainly qualify as "anything." Even so, if you're a believer, you have invented your rationalizations for the ineffectiveness of prayer, instead of thinking critically and accepting the evidence.

Another common rationalization is, "Jesus does answer prayers, but only occasionally, so statisticians cannot detect it." A statement like this is fascinating to anyone who is able to think critically, because it shows a remarkable level of delusion. A critical thinker understands that if statisticians are unable detect the effects of prayer, that inability is the proof that prayers are having no effect. This rationalization is specifically designed to ignore the truth represented by the evidence.

Another common rationalization is, "Jesus didn't mean what he said in the Bible. He's not a vending machine operated by prayer." But this contradicts statements like the one in John 14:14, where Jesus says, "You may ask me for anything in my name, and I will do it." Jesus stipulates here that he is a vending machine operated by prayer. We could convene a conclave of Christian leaders and theologians to try to interpret what Jesus actually meant with his clear, unambiguous statement. But we would run into one big problem that any critical thinker immediately sees: A perfect being who never lies could not make a statement that is untrue. A perfect being would speak the truth at all times, without ambiguity. For example, if what Jesus meant was, "you can accomplish some things if you put your mind to it and circumstances happen to turn out in your favor," then as a perfect being, he would have said that.

God has said in the Bible that we can pray to him and get results. We have seen in this chapter that this simply is not true. You can easily prove it to yourself in your living room anytime you like by praying for things like these:

1. Ask God to let you defy gravity and fly through the air like Superman.
2. Ask God to make a billion dollars in gold bars appear on the floor in front of you.
3. Ask God to write down the next fifteen winning lottery numbers on a sheet of paper for you.

These things are all impossible. Therefore they never happen, no matter what the Bible says and no matter how much you pray.

It does not really matter what you ask for in prayer. Do the experiment, correctly tabulate the results, and see what you discover. If what you pray for is impossible, it will not happen (that is the definition of impossible), despite what Jesus says in the Bible. If it's possible, it will happen at the same statistical rate to you that it would happen to anyone else, regardless of whether or not you pray. In other words, no matter what you pray for or how you pray for it, there will be no measurable effect here in the real, physical universe that we inhabit. If you take the time to track and measure the results of any prayer of intercession in the same way that an unbiased scientist would, you can easily prove the true nature of our world to yourself. Prayers of intercession have no effect in the real world.

OFFICIAL DOUBLE-BLIND TESTING

What about spending the time and money to set up an official double-blind scientific experiment to test the efficacy of prayer in a hospital setting? This has been done many times. One of the most expensive experiments, with a cost of $2.4 million, was done by an organization called the John Templeton Foundation and completed in 2006. The results were widely reported in *The New York Times* and many other credible media sources.

What the Templeton Foundation wanted to explore is the effect of intercessory prayer on surgical outcomes. For the experiment, 1,800 people were divided into three randomized groups, where everyone in all three groups was to have heart surgery. Each group was prayed for in a different way:

1. Group A patients were told they would receive prayers
2. Group B patients were told they could receive prayers, but then again they might not
3. Group C patients were told they would receive no prayer

Then the congregations of several churches were enlisted to deliver the prayers, and specifically to pray "for a successful surgery with a quick, healthy recovery and no complications."

Thirty days after the surgeries were performed and the prayers said, statisticians tabulated the results. What do you expect happened? Just as is the case with coin tosses, there were no differences in outcomes seen between the patients who received and did not receive prayers. But the fascinating thing is that scientists did observe a reverse placebo effect. Not a placebo effect—a reverse placebo effect.

The people who knew they were being prayed for in Group A did worse than the people in Group B. So it turns out that prayer doesn't help anyone, and if you tell a friend you're praying for him, he might actually do worse than if you left him alone. Why might that occur? One hypothesis for the difference between groups A and B is that being prayed for stresses people, and the stress leads to medical complications. Perhaps the people in Group A feel an obligation to get better because of the prayers, and the obligation causes stress. In any case, the study proved conclusively, yet again, that prayer has no effect.

If you think about it, this outcome is obvious to any thinking person simply by looking at the real world around us. Once researchers control for all variables, the real world always behaves in a way that indicates that prayers of intercession are ineffective:

- People who pray do not win the lottery more often than people who do not.
- People who pray do not die less frequently after car accidents than people who don't.
- People who pray do not have home appliances that are more reliable than people who don't.
- People who pray do not experience better weather than people who don't.

What you come to realize, if you're a rational person and a critical thinker, is that the belief in the power of prayer is purely a **superstition**, defined in the dictionary as:

> An irrational belief usually founded on ignorance or fear and characterized by obsessive reverence for omens, charms, etc.

It is no different than believing in homeopathy, and we can prove that prayer is as ineffective as homeopathy using exactly the same kind of scientifically accurate double-blind trials. The only reason people would believe in prayer is because they fall into the normal traps that anyone does if they're unable to think critically. People who believe in prayer, for example, tend to have a problem with confirmation bias and cherry-picking the data. They believe in anecdotal evidence rather than scientific evidence. They fail to look at the world around them honestly, based on actual, unbiased evidence gathered in an honest and scientifically valid way. They refuse to accept the evidence proving that the effects of prayer claimed in the Bible are imaginary.

COMMON FALLACIES

If there is all this evidence showing that the belief in prayer is a meaningless superstition, why do so many people believe that prayers work? Christians and other believers are especially susceptible to something called the **post hoc fallacy**. It is defined as:

> In or of the form of an argument in which one event is asserted to be the cause of a later event simply by virtue of having happened earlier.

In other words, in the minds of uncritical thinkers who are subject to this fallacy, the simple fact that event B follows event A means that event A caused event B. This type of thinking is easily shown to be incorrect. When the post hoc fallacy combines with confirmation bias, where only positive correlation is noted, a person who suffers from the post hoc fallacy acquires a completely erroneous view of what is happening in the real world.

"Correlation does not imply causation"—this is the correct way to understand the world we live in. Just because you do X and then Y happens (correlation), that does not mean that X causes Y to happen (causation). Causation must be proven scientifically. In addition, there must be a reason to expect causation—a mechanism of causation must be evident. This mechanism of causation must make rational sense and survive scrutiny.

We see people falling victim to the post hoc fallacy constantly in the media. It's a staple of politics. And it's a favorite of preachers. Christians are frequently heard to say, "I prayed for X and it happened. Therefore, God answered my prayer!" A very common example is something like this: "I prayed for a cure for my cancer, and my tumor disappeared. God answered my prayer!" If we dig a little deeper, however, we often find that the person making this statement also underwent surgery in a hospital to remove the tumor along with enduring three months of chemotherapy. A critical thinker understands that the surgery and chemotherapy caused the cure, not the prayer. In addition, if God were working a miraculous cure, the surgery and chemo would have been unnecessary. Why waste the money and endure all of the pain and illness associated with surgery and chemo if praying actually works?

Here is a classic example of the post hoc fallacy in action. In the May 2004 issue of *Guideposts* magazine there is a fascinating story about a huge wildfire that swept through San Diego, California. Steve Homel lived in a subdivision engulfed by that fire.

Steve saw the fire approaching and described it as, "An eighty-foot wall of flames rolling down the ridge that overlooks our street." He and his wife evacuated to the home of Steve's grown daughter about fifteen miles away. There, as he watched the news on television, Steve actually saw the flames reaching his neighborhood.

To save his house, Steve decided to try reaching out to God as the Bible prescribes. According to the article, "Suddenly Steve grabbed a piece of paper. 'God bless this house and the firemen who protect it,' he scrawled." Steve then faxed that sheet of paper to the fax machine in his home.

Days later, Steve and his neighbors were allowed to return to their subdivision. What Steve found when he arrived was absolutely amazing. Despite the raging inferno, Steve's house stood unscathed. It was as though there had never been a fire near the neighborhood.

Unfortunately, every other house on Steve's street burned to the ground in the fire. According to the article, "The only things standing were a few brick chimneys. The rest had been reduced to ash." The thirty-nine other houses on Steve's street were destroyed, along with all the possessions, keepsakes, and belongings of the thirty-nine families.

The story in *Guideposts* is about how God answers prayers. The logic used by Christians is: "Steve prayed for his house and his house survived. Therefore God answered Steve's prayers." According to

Christians, God reached down from heaven into our world and worked a miracle. This story about God's blessings gets written up in magazines and sent to millions of believers. There are thousands and thousands of stories like this documented in Christian inspirational literature. To Christians, they all prove that God answers prayers.

In reality, this is a classic example of the post hoc fallacy at work. Just because something happened following a prayer, it does not mean that the prayer caused it to happen.

The first problem with Christian logic is that the same logic can be applied to anything. For example:

- Let's say that Steve had a portrait of Mother Theresa on the wall. The Catholic Church would claim that what Steve experienced is a posthumous miracle brokered by Mother Theresa.
- What if Steve has a mask of good fortune made by a Haitian voodoo doctor on the mantel? The voodoo doctor would say that the mask worked its magic and saved the house.
- Perhaps Steve's daughter claims to be a good witch, and she cast a spell on Steve's house when she saw how distraught he was. According to her, it was her spell that saved the house.
- The manufacturer of Steve's refrigerator could claim that its line of appliances provides supernatural protection against house fires. It was the refrigerator that saved Steve's house.

These alternative explanations all sound silly, don't they? A portrait on a wall or a mask on the mantel does not prevent house fires. And the refrigerator? We know that *Consumer Reports* would do a study to debunk this claim. But if you are a Christian, think carefully about this statement: "Steve sent a faxed message to his house and it saved his house." To any unbiased critical thinker, it sounds just as silly, because it is. Yet Christians readily accept this kind of logic because they lack or ignore critical thinking skills.

In other words, if we can ascribe the event that Steve experienced to a piece of paper in a fax machine, we can just as easily ascribe it to anything else if we are prone to the post hoc fallacy. A critical thinker, on the other hand, doesn't allow the post hoc fallacy to pollute her thinking process.

A critical thinker would look for a rational explanation, or would chalk it up to coincidence. Perhaps the fire department arrived and only had time to hose down one house to protect it before the fire arrived, but this detail has been left out of Steve's story. If you listen to prayer stories as a critical thinker, you will often find that people affected by the post hoc fallacy omit details like these. Many times when a Christian in a hospital claims a miraculous cure from God, a critical thinker recognizes it as the same kind of thing. If God were working a miraculous cure, there would be no need for the hospital and all of the doctors, medicines, and procedures that the hospital makes available.

A critical thinker would also contemplate the logic of the statement being made, and the ramifications of that logic. For example, a critical thinker would consider the nature of Steve's prayer. It's incredibly selfish if you think about it. What if Steve had changed just one word in his prayer so it had said, "God bless this subdivision and the firemen who protect it?" Would all forty homes have been saved? The fact that Steve ignored the needs of his neighbors makes him incredibly selfish, and the fact that God could not see that greater good of saving the whole subdivision makes God rather monstrous. Or what about this: Why didn't Steve pray to immediately extinguish the entire forest fire? That would have helped even more people.

What if Steve had prayed, "God bless this nation and the firemen who protect it?" Would every fire in the entire country immediately extinguish itself? If so, we could save billions of dollars per year by closing every fire station in the nation and relying on Steve and his fax machine to take care of us all.

Most people understand that closing every fire station in America and instead relying on prayer would be irresponsible. Why? It brings up an interesting question: If you believe that God answered Steve's prayer, then why don't you believe that God would answer a nationwide prayer from Steve as well? Keep in mind what Jesus said in Mark 11:24:

> Therefore I say unto you, What things soever ye desire, when ye pray, believe that ye receive them, and ye shall have them.

If Jesus is God, and if God is perfect, why isn't Mark 11:24 true when it comes to house fires? Why can't we rely on prayer to universally protect America's houses from fire? We would no longer need to pay for fire fighters or fire insurance, saving the nation billions of dollars. A critical thinker recognizes the reality of the situation: The reason why we do not rely on prayer in this way is because rational people know, with 100 percent certainty, that it would not work. This fact is another piece of evidence demonstrating prayer is a superstition. Christians who believe in prayer necessarily ignore this evidence, but that does not change the evidence.

Because religious people who believe in prayer have a tendency to congregate, there can also be significant problems with groupthink among Christian congregations. **Groupthink fallacy** is defined as:

> The act or practice of reasoning or decision-making by a group, especially when characterized by uncritical acceptance or conformity to prevailing points of view.

The problem with groups of human beings is that, if they are not critical thinkers, they tend to create echo chambers amongst their members. If a majority of members in a group believe in the "power of prayer," this belief will be uncritically accepted and promoted by the group, despite all of the evidence to the contrary. Psysr.org describes it this way:

> Groupthink, a term coined by social psychologist Irving Janis (1972), occurs when a group makes faulty decisions because group pressures lead to a deterioration of "mental efficiency, reality testing, and moral judgment" (p. 9). Groups affected by

groupthink ignore alternatives and tend to take irrational actions that dehumanize other groups.

Related phenomena include **social proof** and **normative social influence**. Social proof occurs in social situations. Imagine that you are in a new group of people, and you are not sure what to say or how to act. You may look around you, see what other people are doing, and then do the same kinds of things in order to fit in. The idea is that they, being members of the group already, must know what is going on. Social proof is related to ideas like peer pressure and herd mentality. Normative social influence also stems from the human desire to fit in.

Therefore, if the Bible clearly states in a dozen places that God answers prayers, and a group of Christians is talking about prayer, then groupthink will cause the group to conclude that prayer works, often in spite of all rational evidence to the contrary. Combine group-think with social proof, confirmation bias, anecdotal evidence, the post hoc fallacy, etc., and it can be nearly impossible for group members to see the truth about the ineffectiveness of prayer. A new member who joins the group with a different opinion about prayer either will be rejected by the group, will leave the group because of the group's dysfunction, or will start agreeing with the group because of groupthink, social proof, and normative social influence. The group prevents itself from having its ideas challenged and thus loses its ability to see reality clearly.

Billions of people around the world believe in the power of prayer. These people, either through unconscious or willful ignorance, are delusional—for the same reasons that the believers in homeopathy are delusional. In both cases, believers trust in an effect that is completely imaginary, and do so despite both scientific evidence and personal evidence available in the world around them.

What does the failure of prayer say about God? The Bible, which defines God and his attributes and is purportedly written by a perfect God who cannot lie, contains statements about prayer that are clearly and provably wrong. Simple experiments, carefully controlled double-blind tests, and observations of the real world all demonstrate the same thing to critical thinkers willing to examine the evidence without bias: God and Jesus do not answer prayers. The inability of believers to think critically blinds them to the truth of the real world they live in.

Given that prayer is such an important part of the definition of God, the fact that prayer is not working tells us something essential about God. Let's continue exploring...

6:

WHAT HAPPENS IF WE EXAMINE PRAYER STATISTICALLY?

IN CHAPTER 1 WE BRIEFLY DISCUSSED A QUESTION THAT SCIENTISTS FACED IN THE 1940S AND 1950S: ARE CIGARETTES HARMLESS OR DANGEROUS? It was an important question because nearly half of the United States' adult population had started smoking. A combination of big ad campaigns and free cigarette giveaways were encouraging more and more people to smoke.

There are two problems here. The first problem is that we don't really want to set up double-blind tests to answer this question. We know, from common experience, that a person who starts smoking today is not going to drop dead tomorrow, or even next year. Half of the adult population in America is smoking, and they are not dropping like flies. A standard double-blind testing regimen might have to run for a decade or more to see results. It certainly would be helpful to set up a full-scale longitudinal study and have the full results thirty years from now, and in fact scientists regularly do things like that. But it would be much more useful to have results quickly.

The second problem is that, looking at people who are dying today, it is difficult to tell if smoking is definitely the cause of any problems. If a smoker dies of lung cancer today, how can we know for certain that the lung cancer did not come from something else besides smoking? In other words, how do we establish causation?

The key to answering questions like these is to do a statistical study on people who have already been smoking for thirty years. This type of study is typically called a **retrospective study**, which is defined by *Mosby's Medical Dictionary* as:

A study in which a search is made for a relationship between one (usually current) phenomenon or condition and another that occurred in the past.

Scientists do retrospective studies like this all the time, because they are incredibly powerful. For example, in 1999 scientists did a large retrospective cohort study to try to answer this question: Are smokers more likely to get rheumatoid arthritis than nonsmokers? The cohort in this case was female health professionals, and surveys were sent to 377,000 women who had already been enlisted to help study a variety of female health questions.

In order for a study like this to be valid, the scientists doing the survey have to control for noise and other factors so that they are sure to get apples-to-apples comparisons. Therefore, they have to take all sorts of factors into account. For example, older people are more likely to have rheumatoid arthritis than teenagers. Therefore, scientists must control for age when looking at the results. What if pregnancy has an effect on rheumatoid arthritis? What about the length of time since menopause? What about other drugs the women might be taking? Scientists must take all of these factors and many more into account when looking at the survey results. When it was all said and done, this study did produce an interesting outcome: Women who smoke a pack or two of cigarettes per day for twenty years significantly increase their chances of getting rheumatoid arthritis. Scientists had discovered yet another reason to avoid cigarettes.

This kind of study allows scientists to determine the effects of all sorts of things that take long periods of time to manifest themselves. We now know that cigarettes have many unfortunate side effects. We also know that secondhand smoke causes problems for both adults and children. For example, we now know that children whose parents smoke around them get exposed to secondhand smoke at a rate that causes them to get asthma more often than the children of nonsmokers. The parent-child relationship through secondhand smoke is one more terrible side effect of smoking that is revealed through statistical studies.

Because of the results of the statistical analysis of large quantities of data, there have been many efforts over the years to try to reduce smoking and eliminate the public's exposure to secondhand smoke. Many of the problems caused by smoking, like arthritis, are not intuitively obvious, yet they can be teased out of the data. As a result, in America we have banned television and radio advertising of cigarettes, put warnings on cigarette packages, started education campaigns, eliminated smoking in almost all buildings, and have even started eliminating smoking in open public places like parks and beaches. This is an amazing turnaround when you consider that, not so long ago, it was legal to smoke on airplanes and every airplane armrest contained an ashtray. People once smoked freely in restrooms, offices, and restaurants. Not anymore. Statistical analysis has proven the deadly consequences of cigarette smoke.

APPLYING STATISTICS TO GOD

How might a critical thinker apply these statistical techniques to God? It turns out that it's easy to test whether or not prayer works using the same statistical methods that scientists used to decide that smoking is harmful. If prayer actually works, there are a number of things we would expect to see happening, on a statistical basis, in the real world. If God really answers prayers in the way that He promises in the Bible, we would expect Christians who pray to experience measurable effects. Yet it turns out that this is not the case at all.

You don't have to be particularly scientific to see the problem yourself. Simply look at the real world that surrounds you. Please go back and reread the promises the Bible makes about prayer in Chapter 5, on page 63. These are not trivial, flippant, or obtuse statements. They are unambiguous statements like, "Whatsoever ye shall ask in prayer, believing, ye shall receive," and "For with God nothing shall be impossible," and "All things are possible to him that believeth." A critical thinker understands that these statements are either true or false. If they are proven to be false, it's a significant data point.

So, as critical thinkers, we look out at the evidence available, searching for the statistical effects of prayer. For example, if prayer works as God describes it in His Bible, what would we expect to happen with the lottery? We would expect faithful, prayerful Christians to consistently win the lottery. In fact, we would expect that, in every lottery, we would see thousands of devout, prayerful Christians splitting the winning pot. They would all pray, and "Nothing would be impossible for them," and since there are many devout Christians, they would necessarily have to split the pot when they all picked the winning number. In addition, when they prayed repeatedly they would win repeatedly. This is a necessary outcome of what the Bible says about prayer if the Bible is true. Recall that more than half the adult population in the United States believes that the Bible is literally true. If these adults would simply look statistically at lottery results, they would easily see that something is amiss.

Do thousands of devout Christians repeatedly split winning pots in every lottery? It's easy to run the statistics. We see nothing of the sort in the real world. The people who win the lottery follow the normal statistical patterns we would expect to see. We do not see the same devout Christians winning the lottery repeatedly. We do not see Christians winning more often than nonbelievers based on demographics. Instead of what we expect to see after reading about prayer in the Bible, the statistics that we see in real world lotteries exactly reflect what we would expect if the effects of prayer are imaginary.

Think about the many other things that would be statistically true if God really answered prayers. Would hurricanes ever hit the United States? Obviously not—Christians would be able to pray them away. Same thing for droughts and floods. Yet statistics show that hurricanes hit the United States with regularity. Even more curious is the fact that hurricanes, by and large, hit the United States in the "Bible Belt"—the southern area of the United States where Christianity is most widespread and most deeply rooted.

What about infant mortality rates in devoutly Christian congregations that interpret the Bible literally and believe in faith healing? Wouldn't we expect these Christian communities, with all of their prayers and the Bible's unambiguous statements about prayer's efficacy, to have infant mortality rates that are effectively zero? Yes, we would expect that if Jesus' statements about the efficacy of prayer are true. But when we look at the statistics seen in the real world, for example in a Christian sect known as Followers of Christ in the United States, we find the exact opposite. Members of the Followers of Christ sect cut themselves off from modern medical science because of their beliefs. Their children die at alarming rates from easily prevented problems. The infant mortality rate in this sect can be over twenty times higher than normal for the United States. It's an amazing statistic, and demonstrates clearly that prayer is not working as the Bible says it should.

The facts are simple and straightforward. When critical thinkers apply modern statistical methods and use them to understand if prayer works, there is no valid evidence that it does.

FRANCIS GALTON'S STUDIES

The statistical study of prayer goes all the way back to 1872, when a scientist named Francis Galton published a paper entitled "Statistical Inquiries into the Efficacy of Prayer." In this paper, he opens by laying out the methodology of a critical thinker:

> The efficacy of prayer seems to me simple, as it is a perfectly
> appropriate and legitimate subject of scientific inquiry. Whether
> prayer is efficacious or not, in any given sense, is a matter of fact
> on which each man must form an opinion for himself. His decision
> will be based upon data more or less justly handled, according to
> his education and habits. An unscientific reasoner will be guided
> by a confused recollection of crude experience. A scientific rea-
> soner will scrutinize each separate experience before he admits
> it as evidence, and will compare all the cases he has selected on a
> methodical system.

He also points out that prayer's universality does not really have any meaning in a scientific sense:

> A prima facie argument in favour of the efficacy of prayer
> is therefore to be drawn from the very general use of it. The
> greater part of mankind, during all the historic ages, have been

accustomed to pray for temporal advantages. How vain, it may be urged, must be the reasoning that ventures to oppose this mighty consensus of belief! Not so. The argument of universality either proves too much, or else it is suicidal. It either compels us to admit that the prayers of Pagans, of Fetish worshippers, and of Buddhists who turn praying wheels, are recompensed in the same way as those of orthodox believers; or else the general consensus proves that it has no better foundation than the universal tendency of man to gross credulity.

Galton's point is that many people seem to be drawn to the concept of prayer, and they do it regardless of which god they worship. All of these believers seem to ascribe divine power to the practice. This gives us our first clue about the efficacy of prayer—we cannot say that the God of the Bible has any special abilities in this regard, nor that the practice is unique to Him. The general idea is that people can pray to anything and get the same result. As we have been discussing in prior chapters, however, this result is nothing more than an illusion brought on by uncritical thinking patterns. Or as Galton puts it, "gross credulity," where credulity is defined in the dictionary as "readiness or willingness to believe especially on slight or uncertain evidence." George Bernard Shaw has a relevant quote:

> The fact that a believer is happier than a skeptic is no more to the point than the fact that a drunken man is happier than a sober one. The happiness of credulity is a cheap and dangerous quality.

Galton summarizes the general case against prayer with a simple observation that holds as true today as it did in 1872:

> There is not a single instance, to my knowledge, in which papers read before statistical societies have recognized the agency of prayer either on disease or on anything else. The universal habit of the scientific world to ignore the agency of prayer is a very important fact.

This statistical evidence is compelling and in fact crosses all of science. There is not a single scientific law or equation that contains any factor for prayer or God. That absence tells a critical thinker everything we need to know about how the real world really works—prayer has no effect.

One of the most interesting studies described in Galton's paper looks at the longevity of people who are frequently prayed for. Since they receive many prayers, we would expect statistics to show these people living longer. If prayer actually worked, their longevity would be statistically obvious. In reality we see nothing of the sort in the statistics. Galton puts it this way:

> An inquiry of a somewhat similar nature may be made into the longevity of persons whose lives are prayed for; also that of the praying classes generally; and in both these cases we can easily obtain statistical facts. The public prayer for the sovereign of every state, Protestant and Catholic, is and has been in the spirit of our own, 'Grant her in health long to live.' Now, as a simple matter of fact, has this prayer any efficacy?

What do you suppose the result to be? Would we not expect people who are frequently prayed for to live the longest if God is real and he answers prayers as the Bible describes? That is not the case at all:

> The sovereigns are literally the shortest lived of all who have the advantage of affluence.

What a strange result, given the statements in the Bible and the billions of people who believe those statements. Yet we see this same sort of thing all around us and can recognize it easily if we think critically about it. The Pope, for example, should approach immortality if prayer actually had any effect. Yet the Pope dies like everyone else.

HEALTH INSURANCE

Even more interesting is the statistical fact we can glean by looking at the behavior of religious people living in any modern society. For example, by and large, the majority of Christians in the developed world make use of doctors, hospitals, and modern medicines. If prayer actually worked as described by Jesus, why do we observe Christians in the developed world availing themselves of the benefits of modern medical science, rather than trusting the power of prayer to do the healing?

If what Jesus says about prayer in the Bible is true, and if all the stories about medical miracles in Christian inspirational literature are true, and if a Christian's belief in God and the power of prayer is true, and if God has a plan for Christians (see Chapter 9), then why does a Christian ever need to visit a doctor or go to the hospital? Why don't Christians simply pray for a cure whenever they get sick and leave it at that? Health insurance is expensive—why not rely on prayer and avoid this expense?

The reason to ask this is because the statement that Jesus makes in Mark 11:24 is so simple:

> Therefore I say unto you, What things soever ye desire, when ye pray, believe that ye receive them, and ye shall have them.

So is what he says in John 14:14:

> If ye shall ask any thing in my name, I will do it.

In Mark 16–17, Jesus talks about the laying on of hands:

> He that believeth and is baptized shall be saved; but he that believeth not shall be damned. And these signs shall follow them that believe; In my name shall they cast out devils; they shall speak with new tongues;

But even more remarkable is James 5:15, where the Bible says:

> And the prayer of faith shall save the sick, and the Lord shall raise him up; and if he have committed sins, they shall be forgiven him.

These are powerful verses. Keep in mind that these are, supposedly, the words of a real, all-powerful, all-knowing, perfect God. If these words in the Bible are true and perfect, then a faithful person should have no need for health insurance, doctors, or hospitals.

What reason would a perfect God have for making false statements in the Bible? Yet, by owning health insurance, Christians demonstrate reality: They do not believe or have any faith in what the Bible says. This statistical fact is undeniable in the United States, as we can see in the following example.

PRAYING FOR A CURE

When Christians are sick, they often pray to God for a cure. This is especially true in the case of profound, life-threatening illnesses and chronic diseases. We've all heard the stories of amazing cures and medical miracles that have supposedly come through prayer.

If you subscribe to *Guideposts* magazine you can read a new story like this in just about every issue. Even newspapers and national magazines report on these stories now.

There are two questions that a critical thinker would ask about these types of prayers:

1. Why use modern techniques like surgery or pharmaceuticals if God is going to work a cure anyway? Why see a doctor or accept chemotherapy drugs? God is all-powerful, so his cure should be instant and free of side effects.

2. On the flip side, if "God's plan" is for sickness to occur, what point is there praying? God's plan comes from an all-powerful being and it's going to run its course no matter what we do. What good is it to pray in such a situation?

If you think about these two questions critically, and take the time to understand how they interact with each other, you will realize something important. If God is real, and if God answers prayers, and if God has a plan for each of us, then there is no point in ever visiting a doctor. Owning health insurance has to be a frivolous waste of money for any Christian. The reason is easy for a critical thinker to understand: Either God will or will not answer any prayer for healing. If he does answer the prayer, there is no need for a doctor. If he does not, then God's plan is for you to be sick. Since God is omnipotent, no amount of doctoring will change the outcome of God's plan. Seeing a doctor is a waste of time.

One common Christian rebuttal to this thought process is the phrase "God helps those who help themselves." But if, as a critical thinker, you ponder the logic of this statement, you'll realize what it means. A critical thinker realizes that you could replace "God" in that phrase with literally anything. "The sun helps those who help themselves" is just as valid a statement.

The fact is that people who take the time to help themselves are more likely to succeed than people who do the opposite. The phrase should really say, axiomatically, that, "People who help themselves help themselves." Neither "God," nor any other deity, has anything to do with it. People with initiative generally do better than people who lack initiative for obvious, logical reasons. People who have health insurance and who take advantage of doctors, hospitals, and modern medical science do better not because of God's help, but because of the benefits of modern medical science.

A person who is a critical thinker can understand the logic that Christians should be applying if they actually believed in the attributes of God: If God answers prayers as described in the Bible, then a Christian has no need for health insurance. Yet the overwhelming majority of Christians in the developed world live with the contradiction of their health insurance every day. Their inability or unwillingness to apply critical thinking skill renders them unable to process the evidence that they see in their own lives. This evidence indicates that prayer is a meaningless superstition rather than an effective protocol for treating disease.

If you are a Christian, you might take offense at the previous paragraph. In fact, you might be thinking something like this: "I personally know a number of people who God has healed through the power of prayer. There's no denying the evidence I see before my very eyes!" The problem with this evidence is that it has been gathered in a faulty, uncritical, ill-structured, unscientific way. It's anecdotal evidence suffering from confirmation bias, cherry-picking, and the post hoc fallacy discussed previously in Chapter 5. Therefore, your evidence is creating an illusion for you. If you begin thinking critically, you will be able to understand and correctly ignore this illusion.

You can gain a better understanding of the illusion by thinking about the following example. Imagine that there is a nasty form of brain cancer that, statistically, has only a 5 percent survival rate. How do we know the survival rate? Through statistical analysis. Doctors examine thousands of cases, tabulate the survival rates, and determine that only 5 percent of patients survive given the current state of medical science. Now imagine that one hundred devout, prayerful Christians get this form of cancer. They all pray. Despite their prayers, the fact is that, on average, ninety-five of these Christians will die while five survive. It's not the case that all one hundred Christians survive because of their prayers. The 5 percent survival rate applies to everyone equally regardless of whether they pray or not.

In Christian inspirational literature, we will hear all about the few who survive because they are out in public shouting about the power of prayer: "I prayed to God and He healed my brain cancer!" This story may very well get picked up by newspapers and by Christian magazines and websites.

But the fact is that the other ninety-five praying Christians, who prayed just as fervently, all died in the exact statistical proportion expected. Uncritical thinkers completely ignore these dead people—that is the source of the illusion. Because the dead people are ignored, we never see stories in inspirational literature about people who pray and then die. And these dead people are not able to tell their stories about the failure of prayer, because they are dead. Once again, confirmation bias and the post hoc fallacy make it look like prayer works, when, in fact, it did not work at all. Ninety-five people died, which is exactly what we would expect from statistical patterns for this disease. The uncritical thinker who believes in prayer refuses to look at this evidence, however. That omission is what allows him to continue to believe that prayer works, but it also renders him unable to see reality.

We should also reiterate one important point from Chapter 5: note how selfish most prayers are. If someone is going to pray to cure their own cancer, why not pray to cure the whole world of all cancers immediately? Millions of people would benefit from such a prayer. The religious do not pray this way because they know that such prayers never work, in direct defiance to the Bible's statements about prayer.

The fact is, the more we look at prayer, the more evidence against it we can gather and the more obvious it becomes that the belief in prayer represents a superstition fueled by uncritical thinking. We will look at another example of this phenomenon in the following chapter.

7:

DOES GOD CURE RABIES?

HOW DO WE KNOW THAT THE WORLD IS ROUND? Have you ever thought about it? This question would be especially interesting 2,000 years ago, before the advent of things like satellites and the International Space Station. When a casual observer looks at the world, it does appear to be flat. The ocean looks flat. A grassy field looks flat. There certainly are hills and mountains, and they are understood to be punctuations of the basic flat nature of Earth.

But even though it looks flat, the fact is that the earth is a sphere. Most sensible people understand this. Even though "common sense" and simple observation tell a lot of people that the world is flat, this does not make it so.

So imagine that you are able to get in a time machine and go back in time 2,000 years. You meet a man named John, and John is convinced that the world is flat. His eyes tell him it is flat, and that is all the data John needs to make his decision. How might you go about demonstrating to John that the world is really a sphere? This situation gets us to the nature of science, as well as the scientific method. The dictionary defines **science** in this way:

> Knowledge about or study of the natural world based on facts learned through experiments and observation.

> **Scientific Method**: principles and procedures for the systematic pursuit of knowledge involving the recognition and formulation of a problem, the collection of data through observation and experiment, and the formulation and testing of hypotheses.

One of the great things about the scientific method is that it allows us to form hypotheses, from those hypotheses to make predictions, and then to verify whether those predictions are true using experiments.

In talking to John, you could hypothesize that the earth is actually an immense sphere. The sphere is so large that the part we can see appears to be flat to our eyes. Why might you and John develop this hypothesis? One reason might come from your observations of the sun and moon. These two heavenly bodies are definitely spheres, so we might imagine that Earth is similar.

Our spherical hypothesis would enable us to make certain predictions about the nature of the world, and then go test those predictions with experiments. One of the first known people to form and test a hypothesis involving the earth's spherical nature was Eratosthenes, a Greek mathematician who lived more than 2,000 years ago.

Eratosthenes had heard that in the city of Syene (modern Aswan, Egypt) at noon on the day of the summer solstice, a column would cast no shadow. In other words, the sun would be directly overhead at that precise moment every year. He hypothesized that if the earth is a sphere, then on the same day at the same time, the shadow would be different in a city farther north due to the curve of the Earth.

Eratosthenes therefore visited Syene one year and observed that there really was no shadow cast at noon on the day of the summer solstice. The next year he made the same observation on the same day and time at Alexandria, a city approximately 600 miles (965 km) to the north of Syene. As predicted, there was a shadow. From the length of the shadow, Eratosthenes was able to calculate the circumference of the spherical earth within 2 percent of the actual circumference using nothing but a little math, the size of the shadow in Alexandria and the distance between Syene and Alexandria.

There are many other ways to make predictions and see the spherical nature of the planet. For example, what should happen if the world is flat and you stand on shore to watch a tall sailboat sail toward the horizon? The boat should get smaller and smaller but remain visible. If the earth is a sphere, however, then the hull of the boat should disappear while the mast will still be visible. The curve of the earth hides the hull first. Then the mast will disappear as well. This only makes sense if the earth is a sphere. Since the earth is in fact a sphere, the hull does disappear, and then the mast.

In the same way, a person standing on flat ground may not be able to see a tall tree or building in the distance, but it becomes visible after climbing a hill. By climbing the hill, it becomes possible to see farther around the curve of the earth.

The fact that it's possible to sail a boat consistently west and arrive back at the starting point shows that the earth is a sphere. Sure, the journey takes a considerable amount of time (after all, the circumference of Earth is 25,000 miles (40,000 kilometers)), and you have to take detours around Africa and South America, but circumnavigation makes sense on a globe while it makes no sense at all on a flat earth. The fact that there are time zones shows the same thing. So does the change in the angle of the sun as you head from the equator to the poles.

In other words, even though the basic information available to our eyes tells us initially that the earth is flat, the fact is that the Earth is a sphere and we can figure this out with more careful observations and experiments. The evidence is available if we take the time to look for it.

This same kind of scientific process and investigation has made it possible to create the modern world we live in, and all of the medical science we now have available.

CURING RABIES

There are so many examples of situations that appear to demonstrate the power of prayer, but one in particular deserves special consideration because it is so well documented. In December 2004, a girl named Jeanna Giese survived a bite from a rabid bat. Hundreds of newspapers (including the *Raleigh News and Observer* in my hometown) ran stories about her recovery with headlines such as "Rabies girl in miracle recovery." In Raleigh, the headline was "Web weaves global prayer circle—petitions circle the world as girl beats rare case of rabies."

Why was it such a big deal? Because no one had ever survived full-blown rabies before. People can survive if they are vaccinated shortly after being bitten, but no one thought to vaccinate Jeanna. Up until 2004, full-blown rabies had been 100 percent fatal.

The summary of the story goes like this: Jeanna was in a church service in Wisconsin when a brown bat fell into the aisle. She picked up the bat and carried it outside. No one gave it a second thought. But a month later it was obvious that something was wrong. Soon Jeanna had a full case of rabies.

How did Jeanna become the first person ever to survive a full-blown case of rabies? According to the article, a global prayer circle caused Jeanna's recovery. Once she got sick, Jeanna's father called friends and asked them to pray for Jeanna. People around the world heard about her story through the press and by word of mouth. They prayed. They sent e-mails. They passed the word along. Millions of people heard about Jeanna's plight and they all said prayers for her.

And, according to Christians, the prayer circle worked. Through the power of God, Jeanna recovered. Jeanna was the first human to survive rabies without being vaccinated.

Dr. Charles Rupprecht of the Center for Disease Control (CDC) in Atlanta called Jeanna's case a miracle. The family and everyone in Jeanna's huge, global prayer circle believe that God heard their prayers and answered them.

This is amazing stuff. The dictionary defines a **miracle** as:

> An event that appears inexplicable by the laws of nature and so
> is held to be supernatural in origin or an act of God.

What believers are proposing is that God, through an inexplicable and supernatural event, reached down to Earth and personally healed Jeanna's body from a disease that, previously, was 100 percent fatal.

So we, as critical thinkers, must ask a fundamental question: Did an all-loving, all-powerful God hear the prayers from Jeanna's worldwide prayer circle and then decide to cure Jeanna? Did God actually interact with Jeanna's body supernaturally, making the impossible happen and curing her case of rabies through a divine miracle? Or did something else that is completely normal and natural happen without involving God at all? Are we seeing the power of prayer in this case, or is the post hoc fallacy at work again, creating an illusion, as we discussed in Chapter 5 and Chapter 6? And how would we know one way or the other? How would a scientist decide what caused Jeanna's cure?

A critical thinker might approach these questions from three angles:

1. Is there any evidence of a miracle?
2. Conversely, is there any evidence that the cure was normal and natural, part of regular medical science and its consistent advancements?
3. If we believe it to be a miracle, what are the logical side effects of that belief?

Is there any evidence of a miracle? To answer this, we look at the circumstances surrounding the event. Did Jeanna lie at home in her bed without any medical care? Then, suddenly, did she get better? And how did the miracle arrive? Did she get a miracle from God through, for example, an angel's appearance recorded with a video camera? Any critical thinker would ask questions like these instinctively. These are things we would expect if a miracle occurred. What evidence is there that a miracle occurred? The answer is that there is no evidence of a miracle.

Conversely, is there any evidence that the cure was a normal part of medical science? The fact is that Jeanna was in a hospital receiving a radical and experimental form of care. Her cure actually has a name now—it is called the **Milwaukee protocol**. Since being proven for the first time with Jeanna, the Milwaukee protocol has saved several people. In this protocol, powerful medications take the patient deep into an induced coma to slow down the infection, and then advanced antiviral drugs go to work on the rabies virus that causes the infection. When successful, the coma provides time for the antivirals to clear the infection, and the patient survives. What evidence is there that medical science cured her? The evidence is voluminous.

If it had been a miracle, what would be the logical side effects? One side effect is that, if the cure had actually come from God as a miracle, it would not be repeatable except through prayer. But we see that the

Milwaukee protocol is repeatable. Another side effect: No doctors, drugs, or hospitals of any kind would be required for Jeanna's cure if a miracle occurred. But we see that doctors, drugs, and hospitals are used in abundance with the Milwaukee Protocol.

For science to work, God (and everything else supernatural) is considered to be imaginary. The universe is considered to be a rational system where causes and effects can be understood. A scientist looks at a case like Jeanna's and says, "There is a natural cause for what we see here and therefore, potentially, a solution. If we understand the cause and perfect the solution, then we can heal many more people suffering from the same condition. In addition, we may be able to generalize the solution and cure other diseases." This process explains how scientists have invented so many different medical advancements:

- Antibiotics are specialized poisons that kill bacteria cells but not human cells, and there are now hundreds of these poisons that have been developed to clear infections.
- Vaccines are substances that alert the human immune system to a virus ahead of time, so that the immune system learns how to manufacture the right antibodies to attack the virus. When the real virus comes along, the immune system can respond immediately and destroy the virus before it does any damage.
- A stent is a small mesh tube that props open an artery so that blood can flow normally rather than being obstructed.
- And so on.

Each of these advancements starts with a hypothesis, then experiments and observations. No prayer is involved at all. In other words, it's by assuming that the belief in prayer is a superstition and that God is imaginary that science can proceed.

Did the team that treated Jeanna Giese think, "The only possible cure of her rabies is a miracle from God. God must reach down and cure her in response to our prayers. There is nothing we can do!"? Of course not. If they thought that way, then there would have been no reason to try the Milwaukee Protocol in the first place, and it would be unable to cure anyone else. Instead, the doctors completely ignored God and prayer. They determined what was actually happening through experimentation and then created a useful medical protocol that cured full-blown rabies for the first time. Then they applied that protocol to other people. The doctors took a rational approach and many people benefit from the new protocol. Over time doctors improve the protocol or develop new techniques that are more and more effective.

After looking at this case, what is the conclusion of rational people? There is no evidence indicating that a miracle occurred. All evidence indicates that an advancement in medical science cured Jeanna. Therefore, critical thinkers look at the prayer circle explanation with bemusement. It is apparent, based on the evidence, that the people who believe that a prayer circle cured Jeanna are suffering from several forms of delusion. The idea that, "We prayed, Jeanna was cured, therefore the prayer cured her" represents a perfect example of the post hoc fallacy. Believers in this case have also ignored the efforts of the doctors, as well as the new protocol the doctors developed. In addition, these believers fail to recognize the value and power of medical science. Once Jeanna was cured, the protocol could be refined and applied to many other people. If it were actually prayer that cured Jeanna, this would not be the case at all—her cure would not be reproducible except with more prayer. When believers disregard all of these simple facts, and publicly brandish a well-known fallacy, what critical thinkers see is ignorance and thoughtlessness, plus the need for education.

One thing you might hear religious people say by way of rationalization is, "God inspired the doctors to develop this cure." A statement like this perplexes a critical thinker. First, there is no evidence that this is happening. Second, there is plenty of evidence to the contrary. If God "inspired the doctors," then what might some of the logical side effects be?

- Why is it that only trained professionals like doctors
  and scientists are "inspired" in this way? If God were
  providing the inspiration, then, logically, there would

be no need for the years of training doctors receive. Anyone could be inspired if God were involved.

- Why is it that doctors are inspired in the time progression that science would be expected to naturally follow? The Milwaukee Protocol arrived about the time it would be expected in the natural course of scientific discovery. Drugs had to be developed in order to induce comas, and powerful antivirals had to be discovered. Once these medicines existed, then the Milwaukee Protocol arrived. Why didn't it happen 3,000 years ago if a miracle were involved? Why was Jeanna's survival the first such survival in history?
- Why are the prayers always so selfish or tiny? If a giant prayer circle is going to pray about rabies, why not pray to completely cure every case of rabies worldwide tomorrow, thereby eliminating the disease completely?
- Why is it that even the simplest, most basic scientific insights are missing from the Bible?

That last question is telling, and the logic here is sound. If God actually were to be real, is He not a monster for withholding life-saving information from the Bible and for withholding inspiration for thousands of years? Think about it this way: Why would God not provide his inspiration (and the similar inspirations to cure polio, small pox, cancer, etc.) thousands of years ago, saving millions of people from suffering and death? For that matter, why would these diseases exist in the first place? As we've noted before, Christians believe in four important attributes of God:

- God is all-loving
- God is all-knowing
- God is perfectly moral
- God wrote the Bible

Therefore, through omniscience, God would have to know about all diseases and how to perfectly cure every one. Christians also believe in the story of the Good Samaritan, found in Luke 10:30–37 in the Bible:

And Jesus answering said, A certain man went down from Jerusalem to Jericho, and fell among thieves, which stripped him of his raiment, and wounded him, and departed, leaving him half dead. And by chance there came down a certain priest that way: and when he saw him, he passed by on the other side. And likewise a Levite, when he was at the place, came and looked on him, and passed by on the other side. But a certain Samaritan, as he journeyed, came where he was: and when he saw him, he had compassion on him. And went to him, and bound up his wounds, pouring in oil and wine, and set him on his own beast, and brought him to an inn, and took care of him. And on the morrow when he departed, he took out two pence, and gave them to the host, and said unto him, Take care of him; and whatsoever thou spendest more, when I come again, I will repay thee. Which now of these three, thinkest thou, was neighbour unto him that fell among the thieves? And he said, He that shewed mercy on him. Then said Jesus unto him, Go, and do thou likewise.

The point of this story is to demonstrate that a moral person, like the Samaritan, helps other people when they are suffering.

God, if He were to exist and be omniscient and omnipotent, necessarily knows the cure to every disease. And he sees millions of people suffering. God could have easily written all of the cures to every disease into the Bible 3,000 years ago. By doing that, God would have saved untold millions of lives and eliminated massive amounts of human suffering. Instead, God remained silent, and remains silent now. In so doing, God acts like the priest and the Levite in the parable of the Good Samaritan, instead of acting morally.

The logical conclusion here is stark. A critical thinker understands, from the definition of God, that an all-powerful, all-knowing God must know how to eliminate every sickness. However, God refuses to do so. By behaving in this manner, God becomes the author of all human suffering from disease. Why would anyone want to praise and worship such a being?

So what is really going on here? The evidence is straightforward in Jeanna's case: Science cured Jeanna, not prayer or God. By looking at another example, we can add clarity to this situation.

8:

WHY WON'T GOD HEAL AMPUTEES?

BELIEVERS FREQUENTLY APPROACH GOD WITH PRAYERS OF INTERCESSION, IN WHICH THEY ASK GOD TO DO SOMETHING. Millions of people pray to God every day to cure their diseases, solve their financial problems, help them win in Las Vegas, and so on. Christians behave in this way for many reasons: Because so many other people talk about answered prayers; because prayer is a big part of the culture; because of the many statements in the Gospels claiming that God will, in fact, do something as a result of prayer.

The truth that you should now be realizing is that when a Christian prays for God's intercession, and the prayer appears to be answered, the "answer" to the prayer is nothing more than a **coincidence**, defined in this way:

> The occurrence of events that happen at the same time by accident but seem to have some connection.

For example, if a religious person has a cold and prays for relief, the likelihood is that the cold is going to go away anyway. Therefore, the end of the cold is not an answered prayer, but instead a coincidence. If a believer prays to win the lottery and then wins, it is purely coincidence—statistical analysis proves it beyond any shadow of doubt, as seen in Chapter 6. Religious people often misinterpret what is really happening, however, because of things like confirmation bias, the post hoc fallacy, cherry-picking, and groupthink.

Imagine a Christian named Ashley who would like to be intellectually honest with herself. Her desire is to understand what's really happening with prayer—to understand whether God is actually answering her prayers, or whether her "answered prayers" are in reality simple coincidences. For Ashley, there is an easy way to discover the truth: She can pray in a situation where there is no chance for coincidence to occur. Since coincidence has been eliminated, the only way for the prayer to be answered is for God to actually answer it. Let's look at an example.

One of the more forlorn aspects of modern warfare is the rising number of amputees. In the past, soldiers with blown-off limbs were more likely to have died on the battlefield. Today they often survive because of a combination of better body armor, quicker evacuation, better medical techniques on the front line, and better facilities once in a hospital. The United States has several soldiers who have survived quadruple amputations, dozens with triple amputations, and thousands more with an amputated arm or leg.

Let us imagine that we, as critical thinkers, wish to formulate an extremely simple and extremely benevolent experiment to test the efficacy of prayer for Ashley. We take Christian veterans who are amputees and we start a program to actively and intensely pray for them. Christians gather together to ask God to spontaneously restore the lost limbs of veterans. We do not pray for prosthetics, or for surgeons to graft on donor limbs, or for medical science to develop a revolutionary new stem cell therapy or gene manipulation. We ask God to spontaneously replace amputated limbs today using only the power of prayer.

Why would we try this particular experiment? One reason is because believers frequently claim that God is answering their prayers and performing medical miracles. The case of Jeanna Geise, seen in the previous chapter, is just one example, and it was reported through dozens of media channels. Christian inspirational literature is filled with thousands of other examples—everything from cancer tumors eliminated to eyesight restored. A second reason is because Jesus is quite clear in the Bible that God will answer our prayers, as discussed in Chapter 5.

What happens if Jesus, who is supposed to be God incarnate, who is supposed to be perfect, omniscient, and incapable of lying, says, "I will do whatever you ask in my name" in a book that the majority of adults in America claim to be literally true? In that case, a critical thinker reasonably expects Jesus to do what he says he will do. We expect Jesus to regenerate amputated limbs in the same way that Christians claim Jesus is eliminating cancerous tumors. There really is nothing else to expect in this situation unless one or more of God's attributes are false.

Yet we know, with certainty, that prayers for the restoration of amputated limbs will never work. Amputated limbs are never restored through prayer. Every thoughtful, intellectually honest person knows this.

It doesn't matter how many people pray, how sincere they are, how devout they are, how much money they give to the church, or whether a priest is involved. Nothing ever happens when we pray to restore amputated limbs.

Is it because it is too obvious? No. When Jeanna beat rabies, that was completely obvious and self-evident, and millions of people were happy to claim that prayer cured her. Religious people claim that God cures cancer all the time. One day the tumor is there, plainly visible on an MRI scan, then it is gone a few weeks later. The tumor's disappearance is completely obvious. Religious people claim that God helps them get pregnant. One day the pregnancy test is negative, and then a week later the pregnancy test is positive. Nine months later a baby is born. Few things are more obvious than a healthy, crying baby right after delivery.

So why won't God help amputees by restoring their lost limbs? Does God hate amputees? Is God discriminating against amputees? Is there something about amputees that locks them out of God's prayer-answering circle?

These are valid questions, but they are not the correct questions. This is the question a critical thinker asks: Does God answer any prayers? The critical thinker then forms a hypothesis: Every answered prayer of intercession is nothing more than a coincidence. The critical thinker then looks for evidence to support this hypothesis:

- The situation with amputees provides evidence that is clear and unambiguous: Prayers to restore amputated limbs never work. In fact, every prayer fails when the possibility of coincidence has been eliminated like this.
- Try praying big instead of praying small. Instead of praying to cure one case of rabies, pray to God to completely eliminate the rabies virus worldwide overnight. Note that big prayers like these never work. Again, the chance for coincidence is eliminated.
- When the answer to a prayer could be a coincidence, and statistical analysis is performed, it becomes clear that every "answered prayer" is in fact a coincidence. Religious people do not win lotteries more often because they pray to win. Religious people do not get cured of diseases at better rates because their friends pray for them. And so on.

The evidence is concrete, consistent, and unambiguous. There is voluminous evidence indicating that belief in prayer is a superstition, and no valid evidence at all indicating that prayers of intercession work. You can perform experiments yourself, in your own home today, to prove that prayer doesn't work as described in the Bible. Critical thinkers use the evidence to understand the truth about how the world works.

So why do billions of people on Earth today believe that prayer works? Why is religious inspirational literature filled with thousands of examples of "answered prayers?" What's happening is simple: Believers, because they lack or ignore critical thinking skills, do not look at evidence correctly. Or they completely ignore evidence. For example, believers fail to take coincidence into account when evaluating prayer's efficacy, using confirmation bias to make note of the prayers that "work" while ignoring all of the prayers that do not.

How do Christians typically handle the unambiguous evidence that amputees represent? They might come up with rationalizations to try to explain why statements in the Bible are untrue for amputees. Or they might try to explain why amputees are somehow different from other people. Or they might simply get angry and storm away so they can ignore the evidence completely.

To see the reality of prayer, simply read what the Bible says and listen to what Christians say about prayer. Then pray for anything that cannot happen by coincidence. Pray for amputees to see their lost limbs spontaneously regenerated. Pray for an immediate, worldwide end to all cancers and other illnesses. Pray to fly like Superman. If there is no possibility for coincidence to influence the outcome, the number of answered prayers will always be zero.

There is one more faulty line of thinking that tricks religious people into believing that prayer works. We will examine it in the next chapter.

9:

HAVE YOU THOUGHT ABOUT THE YES/NO/WAIT FALLACY?

IMAGINE THAT YOU'RE WALKING THROUGH YOUR LOCAL MALL AND A SALESPERSON APPROACHES YOU FROM A KIOSK. She wants to demonstrate a new Power Bracelet for you. She says that once you see this demonstration, you will definitely want to buy one of these bracelets because it will give you more energy, more vitality, and a better outlook on life from a position of increased power. It will only take a minute.

The first thing she asks you to do is to stand on one leg with your arms outstretched. She pushes down on one of your arms and you immediately fall off balance, which seems completely reasonable. Then she puts a Power Bracelet on your wrist and she asks you to once again stand on one leg with your arms outstretched. This time when she pushes down on your arm in just the same way, you have no problem at all maintaining your balance. It seems amazing—you cannot believe what you are seeing, so you ask for a repeat.

You take the bracelet off and ask her to redo the test. Again you lose your balance immediately. But when she puts the bracelet back on, you have no problem standing firm no matter how hard she pushes. What could the bracelet possibly be doing that makes such a big difference? But there is no question that the bracelet works. She explains that the bracelet is able to set up a resonant power field in your body that increases your strength and vitality. This is what makes it so much easier to balance when you are wearing the bracelet.

She does several other balance demonstrations like this and the results are the same in each case. It seems amazing, but there is no denying what you are seeing with your own eyes and experiencing with your own body.

Then she shows you a flexibility test. She asks you to stand up straight and stretch your right arm out in front of you. Now she asks you to rotate your torso clockwise as far as you can go and hold that position. Then she places the bracelet on your left wrist and asks you how much farther you can now rotate. You are amazed to see that you are able to rotate even farther, although just a few seconds before you were as far as you could go. Once again, the bracelet has proven that it works.

After these demonstrations you are completely convinced. You buy a Power Bracelet on the spot for $20 and put it on. You can feel the power and vitality from the bracelet coursing through your veins. It gives you a whole new outlook.

This demonstration is so convincing because you saw it with your own eyes and felt it with your own body. There is no denying what you experienced. There is also no denying the boost that you feel the rest of the day as you wear your new $20 Power Bracelet. It really does make a difference.

However, if you take the time to do a little searching on the Internet, you will come to realize that the Power Bracelet is a scam that repeats itself every decade or two. The fact that you experienced it yourself does not change the fact that it is a scam. And that feeling of power and vitality? It's the power of suggestion working its way into the brain of an uncritical thinker.

Here's what's happening with the balance tests. It all comes down to a very subtle and undetectable change in the direction of the push. When the saleswoman pushes on your arm when you are not wearing the bracelet, she pushes very slightly outward, away from your body. It feels like she is only pushing down, but the slight outward thrust is enough to instantly tip you off balance. Once she puts the bracelet on you, she changes the push just slightly, so that there is a subtle inward push toward your body. This very slight change in direction, which you cannot detect, allows you to stand firm. This same kind of technique is applied on all of the balance tests.

On the flexibility test, what you see is a simple and natural example of the behavior of your muscles, tendons, and joints. Your body is a flexible, stretchable system. If you pull it to its natural stopping point and then wait a bit—just a few seconds is enough—then your system has a little more give. This is true whether or not you are wearing the bracelet. Try it yourself now if you like, and you will see how the effect works. When she puts on the bracelet and then shows you the extra flexibility, the uncritical thinker falls prey to the post hoc fallacy described in Chapter 5. There is also an element of ignorance at work—most people do not know that this is how the human body works.

If you are not a critical thinker, the balance and flexibility tests look and feel convincing. Then, once you've been convinced of the bracelet's abilities, paid your money, and start wearing the bracelet, the power of suggestion takes over. This is a simple fact about human beings: Our expectations tend to influence our behavior. At its core, the thing that drives the placebo effect is the power of suggestion, and suggestion affects many other things in our lives as well. It's a powerful sales tool.

The ability to recognize scams is an important skill for any critical thinker, and it's also important for consumers in the marketplace. At any given moment there are scam products and scam offers on display all around us. In addition, vendors are overcharging customers or failing to deliver on their promises on a regular basis. How can a person protect himself from these scams? The Internet is your friend. The key is to avoid impulsive decisions and do a little research.

There is one particular scam that's applied consistently to prayer. To a person who can think critically, this scam is so transparent and so obvious that it seems impossible to believe that anyone would fall for it. Yet fall for it they do, by the millions. The scam is known as "Yes, no, or wait."

Let me start by assuming that you're a religious person. Since you're a religious person, you believe in God and you believe in the power of prayer. You probably agree with this kind of statement: "Whatever troubles you are having, whether they be in your love life, your financial life, your family life, your personal life in the form of health problems, addictions, anything at all…the thing to do is pray to God. God has promised in the Bible that he will hear and answer our prayers. God is always listening, always helping, always loving. He is ready to help you right now."

We see these kinds of hopeful messages about prayer all the time. The Bible says that God answers prayers, and millions of people claim that God is answering prayers in their lives every day. The idea is that God really can perform miracles, God really does answer prayers, and God really does care about you and your needs. By praying, you unlock God's blessings.

But believers know that God sometimes does not answer their prayers, and they need a way to explain this kind of failure. So they have come up with an explanation along these lines: "God will always do what He knows is the best thing personally for each of us. God is not a vending machine. He is a thinking being with His own will and an omniscient view of the world. God perfectly understands the past, present, and future. Therefore, God always does answer our prayers, but not always in the way we think He will. Because of God's free will, He can answer our prayers with 'Yes,' 'No,' or 'Wait.' Whatever God's answer is, simply have faith in God's love and omniscience and know that He is doing what's best for you every time."

The fact is that "Yes," "No," and "Wait" may sound comforting, but it is in fact a transparent scam. As with the Power Bracelet, there might be a convincing demonstration that Yes/No/Wait works. But the fact is, this demonstration is meaningless because it's rigged.

Simply think through the logic. If you consider this explanation as a critical thinker would, you realize that Yes/No/Wait covers every possibility. Therefore, we can pray to anything using Yes/No/Wait logic, and anything answers prayers. That's the scam.

For example, imagine that I place a small statue on your kitchen counter and ask you to pray to it. You could really use $1,000, so you decide to ask the statue for $1,000.

Now if I say to you, "The statue answers prayers in the form of 'Yes,' 'No,' and 'Wait,'" what's going to happen? A coincidence might happen—you might get a check for $1,000 in the mail tomorrow. Or you might coincidentally win a raffle or get a tax refund a few weeks later. Or you might not get any money. But no matter what, if the logic is Yes/No/Wait, the statue just "answered" your prayer.

The thing to understand is that Yes/No/Wait is always true. Any person who thinks about it can see how this scam works. It's a bit like saying, "I'm going to pray to God for the sun to rise tomorrow, and I guarantee that God will answer this prayer!" When the sun rises, it has nothing to do with God or praying. The fact is that the rotation of the planet will cause the sun to rise tomorrow no matter what you do or who you pray to. No matter what a person prays to, "Yes," "No," and "Wait" are the only three possibilities. Therefore, like the sunrise, it's guaranteed to happen.

You should, at this point, be able to understand that prayer has no effect, as we have seen in the previous chapters. If we pray for anything that's impossible, it will never happen—it is, after all, impossible. If we pray for something that's guaranteed to happen (like the sun rising), it will of course happen regardless of the prayer. If we pray for anything else and look at the statistics, the thing we pray for will happen at the same statistical rate that it would happen regardless of prayer. Otherwise, mathematicians would have to modify the laws of probability to account for the effects of prayer.

One place where prayer might work is as a placebo. But in that case, prayer does no better than any placebo would. And we saw in Chapter 6 that when rigorously tested in a double-blind clinical trial, prayer can actually backfire and have a reverse placebo effect. Prayer might also work as a form of meditation or self-talk, but it works in the same way that normal meditation and self-talk work. **Meditation** is a centuries-old technique defined as:

> The act or process of spending time in quiet thought; the act or process of meditating.

Self-talk is a common motivational technique prescribed by many motivational speakers and authors. It's defined as:

> The act or practice of talking to oneself, either aloud or silently and mentally.

It's well known from a number of scientific studies that meditation has beneficial results. For example, the Mayo Clinic notes:

"Meditation can wipe away the day's stress, bringing with it inner peace." If we are doing things that really do work (like placebos, self-talk, and meditation) and we are renaming them as prayer, the renaming is dishonest.

This is a simple thing to prove to yourself. If you insist that prayer works, then simply pray for something impossible and watch it not happen. You have proven conclusively that prayer does not work. Or change the object that you are praying to and watch what happens. Pray to the sun, for example. It will work exactly the same way as prayer works when you direct it toward God. Yes/No/Wait works, literally, on everything that you pray to. If you are using prayer as a form of meditation, then call it by its proper name. It is meditation.

OTHER SCAMS

If you're a religious person who has seen other religious people fall prey to the Yes/No/Wait scam, or if you've succumbed to it yourself, you may be wondering if there are other examples of illogical thinking like this in religious communities. Let's take a moment to look at several of them.

Rick Warren is one of the most famous and most popular Christian pastors in the United States. His most popular book is *A Purpose Driven Life*, a *New York Times* best seller that has sold tens of millions of copies. Warren's book depends on the concept of God's plan, so in Chapter 2 of his book we find him discussing how God plans everything. According to Warren, God plans:

- The reason for your existence
- The exact date of your birth
- The length of your life and the exact date and time of your death
- The way each of your days will unfold

Because God is perfect, no mistakes are possible. According to Warren, even each plant has a place in God's plan. God's plan encompasses everyone and there is a definite purpose for each of us in God's plan.

Given that tens of millions of people have purchased Warren's book, these must be very resonant and comforting ideas. The problem is that they create a host of contradictions if they're subjected to any scrutiny. Most importantly, the idea that God plans your exact date of birth and your exact date of death necessarily means that God must preplan all abortions, murders, diseases, accidents, natural disasters, wars, genocides, suicides, and so on. Preplanning all of these events is the only way for God to preplan your exact date of death. If God's plan is for you to die in a war, then God must have preplanned every war.

The idea that God preplans all of your days, including the dates of birth and death, means that people have no free will. A critical thinker can understand that "God's plan" and "free will" are mutually exclusive, and this means that one or the other is impossible. It would also mean that God has preplanned millions of evil acts and atrocities. No one is responsible for any sin if God has a plan—the logic of Warren indicates that God preplanned every transgression. If God's plan is for you to be murdered tomorrow, the murderer is certainly blameless. This contradicts the idea that God is good and loving.

It also means that prayers of intercession are pointless—what good would it do to pray if everything is already planned out?

How is it possible for anyone to believe what Warren says? There is a concept called **doublethink** that makes it possible, defined as:

> The acceptance of two contradictory ideas or beliefs at the same time.

The term was originally introduced by George Orwell in his book *1984*. Doublethink takes place constantly in politics, advertising, talk radio, and especially religion. In fact, it's the only way for the contradictory messages found in any religion to be supported. For example:

- Doublethink allows religious people to believe in the power of prayer in their own lives, while at the same time observing children who die of starvation by the thousands every day.

- Doublethink causes believers to praise God when he supposedly cures one person of cancer through prayer, but then refuse to pray for God to eliminate all cancers worldwide.
- Doublethink allows a Christian to believe in a good, loving, and moral God, while at the same time reading stories in the Bible (e.g. Noah's ark, the massacre of the innocents, hell, etc.—see Chapters 14 and 20) that show God to be absolutely evil.
- Doublethink allows a Christian to see God as a moral being, while at the same time ignoring God's advocacy of slavery, misogyny, genital mutilation, murder, polygamy, etc. in the Bible.
- Doublethink allows Christians to cherry pick one verse from the Bible to support a particular bias or prejudice (for example, death to homosexuals, as in Leviticus 20:13), while ignoring a hundred other adjacent verses that are immoral or ridiculous (such as death to adulterers, as in Leviticus 20:10, or advice on where to buy your slaves, as in Leviticus 25:44).
- Doublethink allows a Christian to post the Bible's Ten Commandments in public buildings, while ignoring the executions that the Bible prescribes for those who violate the Ten Commandments.
- Doublethink allows Christians to proclaim that God is perfect and omniscient, but then ignore that He needed to flood the earth and kill nearly every living thing when He disliked how His creation turned out.

The level of contradiction and absurdity in these cases is astounding to any critical thinker, yet religious believers routinely harbor these mutually exclusive positions.

Let's look at another example of this tendency. Imagine that a Christian is asked to show us God, or to produce evidence that God exists. The reason that this request would be made is because imaginary beings are invisible and provide no concrete evidence of their existence. It's therefore logical to request evidence of God in order to demonstrate that He is real. One common Christian response to the request is to say that God must remain hidden. "If God showed Himself, it would take away faith," is one common statement.

The problem with this line of thinking is that it's impossible for a hidden God to incarnate Himself, write a Bible, answer millions of prayers, or have relationships with people. In addition, both the Old and New Testaments are filled with stories where God did in fact make Himself known in overt, obvious ways—another contradiction when compared with today. A critical thinker is able to easily see all of the contradictions in this "hidden God" line of thinking, while a believer uses doublethink to ignore the contradictions and obscure reality.

We can find another example of doublethink in the basic ideas behind prayer. God is declared to be omniscient. But if God is omniscient, then there clearly is no reason to pray, because God already knows what you want and need. Christians believe that God can read people's minds. This is the mechanism proposed for the transmission of silent prayers to God. Believers also claim that God can "see into our hearts," which is presumed to be the ability to read our deepest thoughts and intentions even if we try to hide them. If God is omniscient and can "see into our hearts" already, then there really is no reason to pray.

But it goes deeper than that. As seen above, a God who is hidden cannot answer prayers without exposing Himself. If Penelope prays to God to cure her cancer and the tumor then disappears, and if Penelope credits her healing to God, God is no longer hidden.

In addition, as we saw in Warren's book, the Bible clearly states that God already has a plan for each of us. If God has a plan, then any prayer that conflicts with the plan is pointless.

If you think about this as a critical thinker would, the logical problems multiply rapidly. On the one hand, the Bible encourages people to pray. However, the Bible also states that God must remain hidden, which He cannot do if He answers prayers. In addition, the Bible states that God is omniscient. If that is true, then there is no reason to pray since God already knows everything we are thinking. And the Bible states that God has a plan that includes everyone. Any prayer that conflicts with the plan must necessarily be ignored, and any prayer that matches the plan is being "answered" strictly by coincidence. Here we have a four-way contradiction that makes prayer meaningless. Yet Christians who are not critical thinkers insist that people must pray and that God will answer their prayers. The fact is that omniscience, prayer, a hidden God, and God's plan collide to create a number of unsolvable problems. Doublethink is the only thing that allows Christians to accept these contradictions rather than seeing that prayer as described in the Bible is impossible.

To critical thinkers who observe Christians who are deep in the throes of doublethink, the mental gymnastics and cognitive dissonance required to harbor their beliefs seem impossible. So why do Christians work so hard to maintain the charade? It appears to be the only way they can hang on to their delusions, as we will see in Chapters 13 and 22. The side effects of delusion then leak out into many other aspects of their thinking.

Or consider the doxology. The doxology is a nearly universal short hymn that begins with this line: "Praise God from whom all blessings flow." The *Catholic Encyclopedia* points out that, "The doxology in the form in which we know it has been used since about the seventh century all over Western Christendom."

This seems simple enough: this sentence in the doxology indicates that all blessings flow from God. Millions of Christians recite this hymn in church every Sunday, and they have done so for over a thousand years, so clearly they believe it. The doxology does not state that some blessings flow from God, or that the majority of blessings do—it states that all blessings flow from God. The dictionary defines a **blessing** as:

A favor or gift bestowed by God, thereby bringing happiness.

A critical thinker listens to the first line of the doxology and then considers the statistical reality of the world we live in. A critical thinker also considers the logic of the statement. If God is the giver of all blessings, then God, by withholding His blessings, would necessarily be the author of all suffering. The fact is that ten million children on this planet die of simple things like starvation and diarrhea every year. Why doesn't God provide some of His blessings to them?

"Imagine that one hundred children are invited to a party. The hostess tells the children that she is about to hand out cookies. For the first forty children, the hostess gets out one cookie and a pizza cutter. She slices the single cookie into forty tiny slivers and gives one sliver to each of the forty children. The next twenty children get one cookie each. The next twenty get two cookies each. Then ten of the children get six cookies each. Nine of the children get two dozen cookies each. Then the last child, who is a very special child, gets 170 cookies. That is an analogy for the way God flows blessings onto the people in the United States today. It is even worse when we look at the world as a whole. If all blessings flow from God, then what are we to make of this unbalanced situation?"

A critical thinker asks: If God is real, and if all blessings flow from God, and if He is a just and moral God who answers prayers, would we expect to see these statistical trends in wealth distribution? Certainly not. A just, moral, loving God would not allow ten million children to die of starvation each year by withholding his blessings, which according to the doxology He solely controls. Christians are able to ignore the logical consequences of something like the doxology through doublethink.

Clearly there are many types of illogical and irrational thinking that influence believers because of a lack of critical thinking skills. Believers completely ignore the myriad logical problems inherent in the doxology, God's plan, prayer, and Yes/No/Wait. The religious mind can appear to be a very strange place because of all of these logical contradictions. For a critical thinker, it's a place that is bewildering in its logical impossibility.

But a critical thinker can gain a foothold by simply noting all of the contradictions and laying them out simply and clearly. In doing so, believers are sometimes able to see and understand the impossibility of what is being proposed, and the invalidity of their thinking patterns. A critical thinker does this hoping that at some point the believer reaches a breakthrough of enlightenment into the world of reality. As delusion and doublethink fall away, a recovering believer is able to think much more clearly about the real universe that we all inhabit.

10:

WHAT DOES PRAYER TELL

US ABOUT GOD?

IMAGINE THAT YOU AND I ARE STANDING ON THE STREET HAVING A CONVERSATION AND WE MEET A PERSON NAMED JOHN SMITH. He simply walks up to us and introduces himself. And then he says something unexpected and remarkable: "If you believe, you will receive whatever you ask of me in prayer. You may ask me for anything in my name, and I will do it. Nothing will be impossible to you." He says this with complete sincerity and conviction.

What might you and I do next? Be honest.

If you're honest, then your next move might be to say something like, "Okay, put a trillion dollars in my hand right now." Why? Because John just told you that he would do what you requested. He didn't put any limits on what you can ask for.

Obviously John is not going to be able to put a trillion dollars in your hand instantaneously. Even though John said that nothing will be impossible and that you can ask for anything, that is not actually true. In fact, with almost anything you ask for, John is not going to be able to deliver unless it is trivial or coincidental. Spontaneously restore amputated limbs? He can't. Right now, with today's technology, no one can. Bring your dead mother back to life? He can't do that either. Make a fair coin land on heads a hundred times? He can't unless it involves a trick two-headed coin. Let you fly like Superman? He can't, unless we use wires and a harness on a theatrical stage to create a crude approximation. Tell you the next thirty winning lottery numbers? He can't. He can't do any of the things that you ask for. Even if you ask for something relatively trivial or benign, like "Make a giraffe walk down the street right now," John isn't going to be able to do it because he cannot materialize giraffes instantly out of thin air. People can't do these things. We know this.

As you think about this small vignette, there are two facts that you may now realize. First, as discussed in the previous chapters of this book, John's performance is exactly the same as God's performance when it comes to prayers. God will not put a trillion dollars in your hands no matter how much you pray for it. He will not regenerate amputated limbs, bring a dead person back to life, cause a fair coin to land heads one hundred times, let you fly like Superman, or provide you with winning lottery numbers. God and John are absolutely identical when it comes to answering prayers.

Second, having heard the statement John made to you, and now having seen what John can't do, what should you conclude about John's performance? Again, be honest. You are going to come to the reasonable conclusion that John is a liar. When he said, "You may ask me for anything in my name, and I will do it," he was lying. There's no doubt about this. John is clearly unable to deliver any of the things you pray for unless you pray for something that's trivial or available through easy coincidence. Just about anyone, critical thinker or not, understands that John is lying about his ability to answer prayers.

As you think about this more deeply, you'll realize that the God of the Bible is lying too. When Jesus talks about the power of prayer in the Bible, none of what he says is true. We have seen dozens of examples in the previous chapters demonstrating that prayer has no effect in the real world:

- Prayer does not affect coins, dice, roulette wheels, traffic lights, etc. This has been statistically demonstrated for many centuries, and is confirmed by the fact that a single law of probability applies for everyone. There is not a separate law of probability for people who pray (see Chapter 5).
- Prayer does not affect disease. Multimillion-dollar studies have proven this. It was even discovered that

prayer can have a reverse placebo effect (see Chapters 5, 6, 7).

- Prayer's effects have never been demonstrated in any valid statistical sense. For example, we can look statistically at lottery winners and we see no effects from prayer (see Chapter 6).
- When praying for anything that is impossible—for example, the spontaneous regeneration of amputated limbs—prayer never has an effect (see Chapter 8).
- The Yes/No/Wait mentality pushed by many Christian authorities has been conclusively shown to be a scam (see Chapter 9).

Given all of this undeniable evidence proving that the power of prayer is imaginary, why would anyone believe in prayer? We have noted that natural human thought processes are notoriously poor unless humans are trained to become critical thinkers. Billions of humans, unfortunately, have never been trained to think critically. These humans who lack critical thinking skills fall into a number of traps and fall prey to many common fallacies in their thinking. These problems have been discussed in previous chapters and include:

- Confirmation bias
- Anecdotal evidence
- Placebo effect
- Superstitions
- Delusion
- Regression fallacy
- Post hoc fallacy
- Yes/No/Wait fallacy
- Groupthink
- Doublethink

When all of these problems combine together, they can create a powerful illusion for uncritical thinkers suggesting that prayer works, even though every piece of actual evidence proves that prayer has no effect at all.

Belief in prayer is a superstition. For a critical thinker, this is a simple and obvious conclusion based on the evidence.

DOES PRAYER'S FAILURE PROVE THAT GOD IS IMAGINARY?

Now let's ask another question: If John Smith says that he answers prayers when in fact he can't, does it mean that John is imaginary? No—of course not. It is easily proven that John is very real despite the fact that John might lie about his ability to answer prayers. John is a living and breathing human being. John has a body that you can touch, a voice you can hear on the telephone, photos and videos that you can see on the Internet. John has parents and a birth certificate. John might own a house, and if so its ownership is a matter of public record. John's fingerprints are probably on file. John pays taxes. If subpoenaed, John will appear in court, and if he doesn't appear, he will likely need to appear in jail. Clearly John exists. He is simply lying about his ability to answer prayers.

But what about God? Given that God doesn't answer prayers, does that mean that God is imaginary? Here the situation is different.

God, unlike you and me, is a hypothetical being. This hypothetical being is said to be invisible, silent, and undetectable by any scientific means. As a result, there is no tangible, measurable evidence indicating that God exists. God therefore has all of the hallmarks of an imaginary being. Lacking any evidence, the default position of any critical thinker is to assume that God is in fact imaginary.

The only thing that we have to define this invisible, silent, undetectable, hypothetical God-being is the Bible. The Southern Baptist Convention (SBC) defines the Bible in its Statement of Faith. According to the SBC, in the Bible God the author reveals Himself to humankind. God also provides His perfect instruction manual. The Bible, contains the truth without any errors, meaning that the Bible is completely trustworthy. When God judges us, He will use the principles laid out in the Bible for His judgment. The Bible is the sole place to go for definitive information about the Christian God. The Bible, according to Christians, is divinely inspired by God and is nothing but the truth.

For the majority of Christians in the United States, the Bible is literally true and without error. The Bible also contains direct quotes from Jesus, who is, supposedly, God incarnated on Earth.

The Bible contains many positive claims about God. It therefore provides a definition of who God is and what He can do, as revealed by the hypothetical God Himself. In Chapter 4, this definition of God has been condensed down to twelve attributes, all of which are supported by the Bible and have widespread acceptance in Christian doctrine across the spectrum of Christian denominations.

Therefore, if this invisible, immaterial, silent, hypothetical God is real, He needs to match His revealed definition. And this God-being has revealed, in no uncertain terms, that He answers prayers. Christians by the millions pray to God. Every Sunday, churches all across America are filled with millions of Christians saying prayers.

An unbiased critical thinker reaches a simple conclusion on prayer, based on the overwhelming evidence available: prayers of intercession do not work as described in the Bible. The belief in prayer is a common superstition that crosses many cultures. Based on this conclusion, what can a critical thinker conclude about a being who is defined, in part, by His ability to answer prayers? A critical thinker sees that the ineffectiveness of prayer is a powerful piece of evidence indicating that the hypothetical God-being described in the Bible is imaginary. But the conclusion goes further than that. We are actually eliminating three important attributes in the definition of God when we demonstrate that prayer has no effect in the real world:

- God does not answer prayers, even though the Bible and God's followers claim that He does.
- The failure to answer prayers makes God a liar because His statements in the Bible about prayer are categorically untrue.
- Since God is a liar, He cannot be perfect.

By proving that the belief in prayer is a superstition, we have eliminated three of the pillars supporting the God hypothesis from Chapter 4. What can we conclude from this? With God there are two possibilities:

- God might be real, and if so He needs to match His definition in the Bible.
- Alternatively, God, like all of the other gods that human beings have imagined over thousands of years, is a mythological being.

By demonstrating that God does not answer prayers, a major part of God's definition is proven false.

A critical thinker comes to the conclusion that the hypothetical God concept portrayed in the Bible now has a serious problem. We have knocked down three of the twelve pillars that define God, as discussed in Chapter 4. These happen to be three very important pillars, so already it's possible to understand that God is imaginary.

What happens when we look at the nine remaining pillars? If we are able to knock them down as easily, then it will be clear that God is imaginary.

Here's another way to approach this conclusion. Imagine an unbiased critical thinker standing on the street. A Christian approaches and states, "God exists. God is real." The critical thinker would reply, "Great—please introduce me to God. Where is He?"

The Christian would say, "I cannot introduce you to Him—God is invisible, silent, and undetectable by any scientific means."

A critical thinker would reply, "What you are describing is an imaginary being. Imaginary beings are invisible, silent, and undetectable by any scientific means. How do you know that this God-being is real?"

The Christian answers, "Here, read this book called the Bible—it will tell you everything about God. God reveals himself to mankind in the Bible."

A critical thinker would read the Bible and compile a list of attributes for this hypothetical being called God based on His description of Himself in the Bible. The Bible clearly states that God is perfect, God never lies, and God answers prayers. However, it's easy to prove that God does not answer prayers, meaning that the God defined in the Bible is lying and thus cannot be perfect. Therefore, for any critical thinker who looks at the evidence without bias, the God of the Bible is imaginary.

Some people at this point might proclaim that God does not need to answer prayers at all, and He still exists in a form that happens to ignore prayers. This argument is easily refuted by reading the Bible and thinking critically. The God defined by the Bible answers prayers. A person who wants to claim that God exists but does not answer prayers is inventing an entirely new god-concept that stands completely separate from the God of the Bible.

If the desire is to imagine a new god-concept who is defined as a being who does not answer prayers, this new being is imaginary until it is named uniquely, defined clearly, and provided with evidence proving that it exists. A person who goes around redefining God on a whim is a person who is inventing imaginary beings. There's no reason to take a person like this seriously—he is making things up out of thin air without any evidence at all to support his claims.

11:

HOW DO WE KNOW THAT
SANTA CLAUS IS IMAGINARY?

IN THE PRECEDING CHAPTERS OF THIS BOOK, WE DISCOVERED SOMETHING IMPORTANT: IF POSITIVE CLAIMS ARE MADE, IT'S POSSIBLE TO PROVE WHETHER THOSE CLAIMS ARE REAL OR IMAGINARY. So if a drug company claims that a new drug relieves pain, that claimed relief either happens or it does not. If the drug does in fact relieve pain for people in a valid double-blind test, then the claimed effect is real. If not, then the claimed effect is imaginary.

This process is actually quite useful to people whose goal is to understand the nature of the real world in which we all live. It makes it possible for us to decide what's true and what's false. It helps us understand how reality works.

Here's an example that you may have experienced yourself. Many children in the United States believe in Santa Claus. They start hearing about Santa as soon as they can understand language. Their parents talk about Santa as though he is real. They see Santa on television and at the mall. There are songs about Santa, Santa posters put up at school, Santa books, Santa decorations, Santa parades…it really is quite remarkable if you think about it.

But as they make their way toward adulthood, the vast majority of these children come to the solid, unshakable conclusion that Santa Claus is imaginary. They do not say to themselves, "Santa Claus might be real or he might be imaginary—I am not really sure." They say, "I know for certain that Santa Claus is imaginary."

How do competent adults come to the conclusion, with complete certainty, that Santa Claus is imaginary? It's because many of the claims made for Santa Claus do not hold up to scrutiny. Here are several examples:

- The Claim is made that Santa has a workshop at the North Pole. Yet we can visit the North Pole and demonstrate that there is no workshop.
- The Claim is made that Santa delivers toys to all of the good girls and boys. We can look at the real world and see that it's actually parents who buy toys for their children. If Santa did it, then we would expect to see logical side effects of his actions. For example, poor children would get the same number and kinds of toys as rich children. That clearly is not the case on Christmas day in the real world.
- The Claim is made that Santa comes down the chimney and delivers the toys. An industrious child can stay up all night, hide so that he is not discovered, and see that nothing of the sort happens. It's even easier for children whose homes lack fireplaces with chimneys.
- The Claim is made that flying reindeer power Santa's sleigh. A child can come to the rational understanding that flying reindeer and Santa's sleigh are impossible. There's no such thing as a flying reindeer, and no plausible reason that there will ever be one—no reindeer in its natural state (i.e. without the assistance of wings or technology) can or will fly through the air in a Superman-like way.
- The Claim is made that the sleigh carries all the toys. A sleigh that can hold all the toys received by boys and girls around the world would be gigantic—much larger than an aircraft carrier. Therefore it could not alight on a rooftop.
- The Claim is made that Santa visits all of his chosen households in one night. Even if we assume Santa only delivers presents to 100 million households in the

United States and he spends just one second at each household, the total is 100 million seconds; 100 million seconds translates into three years' time.

An adult can look at all of these facts, process them intelligently, and come to a simple, obvious conclusion about the reality of Santa: Santa is imaginary.

In other words, thoughtful people look at the positive claims made about Santa Claus. They gather evidence that either supports or disputes those claims. From the evidence they gather, they can draw sound conclusions. In the case of Santa Claus, we can conclusively understand that he is imaginary because none of the claims about him hold up to scrutiny.

What if an adult friend were to visit you one day and tell you that he thinks Santa is real? What would we think of an adult who harbors this belief? You might question your friend, ask for his reasoning, ask for evidence. No valid evidence would come forward, of course, and none of his reasoning would make sense. So you would come to the conclusion that your friend is delusional, or worse. It would be roughly akin to an adult telling you about his firm belief that Earth is flat. You might not be sure what to do with such a person, because there is so much evidence to the contrary. The fact is that nothing a friend says will convince you that Earth is flat, or that Santa is real—we know with certainty that Earth is a sphere and that Santa is imaginary, based on an abundance of evidence.

We can apply that same intellectual process to God, and have done so in the previous chapters around the claim that God answers prayers. We have certainty that the belief in prayer is a superstition based on a mountain of evidence indicating this fact.

It is easy to understand why people who lack critical thinking skills might fall prey to the illusion that God answers prayers. In the preceding chapters we identified a number of fallacies and problems in thinking that create the illusion. Critical thinkers study and understand the illusion—they are able to see why the fallacies are fallacies— and thus they see reality clearly. God does not "answer prayers." And since God is defined as a prayer-answering being in the Bible, this gives us a strong signal that God is imaginary.

A good question to ask here might be, "How do human beings know anything with certainty?" How do we separate knowledge from belief? How do we determine a level of certainty? How do we know with certainty, for example, that aspirin relieves many types of pain? How do we know with certainty that Santa is imaginary? How do we know with certainty that Earth is not flat? How do we know with certainty that the belief in prayer is a superstition? What we have discovered in the previous chapters is that there are a number of techniques that people use. First we assert something. Then we design valid experiments and gather valid data from them to examine our assertions and see if they hold up or not. To create certainty, we perform many different kinds of experiments, gather lots of data, and create an interlocking web of evidence that all points to the same conclusion.

Therefore, if the assertion is, "This drug relieves pain," we can perform valid double-blind clinical trials that prove or disprove the assertion, and from those experiments we can know with certainty whether or not the drug works. If the assertion is, "Santa as defined by a set of attributes is real," we can gather voluminous evidence disproving the assertion and know with certainty that Santa is imaginary. If the assertion is, "God answers prayers of intercession," we can design any number of valid experiments to test this assertion, just like we can in drug testing. The evidence from all of these experiments points to the same conclusion: The belief in prayer is strictly and clearly a superstition.

The ability to answer prayers is just one of the attributes of God. As seen in Chapter 4, there are a number of others. Can these other attributes of God be dismantled as easily? In the next chapter, we will look at the Bible and see how it holds up to scrutiny.

12:

WHAT IS ABSURDITY, AND WHAT IS A MYTH?

> I'm a superhuman being. I have supernatural powers that allow
> me to do things no other human being can do. Today I flew to the
> sun just like Superman would. I dove down into the sun's core and
> pulled out this handful of material. What I hold in my hand literally
> came from the core of the sun today.

In his hand he is holding something that looks like a black rock.

What this person is proposing sounds absurd on many different
levels, doesn't it? As critical thinkers, we know that there is no evidence
that any human can fly like Superman. Similarly, no human can survive
unprotected in the vacuum of space. The distance to the sun is 93 million miles, and it would take many months to get there in a traditional
spacecraft; traveling there in a day is impossible unless an amazing new
technology has been invented. And then there's the searing heat of the
sun itself. No human could possibly plunge into the sun and reach its core
without some startlingly clever equipment that has never been demonstrated. This story of the trip to the sun is not just unlikely, it's absurd.

The easiest thing to do in a situation like this is to declare the
obvious: "Your story is completely absurd. You're lying."

The reason why this is easy to do is because the story contains all
of the elements of absurdity. Think of every fairy tale, every myth that

you have heard. One common denominator of these stories is that they contain story elements that are impossible and ridiculous.

- In "Jack and the Beanstalk," Jack plants a seed that generates a gigantic beanstalk overnight. Jack climbs it and then finds himself able to walk on the clouds, where he discovers a giant and his castle. The beanstalk, the solid clouds, and the cloud-dwelling giant are all absurd.
- Santa has a magical sleigh that is powered by flying reindeer. One of those reindeer has a glowing red nose whose light is able to penetrate fog. The sleigh, the flying reindeer, and the red nose are all absurd.
- Superman is able to fly up in the sky simply by thinking about it, and is able to do things like reverse time and move planets. All of the superhuman feats of Superman are absurd.

We can easily call these things absurd because they each match the dictionary definition of the word **absurd**:

> Utterly or obviously senseless, illogical, or untrue; contrary to all reason or common sense; laughably foolish or false.

But what if the storyteller who claims that he has flown to the center of the sun insists that he is telling the truth? How might a critical thinker approach such a situation? A critical thinker is open-minded. If evidence can be produced—for example, that our sun diver can actually fly like Superman—then that would change things quite a bit. Therefore, the key thing that a critical thinker would request is evidence.

So a critical thinker might ask, "Could you please fly up into the sky right now like Superman would?" That seems like a simple and reasonable request. If the storyteller claims to have flown to the sun like Superman, then the storyteller should be able to fly twenty feet up into the air right now. This seems obvious and trivial, so the request is made. The person replies that he can fly like Superman because he has supernatural powers, but only when it is his will to do so, and it is not his will to fly right now.

"Well then," you might ask, "Can you hold your breath for three hours for me?" If the storyteller is able to fly in the vacuum of space, he must be able to survive there without breathing, so this is a reasonable request. But the person states that he cannot, and asks why the ability to hold his breath is important. "Because you cannot breathe in the vacuum of space, nor in the body of the sun, so you need to be able to survive without breathing. Holding your breath for a couple of hours should be easy," you might say. The person claims that air is not needed to breathe in space. "Well, then why don't you demonstrate that by holding your breath?" you might ask. You are told that it only works in space.

This sort of questioning might go back and forth for several minutes. In each case, the question is deflected or the answer yields no evidence.

"May I please have your rock then, so that I may test it?" The storyteller's answer is no. "Why not?" He explains that the rock is very valuable, coming from the sun's core and all. "I'll give it back to you when the testing is finished, or why can't you just fly up and get another one?" you ask. The person explains that he does not want to waste his time traveling to the sun again.

What would you, as a critical thinker, conclude after this conversation? You would reasonably conclude that the person is lying about the origin of the rock and the trip into the sun. Perhaps you might further conclude that our storyteller is suffering from deep delusions, possibly some form of mental illness or insanity. You would conclude that none of his claims about his trip to the sun are true, since he has no evidence to support any of them. Things such as flying like Superman and surviving the heat of the sun are known to be impossible unless evidence to the contrary can be produced.

The key thing to note is that absurdity is recognizable, and it can be labeled as such. If a person claims to be able to do things that are currently known to be impossible (e.g. flying like Superman), or describes an event that is currently known to be impossible (e.g. retrieving material from the core of the sun by diving into the sun unprotected) then the claims are absurd unless there is solid evidence to prove their veracity. There's no reason for an intelligent person to accept absurdity.

WHAT ABOUT MYTHOLOGY?

Myths are a common feature of many human cultures. They are fanciful stories that primitive people often use to entertain or to explain things that they can't understand. The dictionary defines the word **myth** as:

> A traditional or legendary story, usually concerning some being or hero or event, with or without a determinable basis of fact or a natural explanation, especially one that is concerned with deities or demigods and explains some practice, rite, or phenomenon of nature.

Many of the stories from Greek mythology are still told today. Here is one myth that Greeks used to explain the coming of winter every year.

> Demeter is the goddess of the harvest, giving her power over the fertility of the earth. She had a daughter named Persephone, fathered by Zeus, the king of the gods. But Hades, the god of the underworld, kidnapped Persephone and took her to live with him. Demeter could not find her daughter and, distraught, failed in her role as goddess of the harvest. The earth suffered a terrible famine. When Persephone was finally found and returned, there was much rejoicing. But there was also a problem—Persephone had eaten from a pomegranate, the food of the underworld. Therefore she was forced to return to the underworld each year. Persephone's time in the underworld causes Demeter to enter a period of mourning, which we see on earth as winter. When Persephone returns, Demeter's joy is the cause of spring.

Does this mythical story explain why winter comes each year? No. How do critical thinkers know this? First, critical thinkers—in fact most people today—understand that Demeter, Zeus, Hades, Persephone, and the underworld are all imaginary. Like Santa Claus, there is no evidence that they exist and plenty of evidence that they do not. There is no goddess of the harvest who causes famines on Earth with her distress and mourning. Pomegranates do not force anyone to do anything, and they especially do not compel imaginary goddesses like Persephone to return to an imaginary underworld. All of these facts make it apparent that the Greek explanation of winter is a myth.

Today we understand winter scientifically instead of using myths. We understand that winter comes each year because of the inclination of Earth's rotational axis with respect to its orbital plane around the sun. This is the valid scientific explanation for the phenomenon called winter, supported by many different types of evidence. The inclination of Earth's axis has several easily observed side effects besides winter. For example, the inclination is the reason why the North Pole and South Pole will have periods each year where there are twenty-four hours of daylight or twenty-four hours of darkness (unlike equatorial locations, which have a very even and nearly equal amount of daylight and darkness throughout the year).

With this knowledge about the inclination of Earth's axis, we can make predictions. If we understand that winter results from axial inclination, we would predict that winter in the Northern Hemisphere should correspond to summer in the Southern Hemisphere, and vice versa. And this is in fact the case. When it's winter in the United States, which is in the Northern Hemisphere, it's summer in Australia, which is in the Southern Hemisphere.

Myths fall into the same category as the story of the sun diver in the previous section. Myths are absurd stories, and are easily called out as such. We know they're absurd first because of their fanciful, ridiculous story elements (e.g. mention of a fictional underworld that doesn't exist, constant mention of imaginary supernatural beings, magic, the suspension of the normal laws of nature, talking animals, etc.). More importantly, myths usually conflict with reality. For example, if Demeter's mourning actually caused winter, we would expect winter to occur at the same time in the Northern and Southern Hemispheres. We know this is not the case, and therefore the myth contradicts reality. In addition, the lack of any evidence to support the mythical stories tells us that myths are fictional.

TESTING THE BIBLE FOR ABSURDITY

Given this context of absurdity and myth, have you ever taken the time to think about the story that the Bible tells about God? Have you taken the time to understand what the Bible must mean? If the Bible is to be believed, God Himself—an all-knowing, omnipotent being—wrote this book about Himself. Billions of Christians believe this. The Statement of Faith for the Southern Baptist Convention (SBC) provides a description of the Bible that is believed by tens of millions of Baptists and is representative of Christian dogma in general. The SBC's Statement of Faith states that, in the Bible, God the author reveals Himself to humankind. God also provides His perfect instruction manual. The Bible contains the truth without any errors, meaning that the Bible is completely trustworthy. Similarly, the Catholic Encyclopedia explains that for Catholics, the Bible is the word of God. Specifically, God's authorship of the Bible means that it is inerrant and infallibly true.

Christians believe that: 1) The Bible is God's word, and as such, that 2) the Bible is inerrant and true. This is the case on both the Catholic and Protestant sides of the aisle. And the Catholic and Baptist churches together represent more than a billion people.

A critical thinker therefore asks the obvious question about the Bible: Did an omniscient God author the Bible, or is the Bible another book of myths, just like the myths from so many other human cultures? The way a critical thinker would determine if the Bible is a myth is by examining the story and looking for the markers of myth: absurdity, contradictions, incompatibilities with reality, lack of evidence, and so on. Let's take a few moments to review the story told in the Bible's book of Genesis and see how it stacks up. Is it believable as the product of an omniscient mind, or is it believable as a run-of-the-mill myth created in a prescientific culture?

CHAPTER ONE OF GENESIS

The story in Genesis begins with God creating the universe. The first line in the Bible says, "In the beginning, God created the heavens and the earth." This seems simple enough, and it's quite familiar since we've all heard this line a thousand times. But take a moment to think about it: What is the story of Genesis proposing in this opening sentence? And what is a critical thinker to make of this proposal?

The first thing a critical thinker would note is that this first line is inaccurate. Earth and the universe were not created simultaneously. All available evidence indicates that the universe came to exist in one event approximately 13.7 billion years ago, and then, approximately 9.2 billion years later, the planet Earth formed through an entirely different mechanism. This inaccuracy in the first line of Genesis seems odd given that the author is supposed to be an all-knowing, perfect being who would have access to the same data that scientists have used when determining the age of the universe and Earth.

A critical thinker also notes that there's no explanation given for how God might have performed His creative act, or where God Himself came from. Plot holes like these are standard features of myth. These omissions and discrepancies give this very first sentence of Genesis all the hallmarks of a primitive myth.

A critical thinker would also note a contradiction in the first line. Elsewhere in the Bible, God is defined as perfect and omniscient. Therefore, here is a question that a critical thinker would ask: Why would a perfect, omniscient being need to create a universe in the first place? The dictionary defines the word **perfect** in this way:

1. Conforming absolutely to the description or definition of an ideal type.
2. Excellent or complete beyond practical or theoretical improvement.

A perfect being is perfect—he needs nothing more, nor anything less. Perfection is also defined as "being entirely without fault or defect" and "lacking in no essential detail, complete." If God is complete and without fault, what purpose does a universe serve? Especially a universe that is imperfect—our Earth is certainly a great depository of imperfection. This fundamental contradiction gives a critical thinker another reason to mark Genesis as myth. The problem is exacerbated by the definition of omniscient. An **omniscient** being is defined as:

1. Having infinite awareness, understanding, and insight.
2. Possessed of universal or complete knowledge.

Therefore, an omniscient being will know exactly what will happen upon creating his universe. So why bother? For an omniscient and perfect being, there is no reason to create a universe.

If you think about it a bit further as a critical thinker, you realize that the whole idea of creating planet Earth is odd for an omniscient being. The time that humans spend on Earth is an exercise in suffering for the majority of people on the planet. Miscarriages, infant mortality, the death of children and adults across the globe through disease, starvation, thirst, natural disaster, accident, war, terrorism, rape, parasites, suicide and murder...Life on Earth is fraught with agony and suffering for a great many of its inhabitants. More than two billion people on Earth today eke out a very meager existence on less than two dollars per day.

Why would an omniscient God create a universe that He knew would be a place of suffering for so many? Why not create people and place them directly into heaven, since according to Christians heaven exists and heaven is perfect? It would eliminate the massive suffering found on Earth—something an omnibenevolent, perfect being would strive to avoid. This is another contradiction that a critical thinker immediately identifies, and it makes the story told in Genesis seem silly and mythological from the very first line. A perfect, omniscient, omnibenevolent being would not create an imperfect place that he knows will be filled with suffering—He violates His own definition to do so. The evidence for myth soars.

For all of these reasons, critical thinkers must ask the logical and obvious question: Is it likely that an omniscient, perfect being with perfect access to all scientific knowledge would author an opening sentence like this for the book of Genesis? Or is it more likely that a regular human being living thousands of years ago, with no access to any scientific knowledge whatsoever and no access to omniscience, would write this sentence?

In critical thinking there is a trend toward simplicity known as **Occam's razor**, a.k.a. the principle of parsimony. The idea is that if we are presented with two different explanations for a phenomenon, with one explanation being simple and understandable and the other requiring great leaps of logic, a long series of rationalizations, or lengthy, convoluted explanations of why it could be true, then the simple explanation is preferred. In the case of the first line of Genesis, there is every reason to believe that it was written as the beginning of a run-of-the-mill myth authored by members of a prescientific culture. The line's inaccuracy, its conflict with reality/science, and its contradictory elements all point in that direction. That sort of authorship has been repeated hundreds of times over thousands of years in dozens of human cultures, so it's the default explanation as well. Myths are a standard part of the human experience. There is no evidence at all to indicate that an omniscient supernatural being stepped in to write this sentence, so critical thinkers discard that explanation.

We gather all of this evidence of myth within the first sentence of Genesis. But let's ignore our initial impression and proceed. The next five verses of Genesis are:

> And the earth was without form, and void; and darkness was upon the face of the deep. And the Spirit of God moved upon the face of the waters. And God said, Let there be light: and there was light. And God saw the light, that it was good: and God divided the light from the darkness. And God called the light Day, and the darkness he called Night. And the evening and the morning were the first day.

Again we ask a simple question: Does this section indicate to us that the Bible was written by an omniscient supernatural being, or by a normal human being writing another myth for a prescientific society? It's very difficult for a scientifically literate person to fathom this section. If you understand how the solar system works, you know that daylight comes from a source of light that we call the sun (which is not yet mentioned), and the sun is always on. Night on Earth happens because the Earth rotates and blocks the sun on the dark side of the planet. None of this information, which would be readily available to an all-knowing being, is mentioned. Again, this is the sort of ignorant explanation that we would expect from a person who is scientifically illiterate and creating a myth, not from an omniscient being.

Here are the next few verses of Genesis:

> And God said, Let there be a firmament in the midst of the
> waters, and let it divide the waters from the waters. And God made
> the firmament, and divided the waters which were under the firma-
> ment from the waters which were above the firmament: and it was
> so. And God called the firmament Heaven. And the evening and the
> morning were the second day.

Does this section indicate to us that the Bible was written by an omniscient supernatural being, or by regular people writing another myth for a prescientific society? A critical thinker, in looking at this section, reaches a conclusion very quickly. If the author of the Bible were to have no knowledge of the atmosphere or the phenomena called "Rayleigh scattering" that causes the sky to turn blue in the presence of the intense light of the sun—in other words, if the author were scientifically illiterate—then perhaps the author might guess that the blue of the sky is caused by an elevated lake of water that has somehow been physically separated from the ground by a "firmament" (also described as a "vault" in some translations), or something very strange like that. But this is nonsense from a scientific standpoint. There is no lake in the sky, nor any sort of firmament or vault. The air of Earth's atmosphere is a layer of gas covering the planet, held there by gravity, that blends gradually into the vacuum of space. When sunlight hits this gaseous layer, Rayleigh scattering creates the blue color that we see in the sky during daytime. A person living in a prescientific culture wouldn't know that, while an omniscient being would. More myth, and certifiably so, because this part of Genesis is so absurd.

Genesis continues:

> And God said, Let the waters under the heaven be gathered
> together unto one place, and let the dry land appear: and it was so.

And God called the dry land Earth; and the gathering together of the waters called he Seas: and God saw that it was good. And God said, Let the earth bring forth grass, the herb yielding seed, and the fruit tree yielding fruit after his kind, whose seed is in itself, upon the earth: and it was so. And the earth brought forth grass, and herb yielding seed after his kind, and the tree yielding fruit, whose seed was in itself, after his kind: and God saw that it was good. And the evening and the morning were the third day.

Is the author of the Bible a human being who has no access to any scientific knowledge whatsoever, or an omniscient being who knows everything? There is not an omniscient being anywhere in this picture. As we might expect, the scientifically illiterate author of the Bible has no knowledge of single-celled creatures, nor any knowledge of the arthropods and fish species that proceeded plants in the timeline of life on Earth. In the Genesis story, land plants appear first, contrary to the reality of life's actual progression in Earth's history. In addition, these plants appear before the creation of the sun, which we discover as we continue reading:

And God said, Let there be lights in the firmament of the heaven to divide the day from the night; and let them be for signs, and for seasons, and for days, and years: And let them be for lights in the firmament of the heaven to give light upon the earth: and it was so. And God made two great lights; the greater light to rule the day, and the lesser light to rule the night: he made the stars also. And God set them in the firmament of the heaven to give light upon the earth, And to rule over the day and over the night, and to divide the light from the darkness: and God saw that it was good. And the evening and the morning were the fourth day.

People in a prescientific culture might be expected to see both sun and moon as "lights," but a knowledgeable person knows that the moon is not a light at all. It is a sphere that reflects sunlight, rather than a sun-like object that produces light. A scientifically literate person also knows that these bodies do not "govern the day and the night"—the rotation of the earth along with the orbits of the earth and moon do. Also strangely absent is any knowledge that the sun itself is a star. Or the fact that many of the stars and galaxies we see in the sky existed long before Earth coalesced from orbiting supernova debris. Or the fact that there is no firmament to hold the sun, moon, and stars. Genesis bears no resemblance at all to reality.

Note that this ignorant, prescientific notion of a firmament filled with stars persists throughout the Bible. In Mark 13:25, Jesus talks about the stars falling from the sky, and in the book of Revelation the stars fall from the sky onto earth "even as a fig tree casteth her untimely figs, when she is shaken of a mighty wind" (Revelation 6:13). If you think that the stars are small objects attached to a vault in the sky, and if you have no idea what a star really is, you might believe that stars could fall to Earth like figs. But the reality is that the stars we see in the sky are located many light-years away. They are thousands of times larger than Earth. Real stars cannot possibly fall to Earth. Why is the Bible so divergent from reality? The myths in the Bible have no basis in reality because the people writing the myths had no scientific knowledge, nor any access to omniscience.

The Genesis story continues:

> And God said, Let the waters bring forth abundantly the moving creature that hath life, and fowl that may fly above the earth in the open firmament of heaven. And God created great whales, and every living creature that moveth, which the waters brought forth abundantly, after their kind, and every winged fowl after his kind: and God saw that it was good. And God blessed them, saying, Be fruitful, and multiply, and fill the waters in the seas, and let fowl multiply in the earth. And the evening and the morning were the fifth day. And God said, Let the earth bring forth the living creature after his kind, cattle, and creeping thing, and beast of the earth after his kind: and it was so. And God made the beast of the earth after his kind, and cattle after their kind, and every thing that creepeth upon the earth after his kind: and God saw that it was good.

Here again the author of the Bible remains unaware of the actual chronology of life's advancement on Earth according to millions of discoveries in the fossil record. Arthropods and fish came first, then plants, then reptiles, dinosaurs, and early mammals, followed by birds as we know them today. All of these species developed over millions of years, with countless species arising and going extinct. The author of Genesis knows none of this.

If this story in Genesis were true, and all animals were created on a single day in recent history, then the genetic and fossil record would reflect that. There would not be hundreds of millions of years worth of fossils, all carefully laid out with millions of extinct species in countless layers of earth strata.

And then, in the afternoon of the sixth day, man and woman appear in Genesis:

> And God said, Let us make man in our image, after our likeness: and let them have dominion over the fish of the sea, and over the fowl of the air, and over the cattle, and over all the earth, and over every creeping thing that creepeth upon the earth. So God created man in his own image, in the image of God created he him; male and female created he them. And God blessed them, and God said unto them, Be fruitful, and multiply, and replenish the earth, and subdue it: and have dominion over the fish of the sea, and over the fowl of the air, and over every living thing that moveth upon the earth. And God said, Behold, I have given you every herb bearing seed, which is upon the face of all the earth, and every tree, in the which is the fruit of a tree yielding seed; to you it shall be for meat. And to every beast of the earth, and to every fowl of the air, and to every thing that creepeth upon the earth, wherein there is life, I have given every green herb for meat: and it was so. And God saw every thing that he had made, and, behold, it was very good. And the evening and the morning were the sixth day.

If this were the way man and woman actually arose, there would be plenty of scientific evidence to confirm it. But this sudden instantaneous appearance of a single male and female has no correlation with reality whatsoever. There is no evidence to support the story of human origin told in Genesis, and a plethora of evidence (in the fossil record, in archaeological digs, in human DNA, etc.) to disprove it. Therefore there's plenty of evidence again demonstrating this story in Genesis to be a myth.

So ends Chapter 1 of the book of Genesis. All of this happens in six days in the Bible, and according to Biblical scholars like James Ussher and millions of Young Earth Creationists and Bible literalists across the United States, it happened just a few thousand years ago.

In Genesis there is no knowledge of the billions of years of the universe's actual existence. No mention of the millions of species that came and then went extinct over the course of time. No knowledge of the actual chronology of events as indicated by voluminous evidence in nature. No knowledge of astronomy or cosmology, nor of single-cell organisms invisible to the unaided human eye. To an intelligent, scientifically literate person living in modern society, the Genesis story of creation is like every other creation myth, nothing but a fanciful story filled with errors and contradiction.

The Genesis account fits the definition of a myth perfectly. Therefore it's clear to unbiased observers that the book of Genesis is a myth invented by a person or a group of people living in a prescientific society. Simply read Genesis as a thoughtful, knowledgeable, unbiased person would and you know that this is true. By comparing the Genesis story to scientific understanding available today, the dissonance with reality is unmistakable. There is no evidence that an omniscient being had anything to do with what we read in Chapter 1 of Genesis. There is extensive evidence that Genesis is the product of a prescientific culture, like so many other myths. Any thoughtful person reaches this conclusion immediately upon reading Chapter 1 of Genesis, and the process starts with the problems seen in the very first line of the story.

There is one other thing a critical thinker would notice about the Bible: The book is written by men. If God can create the heavens and the earth, the sun and the moon and the stars, all the plants and animals, etc., why can't God write a perfect book Himself? Why not magically bring the book instantly into existence like everything else He supposedly created, rather than "inspiring" human beings to do it? According to the myths in the Bible, God can do anything He wants through His omnipotence. If God can create a universe, God can write a Bible Himself. The fact that the Bible is written by men provides more evidence that it's a book of myth. We will explore this line of thinking further in Chapter 15.

CHAPTER TWO OF GENESIS

The strange thing is, the more you read, the more bizarre Genesis becomes. We see the first example of this trend as we turn to the beginning of Genesis Chapter 2 and find this verse:

> These are the generations of the heavens and of the earth when they were created, in the day that the Lord God made the earth and the heavens.

Isn't that what Chapter 1 was? Yet here we begin a new account:

> And every plant of the field before it was in the earth, and every herb of the field before it grew: for the Lord God had not caused it to rain upon the earth, and there was not a man to till the ground. But there went up a mist from the earth, and watered the whole face of the ground. And the Lord God formed man of the dust of the ground, and breathed into his nostrils the breath of life; and man became a living soul.

Chapter 2's time line is completely different from Chapter 1's timeline. In Chapter 1, man and woman are created on day six, several days after plants. In Chapter 2 there are no "days" of creation, and humans are described as appearing sometime before plants. Would an omniscient being, if one were to exist, create a contradiction like this and write it in His book? Of course not. But would a group of people living in a primitive society, who are combining a variety of creation myths from the region and making up everything as they go along, create a book with a problem like this? Certainly.

In addition, there is no reference in Genesis to the known evolutionary origins and timeline of humans available in the fossil record. In this second version of the myth, God magically creates a single human being by breathing on some dust. Nothing could be more mythological than that.

Let's ignore all of these obvious problems and take the story at face value. In the context of this myth, since man's creator is a perfect, omniscient being, we must understand that this God-being necessarily created man exactly as He wanted man to be created. And note, in addition, that God programmed this man with a language and an entire body of core knowledge that would be necessary to understand language. This programming would need to be done perfectly. After all, God says to Adam in Genesis 2:15:

> And the Lord God took the man, and put him into the garden
> of Eden to dress it and to keep it. And the Lord God commanded the
> man, saying, Of every tree of the garden thou mayest freely eat: But
> of the tree of the knowledge of good and evil, thou shalt not eat of it:
> for in the day that thou eatest thereof thou shalt surely die.

There is no way for Adam to understand the words God spoke in this myth unless God preprogrammed Adam with the ability to process His language.

Think about how you came to understand language. Human beings learn language from their parents and their neighbors. In this myth, on the other hand, there's only one being available to teach Adam, and this is God. Knowledge is also needed to process language. For example, there is no way to understand the word "tree" without knowledge about trees based on experience. We must understand that God did this language and knowledge programming exactly the way He wanted it, since that is the only way a perfect being could do it.

The admonition in Genesis 2:17 is a bizarre thing to say after stating this in Chapter 1: "Behold, I have given you every herb bearing seed, which is upon the face of all the earth, and every tree, in the which is the fruit of a tree yielding seed; to you it shall be for meat." Why create something that cannot be eaten? Why not leave this tree out of the garden if it is forbidden?

Think about the myths and the classic fairy tales that you have read since childhood. You know how strange these stories can get. They feature things like imaginary talking animals, bizarre characters and scenery, and wild flights of fantasy. How do we know that the tale of "Jack and the Beanstalk" is fictional rather than a representation of reality? Because giant beanstalks do not grow overnight into the sky. Because people cannot build buildings on clouds or walk on them, since clouds are nothing but water vapor. Because there are not giants living in the sky. In the same way, we know how the creation of the universe, our solar system, and life on Earth unfolded based on scientific evidence, and the account in Genesis is nothing like that. For any critical thinker, it is apparent that the Genesis story is as fanciful as the story of "Jack and the Beanstalk." The contradiction of a "forbidden tree" is just one more example of mythology.

In the Genesis myth, the God-being has chosen to leave out the programming for any knowledge of good and evil from Adam and Eve. According to the story, God instead decides to embed that programming in a piece of fruit. This entire proposition—Adam's instantaneous programming with language and knowledge and this omission of the knowledge of good and evil—is telling to anyone who can think critically. It creates another contradiction: For a man to make a value judgment about eating the fruit, he would necessarily need to have the knowledge of good and evil to do it. But the fruit contains the knowledge of good and evil. Therefore, this God-being, who is omniscient and perfect, who could create and program man in any way he likes, has created an impossible situation for the man. This is another piece of absurdity; another marker for myth.

Genesis 2:18 is even more bizarre:

> And the Lord God said, It is not good that the man should be alone; I will make him an help meet for him. And out of the ground the Lord God formed every beast of the field, and every fowl of the air; and brought them unto Adam to see what he would call them:

and whatsoever Adam called every living creature, that was the name thereof. And Adam gave names to all cattle, and to the fowl of the air, and to every beast of the field; but for Adam there was not found an help meet for him.

No suitable helper was found? What is your impression of this God-being at his point? God is supposed to be perfect and omniscient, and He created man, by definition, in a perfect and omniscient manner. Yet God is unable to find a helper for man? God eventually figures this out in Genesis 2:22: "And the rib, which the Lord God had taken from man, made he a woman, and brought her unto the man." The fact that this is a myth is undeniable.

CHAPTER THREE OF GENESIS

A critical thinker ponders the first two chapters of Genesis and there is only one possible conclusion: What we have here is clearly a myth created, like all other myths, by primitive people. In this myth a supernatural being named God—an all-powerful and omniscient being—voluntarily creates the universe, sun, moon, Earth, and every form of life on the planet, including the first man and woman. They all spring into existence instantly, in six days, through magic, with no explanation. In addition, God programs the humans he creates. Adam and Eve are created as sentient beings complete with language, core knowledge, and all of their adult thought processes. All of this is information that a human being normally learns from parents, neighbors, and society. But in the myth of Adam and Eve, there is nobody available but God to do the teaching. Therefore, according to the story, God must do the full programming job at the time of man's creation.

At this point the stage is set. The book has introduced our three main characters, given them a backstory, created a place for events to unfold. It is time for some action. Along comes a talking serpent, and what is its origin? The only possible source of the serpent and its programming is this same God, and the Bible confirms God as the serpent's maker in verse 1.

> Now the serpent was more subtil than any beast of the field
> which the Lord God had made. And he said unto the woman, Yea,
> hath God said, Ye shall not eat of every tree of the garden?

The appearance of this talking serpent authenticates the Bible as a book of mythology. When the talking animals come on stage, we know for certain that we are dealing with myth. Since the god in this myth is perfect, and therefore has created everything just the way he wants it, how would we expect things to unfold here in Genesis Chapter 3? To a critical thinker, the answer is obvious: things will unfold just the way this perfect, omnipotent, omniscient character wants and expects them to unfold.

The serpent, created and programmed by this god, talks to the woman, also created and programmed by the same god. Note that, according to the myth, the woman does not yet know the difference between good and evil, having not yet eaten from the tree of the knowledge of good and evil. So Eve eats the forbidden fruit and shares it with Adam in verses 4-9:

> And the serpent said unto the woman, Ye shall not surely die:
> For God doth know that in the day ye eat thereof, then your eyes
> shall be opened, and ye shall be as gods, knowing good and evil.
> And when the woman saw that the tree was good for food, and that it
> was pleasant to the eyes, and a tree to be desired to make one wise,
> she took of the fruit thereof, and did eat, and gave also unto her
> husband with her; and he did eat. And the eyes of them both were
> opened, and they knew that they were naked; and they sewed fig
> leaves together, and made themselves aprons. And they heard the
> voice of the Lord God walking in the garden in the cool of the day:
> and Adam and his wife hid themselves from the presence of the
> Lord God amongst the trees of the garden. And the Lord God called
> unto Adam, and said unto him, Where art thou?

How can an immaterial god walk in a garden? Why would an omniscient god ask, "Where are you?" How could an omniscient god ever be surprised by anything and need to ever ask any question? A critical thinker sees this turn of the myth for what it is—a contradiction. God isn't omniscient at all. And then what happens? God gets quite upset. God doles out an absurd set of punishments for this situation that He created through His own design. The serpent is sunk, as we see in verses 14-15:

> And the Lord God said unto the serpent, Because thou hast done this, thou art cursed above all cattle, and above every beast of the field; upon thy belly shalt thou go, and dust shalt thou eat all the days of thy life: And I will put enmity between thee and the woman, and between thy seed and her seed; it shall bruise thy head, and thou shalt bruise his heel.

Yet what did the serpent do? He did exactly what God in this myth programmed him to do.

For the lady:

> Unto the woman he said, I will greatly multiply thy sorrow and thy conception; in sorrow thou shalt bring forth children; and thy desire shall be to thy husband, and he shall rule over thee.

If you think about this, Eve is punished with these severe pains and the overbearing husband, and so are all of her daughters. What sort of morality is this? And what, exactly, is Eve guilty of in this myth? She is guilty of behaving in exactly the way God created and programmed her to behave, responding to a serpent that God also perfectly created and programmed. She did so, according to the myth, without any knowledge of good and evil. How could she behave in any way other than the way she behaved?

Adam receives a similarly harsh punishment:

> And unto Adam he said, Because thou hast hearkened unto the voice of thy wife, and hast eaten of the tree, of which I commanded thee, saying, Thou shalt not eat of it: cursed is the ground for thy

sake; in sorrow shalt thou eat of it all the days of thy life; Thorns also and thistles shall it bring forth to thee; and thou shalt eat the herb of the field; In the sweat of thy face shalt thou eat bread, till thou return unto the ground; for out of it wast thou taken: for dust thou art, and unto dust shalt thou return.

Adam and Eve are then banished:

Unto Adam also and to his wife did the Lord God make coats of skins, and clothed them. And the Lord God said, Behold, the man is become as one of us, to know good and evil; and now, lest he put forth his hand, and take also of the tree of life, and eat, and live for ever. Therefore the Lord God sent him forth from the garden of Eden, to till the ground from whence he was taken.

The whole story is so silly—it's like a terrible morality play. If God did not want Adam and Eve eating these fruits, why create them in the first place?

What we have here is certainly a myth, and a pretty crazy one as myths go. Absurdity and inanity stack up on top of one another to a ridiculous degree. What we find in the book of Genesis fits the definition of myth perfectly.

The story is so silly that Rabbi Marc Gellman of the "God Squad"—a newspaper column and television program in the United States that has existed for decades and reaches millions of people every week—put it this way in his August 10, 2012, column: If believers take the Bible literally, accepting things like talking snakes and the parting of the Red Sea as literal truth, it does not work out well. It makes religious people look irrational and unintelligent.

Critical thinkers understand the difference between myth and reality. The story in Genesis is a myth, as is everything in the Bible. Therefore, if you are a Christian, you arrive at a crossroads. What will you do with a book that is purportedly written by an omnipotent, omniscient being, but instead is obviously and easily identified as a myth created by normal human beings in a prescientific culture? No great leap is required to understand the mythical nature of the Bible—a thoughtful hour or two of reading it makes the origin of the Bible apparent to any critical thinker.

What can we say about the God-being that is presented to us in the Bible? What can we say about the book itself? And what does this reading of the book of Genesis tell us about the attributes of God discussed in Chapter 4 (page 56)? Here are several pillars to examine:

1. God is omniscient
2. God is omnipotent
7. God is perfectly moral
8. God wrote the Bible
9. God created everything as described in the Bible

All of these pillars crumble simply by reading the book of Genesis in the Bible. First, the Bible is clearly a prescientific myth, not the work of an omniscient being. God did not write the Bible. Second, the creation myth told in the Bible does not match reality in any way. There is no correlation between our scientific understanding of the universe and the story told in this myth (pillars 8 and 9).

Clearly God is neither omniscient nor omnipotent. So that takes care of pillars 1 and 2 as well.

We can also eliminate pillar 7 based on the Genesis story. Taking this myth at face value, there is nothing moral about punishing people when: a) they are behaving in exactly the way they were created and programmed to behave, b) they have no knowledge of good and evil, and c) the being who is judging them knew, through His omniscience, exactly what would happen when He created them. The logic in this myth is, "I, God, as an omnipotent, omniscient, perfect being, punish you for behaving in the way I intentionally created you to behave." This is no logic at all. God's behavior is immoral and unethical. So pillar 7 is disproved in this instance as well.

This is why, if you are an intelligent, thoughtful believer, you necessarily stand at a crossroads when you read the Bible, or any holy book for that matter. The Bible is no different from any of the other myths humans have created describing thousands of imaginary beings. The myth itself disproves a number of the pillars in the definition of God. There really is no question at this point that God is imaginary, because the book that describes this being is a book of mythology.

The mythology continues in the New Testament. A virgin is magically inseminated. A magical baby is born. Magical angels appear, along with a magical star. The baby grows up and becomes a man, performing all sorts of magical miracles, none of which leave behind any evidence. The man dies, but then is magically resurrected, magically appears to hundreds of people, complete with wounds, and then magically ascends into the sky. This sounds very much like the story of the sun diver described at the beginning of the chapter, doesn't it? It's absurd at every level. In addition, all of this happens with no corroborating physical evidence, nor anything written down by this Jesus-being himself. And all of the New Testament mythology references back to the Old Testament mythology without any apology, making it one continuous myth.

A person who is unable to think critically, who will continue to argue that God is real, might at this point have several responses:

1. "I believe the Bible is literally true, from beginning to end." This would be similar to a person today declaring that the world is flat or that Santa is real. The person who harbors this belief ignores the wealth of evidence to the contrary. People who are unable to discern between fiction and reality seem broken at some fundamental level, completely detached from rationality.

2. "I understand that everything in the Old Testament is myth, but the New Testament is real. Everything about Jesus is literally true." A critical thinker notes how odd this logic is. If Jesus were to be real, he would be the incarnation of an omniscient god. Therefore, one of his first acts would necessarily be to declare the Old Testament to be a myth in order to set the record straight. Yet Jesus does nothing of the sort in the Bible. He exists within the same mythological framework established

by the Old Testament. One simple example: The gene-
alogy of Jesus in Luke 3:23–38 references Adam, Noah,
and David from the Old Testament. See also Chapter 17.

3. "I understand that the whole Bible is myth, but that's
okay." By arriving at this point, the Christian is admit-
ting that the Bible is no different from any other book of
mythology—that the Bible is a collection of fictional stories featuring imaginary beings. To understand that the
Bible is myth is to declare forthrightly that the God and
Jesus of the Bible are fictional, mythological, imaginary
beings just like Zeus or Ra.

For a critical thinker, this is an uncomfortably odd situation. In
addition to the billions of other religious people who believe in some
form of omniscient god, there are more than two billion Christians
on the planet. Hundreds of millions of these Christians are living in
the United States, and a majority of the adult population in the United
States admit that they are Bible literalists (see Chapter 13).

Yet the Bible is undeniably a book of mythology. It was written by
prescientific men who make assertions that can now be disproved by
scientific fact, just like any other book of mythology. Therefore, the
God-being described in the Bible is mythological. And all mythological
beings are imaginary.

There is one other position a Christian believer might take: the
believer claims to know that the Bible is myth, but still believes
in a god. In other words, the believer invents his own god, cherry-
picking features for this god from a variety of sources. In a critical
framework, any god imagined by a person of this mindset is a new
God-being, completely separate from the mythical Biblical God and
Biblical Jesus. This new God-being truly is imaginary—his aspects
have been arbitrarily determined based on the believer's imagination. If the believer wishes to maintain that his new god is real, then
that god would need to be defined and then proven to be real. There
is no more of a reason to believe in this single believer's god than to
believe in Santa.

What are we to make of this situation? How can billions of people separate themselves from reality ? We will explore the answer to this question in the next chapter.

13:

IF GOD IS IMAGINARY, WHY IS CHRISTIANITY SO COMMON IN THE UNITED STATES?

WHAT WE DISCOVERED IN THE PREVIOUS CHAPTER IS STRAIGHTFORWARD. If we read the Bible as a critical thinker would, it's easy to see that the Bible is a book of mythology. And yet, it's surprising to find that a large majority of adults in America believe that the Bible is literally true. For example, polls such as those performed by ABC News and Rasmussen Reports find that 63 percent of adults in the United States believe that the Bible is literally true. They believe that Noah's ark, the story of Exodus including the parting of the Red Sea, the creation story, Adam and Eve, the talking snake, and so on are absolutely, literally true. Sixty-one percent of American adults—it's an amazing statistic by any measure. In some parts of the United States, such as the deep South, the percentages go even higher. A majority of Americans believe in the literal truth of the Bible.

It's difficult to believe that any thinking person would swallow stories that are unambiguously mythological like this and declare them to be literal truth. Yet it appears that the majority of Americans are doing it. How can this be happening?

One part of the explanation rests on the fascinating way that most Americans acquire their religion. The progression goes something like this:

1. A typical child in America grows up in a deeply religious culture. As we've just seen, a sizable majority of adults in America believe that the Bible is literally true. Even more Americans believe in God and Jesus.

2. Therefore, from day one, the typical American child is hearing about God, Jesus, and the Bible as though they are absolute truths.

3. In many households and public contexts, it is considered unacceptable or rude to question the reality of God or the stories in the Bible.

4. The child also learns a set of things that instill fear. For example, the child learns about hell, God's wrath, God's retribution, etc. The child hears murderous, frightening stories about God involving massive floods, destroyed cities, plagues, and dead babies. Therefore the child is likely to come to the realization that there are big penalties associated with stepping out of line.

5. At the same time, the child learns that there are rewards for adhering to the rules. Eternal life and heaven are the biggest of these rewards, along with reunion with dead loved ones. Answered prayers and God's continued blessings also factor in heavily.

6. The concept of heaven and hell provides some solace in unjust situations. For example, if you are being harmed or oppressed, you can derive hope from the idea that you will be rewarded by heaven while your oppressor will be punished with torture in hell for eternity.

7. There is the huge ego boost and reassurance that comes from the belief that the all-powerful creator of the universe is on your side. If you ignore critical thinking and accept the illusion that God answers prayers, it feels as though this all-powerful entity will listen and respond to some of your requests and whims. In emergency situations, it feels as though God might reach out and help. In sporting events, it feels as though God might be aiding your team. At home or at work, it feels like God is by your side. Many believers take the illusion even further, believing that they have a personal relationship

with this all-powerful being. In their minds, they believe they can speak to and hear responses from an omniscient, all-powerful being. See Chapter 18 for further discussion.

In this way, all of the religious patterns of thought are deeply ingrained in the child's mind long before the age of rationality. The child's worldview becomes wrapped up with the notion of God, the Bible, and Jesus. Some of the child's deepest primal fears, such as the fear of dying and the fear of abandonment, are tied into this mental framework. Lack of critical thinking skills leads to reinforcement of the beliefs. In addition, there are significant social pressures from human tendencies like in-group psychology, tribalism, and belonging that come into play. It's a huge, potent ball of emotional and psychological dependence that binds people to religion.

There are other touch points with religion that can be just as powerful, especially if the person is experiencing it as an adult convert. Although a child's worldview can become deeply interconnected with religious teachings she learned at an early age, the adult who finds his way to religion, often in response to a traumatic event, can also develop a passionate connection to belief. This leads us to the phenomenon of the "born again" Christian. For example, imagine a person who experiences some sort of life trauma. The person prays about it, and things happen to work out well through coincidence, as they often do. This "answered prayer" can create a strong positive bond to religion. There are many life events that might fall into this category:

- The person gets cancer, prays, and coincidentally survives.
- The person gets in a car accident, prays, and coincidentally survives.
- The person's mother/father/brother/sister/spouse/friend gets very sick, prayers are said, and then that person coincidentally survives.
- The person's dog gets hit by a bus, prayers are said, and the dog coincidentally survives.

- The person is in a battlefield situation or gunfight, prays, and coincidentally survives.
- The person hits rock bottom, say with a drug or alcohol addiction, or job loss and homelessness. The person "finds Jesus," and coincidentally emerges from that rock bottom position.
- A college student gets drunk and has promiscuous sex, regrets it, prays, and coincidentally does not get an STD.
- A student forgets to study for a test, prays, and coincidentally happens to pass.
- A person is frightened walking in a bad part of town, prays, and coincidentally does not get mugged.

For a susceptible believer, the coincidental success in situations like these is confirmation that "God loves me" and "prayer works," and it can be quite uplifting. Because the situation was stressful and caused deep concern, the uplift is even more impactful. The effect is that the person now "knows" that God is real and the person is "special in God's eyes." For a susceptible believer, nothing will shake that belief even though it's clear (as seen in previous chapters) it is a coincidence. Through confirmation bias, the delusion is reinforced.

Now the person starts going to church with renewed vigor. She wants more of these "blessings from God."

With all of this programming and illusion deeply entrenched, and with significant social pressures arriving from every angle to follow along with the rest of the crowd, a Christian believer is born. Also keep in mind all of the fallacies and errors in thinking that support, for example, the belief in prayer. These errors and fallacies lend significant support to the notion that God exists, despite the fact that they are errors and fallacies. If someone never gets exposed to critical thinking, the errors and fallacies go unrecognized.

In Chapter 22 we will discuss an additional factor: the special irrationality in the human brain that supports religion. This special irrationality rivets believers to stories and myths in a religion, as though they are true. It adds to the binding effect.

The problem is exacerbated by the huge number of churches in the United States and the subtle or overt pressure on Christians to attend church. There are approximately 350,000 religious congregations in the United States—nearly three times as many churches as there are gas stations. Why so many churches and why the pressure to attend them? These churches exist, in large part, because they provide a way to make money. The Bible suggests that people should give 10 percent as a tithe to the church (Leviticus 27:30–32, Genesis 28:22, Numbers 18:26–29), and many Christians do all or part of that. **Tithe** is defined in the dictionary as:

> The tenth part of agricultural produce or personal income set apart as an offering to God.

Many Christians believe that giving money to the church will appease their God, making it more likely that prayers will be answered and that blessings will be bestowed. In addition there are large factions of the Christian church based in whole or in part on **prosperity theology**, defined by Wikipedia as:

> A Christian religious doctrine that financial blessing is the will of God for Christians, and that faith, positive speech, and donations to Christian ministries will always increase one's material wealth.

The church is a profitable, tax-free business model in the United States. The assets of the Mormon Church, to take one example, are said to be $30 billion, with revenues of $5.9 billion per year. The Catholic Church is said to make $30 billion per year from real estate investments alone.

The church also provides a community, which many people find appealing because humans tend to be social animals. The thought of leaving the church carries with it the pain of losing this community, along with the possibility of being publicly ostracized by former friends.

One of two things happens in adulthood to a Christian who is indoctrinated this thoroughly. Either the adult learns about critical thinking and becomes a critical thinker, for example, in college. Or, more likely, the typical American adult never learns about critical thinking. The majority of Americans never graduate from college. A surprising percentage of American adults never graduate from high school—in America's largest cities, the high school dropout rate can be as high as 40 percent. For these people, the ability to think rationally and critically can be impaired. The Christian indoctrination therefore sticks—in fact, it's likely to increase in strength over time, because it's never questioned. The indoctrination process started with the person's earliest consciousness and it remains throughout life through decades of constant exposure.

For adults who learn to become critical thinkers, there are two choices. The first is to try to be a critical thinker in most parts of life, but to compartmentalize religious topics so that critical thinking in that realm is forbidden. Wikipedia defines **compartmentalization** as:

> An unconscious psychological defense mechanism used to avoid cognitive dissonance, or the mental discomfort and anxiety caused by a person's having conflicting values, cognitions, emotions, beliefs, etc. within themselves. Compartmentalization allows these conflicting ideas to coexist by inhibiting direct or explicit acknowledgment and interaction between separate compartmentalized self states.

Cognitive dissonance is defined as:

> Psychological conflict resulting from incongruous beliefs and attitudes held simultaneously.

The problem a critical thinker faces as a Christian is that applying critical thinking to Christian dogma can create severe cognitive dissonance, and it's painful. To apply critical thinking to the religious compartment, a worldview deeply embedded throughout a lifetime must be shattered. It can be difficult and depressing to shatter because the worldview of Christianity can be very comforting. A Christian may have been praying to God and Jesus for decades, believing that she hears God's voice and has a personal relationship with God, believing that she will live on after death, go to heaven, and be reunited with loved ones, etc.

The progression that a Christian might traverse when applying critical thinking to her religion goes something like this:

1. Read the Bible in an unbiased way, applying critical thinking skills.
2. Realize that the Bible is clearly a book of mythology.
3. Apply critical thinking skills to prayer.
4. Realize that the belief in prayer is a superstition.
5. Analyze other aspects of the religion critically.
6. Understand that God is imaginary.

The problem is that coming to that point can be difficult, even though it's true. There is the embarrassment of having talked to an imaginary friend for decades. For some, the feeling of embarrassment and betrayal is similar to having a beloved spouse admit an affair—it can be that traumatic. There are also tremendous social costs—a non-believer may be ostracized and rejected by religious friends, will likely face expulsion from the religious community she belongs to, and may also face job loss, an inability to run for public office, etc. Then there is the loss of beloved ideas like heaven and reunion in the afterlife. These costs are the reasons for compartmentalization. It can simply be too heart-wrenching and socially difficult for many people in today's American culture to apply critical thinking skills to their Christianity.

For an honest, thoughtful person who wishes to understand the truth of the world we live in, however, the compartment that holds religion must be opened and examined.

14:

IS GOD LOVE?

IMAGINE THIS SCENE IN A LOCAL PRESCHOOL: A YOUNG, INNOCENT CHILD IS PUTTING TOGETHER A SIMPLE PICTURE PUZZLE. The pieces are thick slices of wood, each piece with a little knob so young fingers can easily fit the puzzle together. What is the scene on the puzzle once it is assembled? It is Noah's ark, filled with pairs of happy giraffes, happy elephants, happy zebras, and happy lions. Rain clouds are receding in the background and a bright yellow sun and rainbow appear in the foreground.

Think about what is happening here. If Noah's story were true, it describes the most horrific mass genocide in the history of the world, a story where nearly every living man, woman, and child—millions of people—along with nearly every living animal, is murdered in cold blood. Yet this appalling story is happily told to children as young as toddlers, and told as though it's true. It's one of the most bizarre rituals that an objective, nonreligious observer could imagine, and it happens every day in the United States.

Noah's story is deeply resonant in the United States and the majority of American adults take Noah's story to be literal truth. So most people who relate this story to children believe that it is true and that it actually happened. Go to Amazon.com and type in "Noah's ark" as the search term. There are thousands of products across all departments with a Noah's ark theme. Mass murder is a big topic in the United States.

It turns out that Noah's story is one that conclusively proves the Bible to be a book of myths. But it goes deeper than that—not only is the story an undeniable myth, but it lays bare the true nature of the mythological god portrayed in the Bible. Let's open this compartment and take a look at what's happening.

How do we know that the story of Noah's ark is a myth? We simply read it. This Bible story is filled with absurdity from beginning to end.

Genesis Chapter 5 indicates that 1,556 years pass between the time that the mythical Adam and Eve appear and the time that Noah has three sons named Shem, Ham, and Japheth. And God is not happy at all with the turn of events during those 1,500 years. The Bible says in Genesis 6:5–8:

> And God saw that the wickedness of man was great in the earth, and that every imagination of the thoughts of his heart was only evil continually. And it repented the Lord that he had made man on the earth, and it grieved him at his heart. And the Lord said, I will destroy man whom I have created from the face of the earth; both man, and beast, and the creeping thing, and the fowls of the air; for it repenteth me that I have made them. But Noah found grace in the eyes of the Lord.

In this story, we see another instance of a contradiction first pointed out in our review of Genesis in Chapter 12. We have a perfect, omniscient, all-loving being who is, supposedly, the universe's gold standard for morality and ethics. He has created the world from a blank sheet of paper exactly as he wanted—being omniscient and perfect, this would have to be the case. But He is not at all satisfied with His creation.

How should a perfect, omniscient, all-loving being solve the problem that He Himself has created? Does God create and program humans so they act the way He intends? No. Does God choose to come down to Earth to educate the humans in how they are supposed to behave? No. Does God take any action whatsoever to ethically remediate the planet and people that He has created? No.

Instead, God formulates a plan to enact the most heinous, monstrous, morally repugnant act of all time. God decides to kill nearly every living thing on Earth. Remember that if the Bible were true and God were real, this story is autobiographical. This perfect, omniscient, all-loving being is proposing the homicide of nearly every man, woman, child, and baby on the planet, along with nearly every animal, as we see in verses 11–17:

> The earth also was corrupt before God, and the earth was filled with violence. And God looked upon the earth, and, behold, it was corrupt; for all flesh had corrupted his way upon the earth. And God said unto Noah, The end of all flesh is come before me; for the earth is filled with violence through them; and, behold, I will destroy them with the earth. Make thee an ark of gopher wood; rooms shalt thou make in the ark, and shalt pitch it within and without with pitch. And this is the fashion which thou shalt make it of: The length of the ark shall be three hundred cubits, the breadth of it fifty cubits, and the height of it thirty cubits. A window shalt thou make to the ark, and in a cubit shalt thou finish it above; and the door of the ark shalt thou set in the side thereof; with lower, second, and third stories shalt thou make it. And, behold, I, even I, do bring a flood of waters upon the earth, to destroy all flesh, wherein is the breath of life, from under heaven; and every thing that is in the earth shall die.

And then God carries out His plan. According to the Bible, the earth is wiped clean in a massive flood:

> And the flood was forty days upon the earth; and the waters increased, and bare up the ark, and it was lift up above the earth. And the waters prevailed, and were increased greatly upon the earth; and the ark went upon the face of the waters. And the waters prevailed exceedingly upon the earth; and all the high hills, that were under the whole heaven, were covered. Fifteen cubits upward did the waters prevail; and the mountains were covered. And all flesh died that moved upon the earth, both of fowl, and of cattle, and of beast, and of every creeping thing that creepeth upon the earth, and every man. All in whose nostrils was the breath of life, of all that was in the dry land, died. And every living substance was

destroyed which was upon the face of the ground, both man, and
cattle, and the creeping things, and the fowl of the heaven; and they
were destroyed from the earth: and Noah only remained alive, and
they that were with him in the ark. And the waters prevailed upon
the earth an hundred and fifty days.

At this point, critical thinkers can ask a question: What man or
woman on earth would worship this being called God? What intelligent
human being would claim that this God is loving or moral? Who would
have anything to do with a God-being such as this? Who would want to
have a relationship with it?

Even more obvious: In this myth, why did God, who is supposed to
be omniscient, start by creating Adam? Why not start with Noah and
avoid the mass homicide?

Even taking the story of the ark as purely allegorical, mythological
fabrication, who would read this myth and then want to worship the
God of the Bible?

God floods the earth, kills everything, the waters recede. Then we
come upon two more unexpected notions in Genesis 8:20–21:

And Noah builded an altar unto the Lord; and took of every
clean beast, and of every clean fowl, and offered burnt offerings on
the altar. And the Lord smelled a sweet savour; and the Lord said in
his heart, I will not again curse the ground any more for man's sake;
for the imagination of man's heart is evil from his youth; neither
will I again smite any more every thing living, as I have done.

Here we have a God who demands burnt animal sacrifices. Billions of
dead carcasses would be littering the planet if the flood myth were true,
and now Noah has to burn a few more. We also have the contradiction of
an immaterial God who possesses nostrils that can smell things—and he
enjoys the pleasing aroma of burnt animals. And we have an admission
that God is imperfect: "For the imagination of man's heart is evil from his
youth." How can humans behave that way unless God designed it thus?
God, according to Biblical mythology, created everything in the universe

exactly the way He wanted it. If every inclination of the human heart is evil from childhood, it would have to be that way because the perfect, omniscient, omnipotent God in the myth created it that way.

In addition, so many aspects of the Noah story are impossible. A critical thinker understands that if an event such as this actually happened as described, it would leave behind massive amounts of irrefutable scientific evidence all over the globe: archaeological evidence, geological evidence, genetic evidence. None of this evidence exists, most notably all of the water. The Bible states that the water "prevailed exceedingly upon the earth; and all the high hills, that were under the whole heaven, were covered. Fifteen cubits upward did the waters prevail; and the mountains were covered." This means that Mount Everest, at 29,000 feet (9,000 meters), would have been covered in water. Where did all of this water come from, and where did it all go? In the myth, it magically materializes into existence and later it magically disappears.

In logic there is a principle called the Law of Noncontradiction that is one of the three Classic Laws of Thought. The Law of Noncontradiction, according to Aristotle, says that "One cannot say of something that it is and that it is not in the same respect and at the same time."

Using this law, we can see that the book of Genesis violates the Law of Noncontradiction in many different ways. A perfect God cannot make mistakes. An omniscient God cannot be surprised. A moral and all-loving God cannot dole out absurd punishments upon others for mistakes He Himself made, nor commit mass homicide. The contradictions show us that the God in the Bible is impossible—that He is pure mythology.

In this way, intelligent people who are able to think critically conclude that the stories told in the Bible are myths, identical to all of the other myths humans have written over the millennia. And thus, God is imaginary, just like Zeus, Ra, and Thor.

So now we look at the sixth and seventh pillars of God described in Chapter 4:

7. God is all-loving
8. God is perfectly moral

Is the God-being described in the Bible all-loving and moral? We simply quote a sentence directly out of Genesis 6:17:

> And, behold, I, even I, do bring a flood of waters upon the earth, to destroy all flesh, wherein is the breath of life, from under heaven; and every thing that is in the earth shall die.

Clearly this God-being is neither loving nor moral. This God-being is a monster. To come to that conclusion, simply look at the definition of **love**:

1. A profoundly tender, passionate affection for another person.
2. A feeling of warm personal attachment or deep affection, as for a parent, child, or friend.

Then look up the definition of **evil**:

1. Morally wrong or bad; immoral; wicked
2. Harmful; injurious
3. Characterized or accompanied by misfortune or suffering; unfortunate; disastrous

A being who set out to murder nearly every living thing on an entire planet is evil, plain and simple.

Imagine a person who commits a single premeditated murder. He would be convicted and sent to prison for a very long time. Imagine a mother who premeditates the murder of a child. She too would be imprisoned, possibly for life. Imagine a person who drowns one puppy, one kitten. He would be excoriated in the public forum and probably sent to jail. They receive these punishments because their actions are evil. God premeditated the murder of millions of people and animals, children, and babies in the myth of Noah's ark. The magnitude of evil seen in God is indescribable.

If you are a Christian, you once again stand at a crossroads. Perhaps you have never thought carefully about the God of the Bible. Perhaps you have never actually read the Bible. But take a moment now to ask yourself: Why would you worship such an appalling being? Why would you want a personal relationship with a being like this? And then, one level deeper, why would you believe in a being that is so obviously mythological, and therefore imaginary?

What are we to make of the billions of people who worship the horrific God described in the story of Noah's ark? They seem to have thoroughly compartmentalized their God and their religion, to the point where they have completely separated faith from reason. The ramifications of this separation are disturbing. There's nothing comfortable about the idea of billions of people who willfully turn off their ability to think critically; whose most deeply felt convictions have been built on a foundation of unexamined contradictions; whose world view involves the worship of a being so monstrous, while at the same time declaring this being to be loving and moral.

How does God work? The story of Noah's ark demonstrates that the only way God can exist in the minds of his followers is through impressive levels of compartmentalization, irrationality, and doublethink, for the contradictions and impossibilities seen in the story of Noah's ark are irresolvable to anyone who looks at the story in a critical, open, intelligent, unbiased way. It seems like Christian believers are separated from the world of rational thought; disconnected from reality and the absurdity of their beliefs. We will examine why this happens in Chapter 22.

Let's continue this line of thinking by looking at the author of the Bible.

15:

WHO IS THE BIBLE'S AUTHOR?

IMAGINE THAT YOU'RE SITTING ON THE COUCH TO WATCH THE NEWS. Your favorite news announcer appears on the screen with the lead story. She says:

> Bob Johnson announced today that he has written a new book of the Bible, completely inspired by God. In a news conference held in Washington, D.C., at 3:00 p.m., Mr. Johnson made the announcement and distributed excerpts from the Bible's new book. When asked why God chose to create a new book for the Bible, Johnson replied: "It's been many centuries since the sixty-six current books of the Bible were written. God feels it's time to update the Bible for the modern audience. He divinely inspired every word that I wrote." When asked why God had chosen Bob Johnson to be the author, Mr. Johnson replied, "Many books of the Bible were written by ordinary people." Mr. Johnson's new book of the Bible is available on his website for $19.95 and Mr. Johnson welcomes the entire human family to read God's word.

What do you suppose would happen if this story were to appear on the evening news? Almost immediately, millions of people would have one simple question: How do we know that this new book of the Bible actually came from God? It would be completely reasonable for people to demand unambiguous, independently verifiable proof that authenticates God as the author of Bob Johnson's new book of the Bible.

How might Bob Johnson provide such authentication?

Think about this problem. What would God have to do to convince humanity that this new book of the Bible came from Him through Bob Johnson here in the modern age?

The most obvious way would be for God to appear and proclaim that yes, God did inspire Bob Johnson to write this new book of the Bible and that, yes, what Bob Johnson wrote is God's word. That would be the simple, straightforward solution. This solution, however, would raise at least two immediate questions of its own. First, how would we know that the being who appeared is actually God? He would have to prove it in some verifiable, unambiguous way. He would have to authenticate Himself, since God has never appeared before. If God simultaneously took over every single television station, radio station, and website, would that be proof? If God's radiant face were to replace the sun for twenty-four hours, repeating the same message over and over in a booming voice, would that do it?

The second question is more important: If God is going to appear, why did God need Bob Johnson? Why didn't God write the book Himself if He is going to be writing books? Why does an all-powerful God need human authors to do the writing when he could do it just as easily Himself using His omnipotence? If a being can create a universe, writing a Bible is trivial.

We can safely say that God is not going to appear on television to vouch for Bob. Therefore, Bob is going to have to provide something else to prove that his new book of the Bible is God's word.

The most obvious way for God and Bob to accomplish this is for the book itself to be the undeniable product of an all-powerful, all-knowing being. This is probably the only proper approach to solving the problem. People in the future might one day disbelieve that God's face replaced the sun—they might chalk it up to mass delusion. The best part of having the book authenticate itself is that this approach is foolproof—it would be provably authenticated in this way for time immemorial.

As you ponder this, you might ask yourself: What would a book look like if it were actually written by a being who is supposed to be the all-powerful, all-knowing creator of the universe? It is a profound question that sparks the imagination. What would the all-powerful, all-knowing creator of the universe say? How would the all-powerful, all-knowing creator of the universe say it? How would the words of the all-powerful, all-knowing creator of the universe change your life and the lives of the people on Earth?

The first thing you realize is that a book that really came from the all-powerful, all-knowing, perfect creator of the universe would be unimaginably brilliant. Each word would be perfect in its placement and meaning, and the words taken together would absolutely astound every reader with their wisdom, insight, and beauty. Each point made, each idea expressed would be inarguable and stunning. Each of us might approach the book as a skeptic, but we would leave deeply moved by the experience of reading it. It would blow us away. It would be impossible to put down. It would touch each of us personally, regardless of our ages, our educations, our experiences. How else would a book written by a perfect, omniscient being be? Would it contain stupidity? No, obviously not. Would it contain ridiculous stories about people committing incest and barbaric acts? No. Would it advocate misogyny, slavery, genital mutilation, etc.? No. Would it contain factual errors? No. Would it contain lies or half-truths? No. Would it contain hate and ugliness? No. Would it contain mistakes or ideas that are obviously contrary to known, undeniable scientific facts? No—unless it were to offer evidence that what we think we know scientifically is actually incorrect or unrefined. Would it contain ambiguity? Absolutely not. None of these could exist in a book written by a perfect being—otherwise he would not be perfect.

A necessary side effect of such a brilliant book is that it would be obvious to every man, woman, and child that the book came from the one true God who created the universe. There would not be multiple religions on Earth any longer, nor multiple denominations within each religion. A book from a real God would unite us all because it would be obvious, without any doubt whatsoever, that the book came from the omniscient, omnipotent creator of the universe.

A second hallmark of this new book of the Bible would be accessibility. It would be immediately and simultaneously available in every single language and dialect currently used by mankind. Spoken versions in every language and dialect would also be available for the illiterate and the blind. Approximately 7,000 languages and 40,000 different dialects would be represented in different versions of the book. All 40,000 versions would be ready simultaneously at the book's launch. When linguists examined all the different versions in all of the different languages, they would be stunned to find that the translations are absolutely perfect.

A third hallmark of a book written by an omniscient being is that it would necessarily contain things that human beings would not already know. God, after all, has access to every knowable thing, while humans are woefully lacking in that regard. The whole point of science is to discover things that we do not yet know about the universe, and there are millions of gainfully employed scientists working all around the world. That's not to say that there would be incomprehensible things in a new book of the Bible—an omniscient, all-powerful being would know how to explain things so that they can be understood. But, of necessity, there would be things in the book that we don't know yet. In fact, this would be an obvious way for an all-powerful, all-knowing being to sign his work.

For example, an omniscient being knows the definitive cure for every form of cancer and every single disease on the planet. If God has a cure and withholds it from the Bible, that would make God the author of immeasurable suffering for millions of people. In other words, withholding such information would be evil.

Withholding the cure for cancer would certainly be harmful and injurious. It would most definitely cause suffering. An all-loving, perfectly moral being cannot also be evil—that would be a contradiction. Clearly, if an omniscient being writes a book and leaves out things he knows about curing disease and ending other common, preventable avenues to human suffering, that being is immoral.

Another thing that an omniscient being would do: He would make sure that there could be no copying errors in his book as it is reproduced over the years. In computer science, there are techniques called error-correcting codes that guarantee that copying errors can be unambiguously corrected. Surely a perfect god would want to employ perfect techniques to prevent anyone from omitting material, changing material, or adding material to his perfect book.

Finally, a book of the Bible created by an omniscient and perfect being would necessarily contain zero ambiguity. So if someone were to sit down to read Bob's new book of the Bible and say, "Now wait a minute, does God mean X or Y when he says that?" then God would have failed. An omniscient, perfect being would have anticipated that problem in every case and solved it. An omniscient being would be able to communicate in such a way that everyone would know perfectly and exactly what He means. There would be no way for two people to argue over what God means—the meaning would be perfectly obvious to everyone.

The features described above for Bob's new book of the Bible are all logical and straightforward. They all make sense. We would expect nothing less from a new book of the Bible. But when you compare these features with the Bible we have, you immediately see the problem. The current Bible contains none of these features. This is one more way to know that the Bible is a book of mythology.

INTELLIGENT CONCLUSIONS

As you think about all of this and review what we've covered above, you will probably realize several things about the current Bible if you are thinking critically.

First, is the existing Bible obviously the product of a perfect, omniscient mind? No—it's filled with nonsense, mythology, ambiguity, factual errors, irrelevant stories, scientific misunderstandings, and contradiction. The problems with the Bible start with the very first line of Genesis, as discussed in Chapter 12.

Second, does the Bible we have stun us with its brilliance, wisdom, and beauty? Does it leave us breathless, with tears of joy and understanding streaming down our faces? No—a quick read of Noah's story instead produces confusion and alarm, as seen in Chapter 14. Many other parts of the Bible have the same effect, as we will see in Chapter 20.

Third, was the Bible we have simultaneously available in every language? No, obviously not. This single piece of evidence alone should tell us it's the product of normal people and not an omniscient being. Why would God want to leave anyone out?

Fourth, is our existing Bible immune to copying errors, omissions, or additions? No—it's filled with problems of this sort. The so-called "Wicked Bible," published in 1631, is just one example of a common phenomenon. It was missing the word "not" from the seventh commandment, so it read, "Thou shalt commit adultery."

Fifth, is the existing Bible free of ambiguity? Not at all. Ambiguity can be found from beginning to end in the existing Bible. This is the source of the thousands of denominations in the Christian church.

Sixth, does the Bible we have tell us things that humans do not already know? No. Instead, the Bible looks primitive, constantly conflicting with modern knowledge. There's nothing in the Bible but the things we would expect to find inside the heads of people living in a prescientific society.

And finally, does the Bible we have make it obvious and undeniable that it comes from the one true, omniscient God who created the universe and everything in it? Has the Bible we have caused everyone to align on a single religion and a single denomination because of its undeniable author and the truth and beauty it contains? Clearly not. We can look at the world we live in and see how badly the Bible fails in this regard.

In other words, the existing Bible looks nothing like we would expect it to look if it came from an omniscient, perfect God. Bob Johnson's new book of the Bible would have to scream its authorship as soon as someone started reading, or no one would take it seriously. It would need to be brilliantly obvious in every way that an omniscient, perfect God is in fact the author of Bob's book, or we would know it to be a forgery.

The thing is, the existing Bible looks like a forgery. The Bible we have, as well as the other sacred books such as the Qur'an and the Book of Mormon, contain none of the markers we would expect to find in books purported to be written by divine beings or channeled by them. It's easy for critical thinkers to understand that these books were written by regular human beings, just like all the other books of mythology that people have created through the centuries.

Looking at the Bible, we ask ourselves a simple question as critical thinkers: Does the evidence convince us that it's written by an omnipotent, omniscient being? To cut to the core issue, does the existing Bible have any of the characteristics of omniscience and perfection described in this chapter? The answer is simple: No. The Bible is lacking in these characteristics and, as discussed in Chapter 12, is undeniably a book of myths. Therefore it's easy for critical thinkers to conclude: Normal human beings created the book of mythology known as the Bible without any access to supernatural omniscience.

16:

IF GOD EXISTS, WHY DON'T WE ASK GOD TO APPEAR?

IMAGINE THAT TWO PEOPLE HAVE AGREED TO A DEBATE ON TELEVISION. One is sure that God is real, and the other is sure that God is imaginary. The latter starts the debate by asking the believer an opening question: "Do you believe, as most Christians do, that God is real, that He is omnipotent, that He loves you, that He answers your prayers, and that you have a personal relationship with Him?" The believer answers in the affirmative, states that he has a loving relationship with the Lord, and that God frequently answers his prayers. The next question is then straightforward: "Can you please pray for God to appear for us right here on stage?"

This is an important question for two reasons. The first is simple: Real beings can appear when asked to do so. And for an omnipotent, omnibenevolent, omnipresent being who answers prayers, the appearance should be immediate and unambiguous. It's not like God needs to catch a flight to appear on stage, or that He has something more important that He needs to do. If God really is omnipotent, omnibenevolent, and omnipresent, then He should be able to appear whenever asked to do so. An imaginary being would not appear, obviously—because it's imaginary. But any real God should appear.

The believer might make the following statement: "God is real, but he cannot appear. He must remain hidden." But this contradicts the believer's initial statement. If God is able to answer prayers and enter into personal, loving relationships, he's not hidden at all (see also Chapters 9 and 18). In addition, there's no way for a hidden God to inspire Bibles, incarnate Himself, dictate commandments, and so on. Doublethink, as discussed in Chapter 9, is the thing that allows a believer to harbor this contradiction.

The second reason it's important is because of a fascinating but little-known passage in the Bible. This passage demonstrates that gods need to appear on demand. Recall from Chapter 12 that the Statement of Faith for the SBC states that, "All Scripture is totally true and trustworthy," and the Catholic Encyclopedia states that, "The inerrancy of the Bible follows as a consequence of this Divine authorship." Therefore, if the Bible requires that gods appear on demand, then the God in the Bible should be able to meet the same requirement.

This passage appears in 1 Kings 18. Elijah, a famous prophet in the Bible, is debating with an important king of the time named Ahab. Ahab and his people have decided to follow a god named Baal, and Ahab has 450 prophets of Baal. Elijah asks that everyone gather together for a test to see which god is real: Baal or God. At verses 22–24, Elijah demands that Baal appear and prove that he is real:

> Then said Elijah unto the people, I, even I only, remain a
> prophet of the Lord; but Baal's prophets are four hundred and fifty
> men. Let them therefore give us two bullocks; and let them choose
> one bullock for themselves, and cut it in pieces, and lay it on wood,
> and put no fire under: and I will dress the other bullock, and lay
> it on wood, and put no fire under: And call ye on the name of your
> gods, and I will call on the name of the Lord: and the God that
> answereth by fire, let him be God.

This is a very simple test that Elijah is proposing. The prophets of Baal will set up a bull on an altar, and so will Elijah. Then the two parties will call on their respective gods. Whichever god manifests himself is a real god. In verse 26, Elijah lets the prophets of Baal go first:

> And they took the bullock which was given them, and they
> dressed it, and called on the name of Baal from morning even
> until noon, saying, O Baal, hear us. But there was no voice, nor any
> that answered.

This is such a simple and obvious thing: If Baal is real, then according to the Bible, Baal needs to appear. When Baal's absence becomes obvious, Elijah begins mocking the prophets of Baal in verse 27:

> And it came to pass at noon, that Elijah mocked them, and said,
> Cry aloud: for he is a god; either he is talking, or he is pursuing, or
> he is in a journey, or peradventure he sleepeth, and must be awaked.

The meaning of this mockery is clear. A god like Baal does not get to have any excuse for not appearing. When people ask him to appear, he must. The believers of Baal do not get to hide behind excuses or rationalizations. They cannot claim that Baal is talking with someone else, or that he is on a journey, or that he is asleep. This situation is quite clear-cut. The Bible says that if a god like Baal is real, he must appear and he must do what is requested of him on demand and on time. If he does not appear on command, then the god is imaginary.

When people on Earth call Baal's name, Baal *must* appear.

What happens, according to the Bible, if the god does not make an appearance? In verse 40 the Bible says that the prophets who follow the imaginary god should get the death sentence:

> And Elijah said unto them, Take the prophets of Baal; let not
> one of them escape. And they took them: and Elijah brought them
> down to the brook Kishon, and slew them there.

The Bible is stipulating a test for existence. If a god is real, he must appear, and he must do as told. If he does not appear, then it must be a false god. The Bible then prescribes the punishment for the false god's representatives: death.

Meanwhile, what happens when Elijah calls on God to appear? In verse 36–39 God makes Himself known in an unambiguous way:

> And it came to pass at the time of the offering of the evening
> sacrifice, that Elijah the prophet came near, and said, Lord God
> of Abraham, Isaac, and of Israel, let it be known this day that thou

art God in Israel, and that I am thy servant, and that I have done all
these things at thy word. Hear me, O Lord, hear me, that this people
may know that thou art the Lord God, and that thou hast turned
their heart back again. Then the fire of the Lord fell, and consumed
the burnt sacrifice, and the wood, and the stones, and the dust, and
licked up the water that was in the trench. And when all the people
saw it, they fell on their faces: and they said, The Lord, he is the
God; the Lord, he is the God.

This Bible story is so simple. If a god is real, he appears on command in an unambiguous way. If a god is imaginary, he does not appear.
What is a critical thinker to make of it? A critical thinker looks at evidence, then evaluates it.

The first conclusion that a critical thinker reaches is that this story
is obviously a myth, as explained in Chapter 12. The story is absurd. If
it were not a myth, then we should be able to repeat the experiment. If
we call on God today to appear in a manner similar to Elijah, we would
expect that God would appear. Yet we know that nothing of the sort happens. Everything about this story identifies it as a myth.

An argument could be made that God does not appear today because
God is the almighty ruler of the universe and there is nothing we can do
to compel God to appear. Or because God must remain hidden. But that
is illogical in the context of the story: If true, the same should be said of
Baal. We saw that Baal's failure to appear meant that his representatives
were slaughtered. Clearly this myth in the Bible does not offer gods any
sort of leniency for having better things to do or for needing to hide.

This myth is quite interesting if you think about it critically. The
myth lays down the test that a god must pass to prove that he is real. If
we call on God to appear, nothing happens. So, in a quite self-referen-
tial way, the myth proves that God really is a myth.

And then the myth goes one step further and proves that the mythological God of the Bible is immoral and repulsive. There is no other
way to describe the slaughter witnessed in this myth—it is repulsive.
Any loving god would simply re-educate the wayward priests rather
than murdering them.

The immorality further proves that God is imaginary because it violates one of God's most important pillars.

Again we are forced back to a question that has been asked a number of times in this book: How can any rational, thoughtful person believe in God, and worship a mythical being who is described to be immoral and evil?

17:

WHY DON'T WE ASK
JESUS TO APPEAR?

ANYONE WHO READS OR RECITES THE APOSTLES' CREED KNOWS THE SUMMARY VERSION OF JESUS' TIME ON EARTH:

> [Jesus] was conceived by the Holy Ghost,
> Born of the Virgin Mary,
> Suffered under Pontius Pilate,
> Was crucified, dead, and buried:
> He descended into hell;
> The third day he rose again from the dead;
> He ascended into heaven,
> And sitteth on the right hand of God the Father Almighty;
> From thence he shall come to judge the quick and the dead.

In Christianity, it's Jesus' miraculous resurrection that proves him to be the son of God.

How did Jesus let people know that he had been resurrected? He had to appear to people in resurrected form. There are several sections of the Bible that describe these appearances, including:

- Matthew Chapter 28
- Mark Chapter 16
- Luke Chapter 24
- John Chapters 20 and 21

And then there is 1 Corinthians 15:3–6, where Paul summarizes Jesus' appearances:

> For I delivered unto you first of all that which I also received, how that Christ died for our sins according to the scriptures; And that he was buried, and that he rose again the third day according to the scriptures: And that he was seen of Cephas, then of the twelve: After that, he was seen of above five hundred brethren at once; of whom the greater part remain unto this present, but some are fallen asleep.

The question that a critical thinker would ask is, why did Jesus stop appearing? If Paul supposedly deserved a personal visit from Jesus to prove that the resurrection is real, why don't you?

If you think about this, you realize that the logic is so simple. Paul needed to see evidence to prove that Jesus was resurrected. The evidence is an appearance from Jesus himself.

In the Christian concept of the trinity, Jesus is one of three elements that comprise God. Therefore Jesus, as God, is omnipotent, all-loving, timeless, eternal, omnipresent, and all the rest. In the previous chapter, we saw that, when we call on a god, then the god should appear. Jesus should appear when requested as well, since he is God.

The other reason that Jesus should appear is because we can fit together several statements that Jesus supposedly made in the Bible, creating a call for Jesus to materialize. The Bible is claimed to be the inerrant word of God, and more than half of adults in America believe the Bible is literally true. For a critical thinker, the logic here is solid. Let's look at the steps that a Christian should be able to take to make Jesus appear.

Step 1 is to read 1 Corinthians 15:3–6, as we did above. This passage proves that Jesus can appear and that there is no harm in Jesus appearing. There's no reason for Jesus to remain hidden, because quite clearly it doesn't take away a person's faith or free will to see Jesus. According to the Bible, hundreds of people saw the resurrected Jesus.

Step 2 is to read Matthew 18:19–20, which says:

Again I say unto you, That if two of you shall agree on earth as touching any thing that they shall ask, it shall be done for them of my Father which is in heaven. For where two or three are gathered together in my name, there am I in the midst of them.

This is fantastic. It states that Jesus is already with us, but apparently in an invisible, immaterial form. It also states clearly that we can ask for anything.

Step 3 is therefore very simple for a critical thinker. We simply ask Jesus to materially appear. Jesus is already here, and he has promised to do anything, and he has already appeared to many people. So we simply pray like this: "Dear Jesus, please appear to us in material, bodily form, as you did to Paul and the five hundred brethren, so that we can see the evidence of your resurrection for ourselves. In your name we pray, amen." If the Bible is literally true, then this prayer should work, shouldn't it?

So we pray to Jesus in good faith, and what happens? Nothing. Absolutely nothing.

As critical thinkers we're compelled to look at the evidence. And the evidence makes it obvious: Jesus' failure to materialize provides the evidence to show that Jesus is imaginary.

Jesus does have a verse in the Bible in John 20:29, where he says, "Blessed are they that have not seen, and yet have believed." The full context of that verse is seen in John 24–30:

> But Thomas, one of the twelve, called Didymus, was not with
> them when Jesus came. The other disciples therefore said unto him,
> We have seen the Lord. But he said unto them, Except I shall see in
> his hands the print of the nails, and put my finger into the print
> of the nails, and thrust my hand into his side, I will not believe.
> And after eight days again his disciples were within, and Thomas
> with them: then came Jesus, the doors being shut, and stood in the
> midst, and said, Peace be unto you. Then saith he to Thomas, Reach
> hither thy finger, and behold my hands; and reach hither thy hand,
> and thrust it into my side: and be not faithless, but believing. And
> Thomas answered and said unto him, My Lord and my God. Jesus

saith unto him, Thomas, because thou hast seen me, thou hast believed: blessed are they that have not seen, and yet have believed. And many other signs truly did Jesus in the presence of his disciples, which are not written in this book.

In the ideal case, every human being would be a critical thinker and they would act like Thomas, demanding evidence. And if Jesus' statements in the Bible are true, Jesus should be happy and willing to provide the evidence. If Jesus would appear to Thomas and Paul, why not you? There really is no reason for Jesus to ignore you, and plenty of reasons why he should appear.

How do we know that something is real in our universe? It is very simple: There must be evidence demonstrating it to be real. With Jesus, we have a special case: The Bible states that Jesus does appear to people, Jesus claims to be an omnipotent God, and Jesus claims he will answer prayers for anything. If there is any being who should be able to provide solid, irrefutable evidence of his existence on demand, it is Jesus. The fact that Jesus provides zero evidence of existence is therefore especially interesting. A critical thinker can therefore conclude that Jesus is imaginary.

Critical thinkers understand how delusion works, as described in Chapters 3 and 5. One of the hallmarks of religious delusion is a refusal by believers to process straightforward evidence and reach logical conclusions from that evidence. Instead, a religious person will generate excuses and rationalizations to cover over missing evidence. In the case of Jesus' failure to appear, the excuses are many and varied. Let's examine several of those excuses here:

> Excuse #1: "Jesus doesn't need to answer prayers." This excuse
> is obviously incorrect. As discussed above and in Chapter 5,
> Jesus' promises about prayer are crystal clear. And as discussed in
> Chapter 4, answering prayers is part of the definition of God.

> Excuse #2: "Jesus is an independent, all-powerful being with
> his own will. If he doesn't want to appear he does not have to."

See excuse #1. This being has promised to answer prayers, and materialization is trivially easy because Jesus claims to be in our midst already. In the previous chapter, Baal's failure to appear meant death to hundreds of people. The Bible stipulates, as seen in Chapter 16, that gods who do not appear are imaginary.

Excuse #3: "In the Bible, in Matthew Chapter 4, it says that you shall not put the Lord your God to the test." This verse is a contradiction. A believer cannot claim that Jesus will answer prayers, and also claim that Jesus cannot be tested. Every prayer is a test. If you look back at Chapter 8, you can see what the request for Jesus to appear is actually doing—it's creating an unambiguous situation. The fact that Jesus fails to appear is proof that he is imaginary.

Excuse #4: "Jesus' appearance would destroy free will!" If this were true, then Jesus could not be incarnated and appear to anyone on Earth. The faulty logic in this statement is painful to a critical thinker. It's a perfect example of doublethink. If Jesus could appear to everyone in the Bible, there is no reason why he can't appear to everyone today.

Excuse #5: "Jesus does appear!" If this were true, there would be evidence for all to see. For example, there would be televised news reports that show Jesus appearing. Jesus would be available, unambiguously, for talk show appearances. Jesus would be all over YouTube. And so on.

Excuse #6: "Jesus appears to me. I can feel him in my heart and I talk with him every day because we have a loving, personal relationship." A critical thinker understands this to be a hallucination. We will see why in the next chapter.

18:

DO PEOPLE HEAR GOD'S VOICE?

THERE ARE MILLIONS OF PEOPLE WHO CLAIM TO HEAR GOD'S VOICE. They also claim to have a "personal relationship with God." Many of these people claim that God is talking to them all of the time. Rick Warren, who has sold tens of millions of books to Christians, notes that the Bible is filled with phrases like "And the Lord said..." (Exodus 3:7). Therefore, according to Warren, God seeks out personal relationships with Christians today, and a central part of the relationship is communication, where God speaks directly to Christians. This sounds fantastic, doesn't it? A being who is supposedly omnipotent, omniscient, and omnibenevolent has chosen to speak to us.

And a wide swath of Christians believes this to be true. We can see that by watching the behavior of Christian politicians in the United States. They will frequently, in public, talk about their conversations with God. In the 2012 election cycle, a number of Republican candidates claimed to hear a calling from God in one way or another. Michele Bachmann is one such person. She said: "Every decision that I make, I pray about, as does my husband, and I can tell you, yes, I've had that calling and that tugging on my heart that this is the right thing to do." She then spoke about a similar experience in her run for Congress in 2006: "God then called me to run for the United States Congress. And I thought, what in the world would that be for? And my husband said, 'You need to do this.'"

Herman Cain had a similar calling. He said: "That's when I prayed and prayed and prayed. I'm a man of faith—I had to do a lot of praying for this one, more praying than I've ever done before in my life. And when I finally realized that it was God saying that this is what I needed to do, I was like Moses. 'You've got the wrong man, Lord. Are you sure?'"

Rick Perry experienced the same kind of thing. In one of the most famous stories of this nature, President George W. Bush claimed to hear God speak on many occasions. For example, Nabil Shaath, a high-ranking Palestinian official, quoted Bush as saying that God said to him, "George, go and fight these terrorists in Afghanistan" and "George, go and end the tyranny in Iraq."

In order for politicians to make claims like these and still be able to win elections, a very wide swath of America must believe that God speaks to people. If voters did not believe that God speaks to people, these politicians would be laughed off the stage.

How might a critical thinker approach a situation like this? Either God is speaking to people, or He's not—how do we decide whether God really is speaking?

What if you are a thoughtful Christian who asks questions about your faith? You hear all of these other Christians claiming that God is speaking to them. Any thoughtful person would ask, "How do you know that you are really hearing God's voice, and not something else?"

A person who is a critical thinker would first do some research to answer this question: When do people hear voices in their heads? There are at least five known and well-studied possibilities when a person hears the voice of another person in her head. The possible sources of inner voices include:

1. The voice of psychosis or insanity. For example, people with schizophrenia often hear voices. These voices are often unfriendly or demand antisocial behaviors from the sufferer.

2. Friendly voices, usually triggered by some sort of trauma or accident.

3. Voices caused by Third Man Syndrome, usually brought on during episodes of extreme physical or psychological stress.

4. Hallucinations that might be brought on by things such as lack of sleep or drug interactions.
5. A misinterpretation of your own internal voice or the feelings brought forward by your own subconscious.

We should also acknowledge the possibility of fraud. People can easily claim that they're hearing God's voice inside their heads even if they are not. They might do this because so many Americans believe in the phenomenon. Perhaps a politician looks like he does not have God's blessing if he doesn't claim to hear God's voice, so the politician fabricates a conversation with God. Or perhaps a politician can add authority to his ideas by claiming God's support. In cases like these, people might very well have a motive to make fraudulent claims about God's voice. We'll return to this idea shortly.

What's the best way to analyze a situation like this? One thing that a critical thinker might do is think about what's being claimed, and then think about side effects that would necessarily surround the claim if it were true. These side effects would be easy to test. If a real God is really speaking to people on Earth, there's no question that there would be many consequences.

For example, God is supposed to be omniscient. Therefore, if God is actually speaking to believers, God should be able to tell believers things that they do not already know. In fact, God should be able to tell them anything they ask. An honest person who thought that God might be speaking to him would ask God to tell him something that he does not already know as a way of authenticating whether or not it's really God's voice.

The authentication would need to be something clear and unambiguous indicating without question that God is the source of the voice. How might this work? Here's one idea that a critical thinker might develop for confirming the identity of God's voice: Ask God to give you the first one hundred digits of pi, and then write them down as God recites them to you in your head. Then you can compare the digits you wrote down with the digits of pi easily found on the Internet. If you're the kind of person who has already memorized the first one hundred digits of pi, you might ask for the second one hundred digits of pi, or one hundred digits of pi starting at the millionth digit.

This is not definitive—if a human being has perfected a device that reads minds and transmits messages into minds, then it's possible for that human being to impersonate God. While there's no evidence that such a device exists, it would be nice to rule out this possibility. If it really is God talking to you, He would have no trouble producing any string of digits you request, and in addition He should be able to tell you things that no human being knows. You might ask God to reveal to you next week's winning lottery number. When it is confirmed, you'll know that you are talking to God.

All of these things would be easy for an all-powerful, omniscient God to do, especially if He is forming personal relationships and having loving conversations with millions of Christians. But it would go much further in practice. If God actually were speaking to human beings, those human beings would appear to be incredibly intelligent because they would have open access to omniscience.

A second side effect of a relationship with God would be intercommunication. Think about it this way: Imagine that you and I are siblings, and our mother calls me. I might ask our mother to relay a message to you the next time she talks to you. This is an extremely common interaction for people with mutual friends. Why wouldn't God exhibit the same kind of behavior? If God were actually involved in personal relationships with millions of His followers, it would be quite reasonable to expect that He would serve in the same message-passing capacity. God would act like an omnipotent switchboard delivering messages for all of his followers.

Therefore, when God spoke to a Christian, the Christian might say, "God, can you tell George to pick up a loaf of bread and some milk on his way home from work?" God would relay the message to George. Why wouldn't that happen? If God is speaking to people already, why not provide the messaging service between people as a courtesy? This would be an easy test for any two believers to perform—one of them simply asks God to relay an unknown message to the other. Of course, if two believers tried this right now, it wouldn't work. The fact that this never works tells us something.

A third side effect that we would expect from a speaking God is that all of the people to whom God is speaking would be getting the same message. In this way, we would expect to see complete uniformity of belief across all Christians who have personal relationships with God. The fact that we see so little uniformity (e.g. there are thousands of Christian denominations instead of one) tells us that something is amiss here. Christians can have wildly divergent beliefs about God's will.

If God actually spoke to Christians, imagine how differently church services would unfold in our world today. Everyone would file into church and take their seats. There would be no need for any pastor, priest, or preacher. Everyone would simply sit quietly and let God speak to all of them together. When finished, they could all compare notes and they would have all heard the exact same thing from God. The fact that this doesn't happen tells us that God is not speaking to people. The fact that we need pastors, priests, and preachers to speak for God clearly shows us that God is not speaking Himself.

Why don't we see uniformity, message passing, or omniscience in the followers of any god? Why do we see no evidence at all that any of these reasonable side effects are occurring? The primary reason is because God is not speaking. All available evidence confirms this conclusion. A secondary reason: It's because there's an important element missing from God's speech: authentication. Two Christians can stand up and say two different things that are diametrically opposed to one another. Both can claim to hear God's voice and both can claim that God confirms what they're saying. Yet neither of them can prove that God said anything. Compare this to how things work in the real world of normal human beings.

AUTHENTICATION IN THE REAL WORLD

Imagine that you're the leader of a large organization. It might be a nation, a nonprofit institution, or a worldwide corporation. For example, imagine that you are the president of the United States. This position is largely regarded as the most powerful position that a person can hold on Earth.

Now imagine that you have an important message that you need to communicate to someone. Because the message is important, you want to make sure of at least three things. First, you want to make sure that the correct message is delivered—that it's not tampered with or modified en route. Second, you want to make sure the recipient receives the message—that the message is not lost before it arrives. Third, you want to make sure that a false message can't be forged by an impostor. Given these three criteria, how might you deliver your message?

One way would be to call a televised news conference in the White House and deliver a speech. In this way, your image and your message are transmitted in real time to every person who cares to hear it. If the message is important enough, every major television channel would interrupt their regular programming to broadcast your message worldwide. All major newspapers and magazines, as well as thousands of blogs and Internet news sites, would report on your message as well. There are many other less expansive ways to deliver a message: Invite the recipient to the White House and talk to her, invite the recipient to ride on Air Force One and talk there, etc.

The point is, if the president wishes to deliver a message to someone, there are many ways to do it, and all of them can be authenticated.

What if you make a mistake during your delivery, or what if you feel that people are misinterpreting what you said? Then you could make another speech or send another message to correct the mistake or to clarify your intent.

What if an impostor were to try to speak on behalf of the president? First, it's unlikely that an impostor could infiltrate the White House pressroom and present a speech without anyone noticing that he is an impostor. But if this somehow were to happen, the impostor would be caught and prosecuted and the president would deliver another speech to set the record straight.

What if the president needs to send a message indicating that the Air Force should launch fifty intercontinental ballistic missiles armed with nuclear warheads at an enemy state? The United States absolutely cannot afford to have this message forged, interrupted, intercepted, modified, or misinterpreted. Therefore, the nation creates an elaborate, secure communications network to deliver the message through multiple communication mediums. The nation also has elaborate, secure protocols to handle the message when it arrives. For example, no single person can launch a nuclear bomb. If two people agree to launch a missile but do not have the launch code delivered by the president, they cannot go rogue and launch the missile themselves. If the president sends the message but then dies a minute later in a nuclear explosion, that will not stop the missiles from being launched. And so on.

Is the system that the United States has designed for launching nuclear missiles perfect? Of course not. Human beings make mistakes and we all know it. But it's a system that has been given a great deal of thought, and a huge amount of engineering talent has been applied to make sure that the message gets through and that the message cannot be corrupted or forged.

The point here is simple. If a human leader wishes to convey a message to her followers, human beings create systems to get the message through unambiguously and with a way to verify who sent the message. If the leader of a major corporation wishes to get a message out to her employees or customers, it's easy to do that and there will be no confusion about what's being said or who's saying it. And it must be this way. Imagine what would happen if an employee could pop up whenever he felt like it and proclaim, "The CEO spoke to me in a dream and told me to shut down this factory," and then other employees listened. There would be chaos. Instead, if an employee were to say this, no one would believe him and no one would respond. To shut down the factory, employees require a real, authenticated message from the CEO.

On the other hand, we constantly see God's messages proclaimed by human beings without any way to verify that the message unambiguously comes from God, or that it's true. A minister can stand up in his congregation and proclaim that God spoke to him in a dream. He can claim any statement from God that he chooses, and there is no way for anyone to verify it. This is why we constantly see different people in the same religion claiming opposite positions for God. It's a ridiculous situation.

The fact that there is ambiguity about God's messages and God's intent, along with the fact that there's no evidence that God is speaking to people and plenty of evidence that He's not, tells us one of two things. Either: 1) The people who claim to hear God's voice are hallucinating, and should therefore be seeking medical attention, or 2) these people are lying about the fact that God is speaking to them for personal gain, and should be called out on their fraud. The dictionary defines **hallucination** as:

> A sensory experience of something that does not exist outside the mind, caused by various physical and mental disorders, or by reaction to certain toxic substances, and usually manifested as visual or auditory images.

If God were real and actually speaking to people, He would authenticate His real messages in order to prevent fraudulent statements from being attributed to Him. In addition, the messages would all align, and there would be a need for only one religion on Earth with only one denomination. The fact that God never does this is another indication that God is imaginary, and that the messages and relationships attributed to God are hoaxes or hallucinations.

19:

WHAT WOULD OUR WORLD LOOK LIKE IF THERE WERE NO GOD?

AS HUMAN BEINGS, WE FIND OURSELVES LIVING ON A SMALL PLANET THAT'S FLOATING WITHIN A UNIVERSE OF NEARLY UNIMAGINABLE PROPORTIONS. Each day we are witness to the reality that our planet and universe present to us. A critical thinker looks at this reality with an understanding that there are two possibilities when it comes to God: God is real, or God is imaginary. If God is real and if God does anything active in our universe (answers prayers, performs miracles, has personal relationships with people, interacts with humans, etc.), then there would be evidence.

So critical thinkers ask: What would our universe look like if there were no God—if God were imaginary? How would that compare to a universe where God is real and interacting with humans as the attributes of God presented in Chapter 4 suggest?

First and foremost, if God were imaginary, our universe would have this quality: We would never be able to see or sense God. He would be undetectable in every way, because this is the nature of imaginary beings. This is, in fact, the state of our universe. We never see or hear or in any way have ever detected the presence of any god in a scientific way.

If God were imaginary, there might even be plenty of stories about God from the distant past, where God was frequently and obviously interacting with people. Things like burning bushes, parted seas, stone tablets, planet-wide floods, people turning to salt, voices booming down from the skies, destroyed cities, plagues, trumpet blasts, angel appearances, pregnant virgins, incarnations, etc. would be very common in the tales of old, where they cannot be verified. But none of those things would be happening in the modern world. And none of the ancient events would leave any physical evidence behind to prove that they really happened. If a story of old describes an event that should have left evidence, the evidence would be long lost or strangely absent. For example, if God supposedly created stone tablets written with the finger of God (Exodus 31:18), the tablets would be missing. When scientists looked for evidence of a worldwide flood, none would be found in the archaeological record, the geological record, the genetic record, the record available from ice cores, etc. This is exactly the situation that we see in our world today. There is no evidence that God exists today, or that God did anything in the past.

If God were real, we would expect people who were inventing religions to align on the one real God. If God were imaginary, we would find that people all through time, when inventing gods to worship, would come up with thousands of completely different, bizarre imaginings for their gods. One group of people would worship the sun. Another group would imagine superhuman beings living on top of a mountain. Another group would imagine a being ten stories tall with the face of a monkey. Another would have a thousand little gods that control all different aspects of life. Another would have a single big omnipotent god that controls everything. Another would have three beings that combine together to act like one god. One imaginary god might require human sacrifice, another sacrifices of livestock, another sacrifices of dogs, while another would require no sacrifices. Gods might even change their minds, demanding sacrifices of animals at one time, then a human sacrifice, and then no sacrifices after that. Some gods would want to see giant stone pyramids, while others want graceful, pillared temples, while others need stone cathedrals. There would be no agreement at all. A billion people who worship a single god might laugh out loud at a different billion people who worship a thousand little gods, and vice versa, and each group would vehemently cling to and defend their view of their god(s) even though the two perceptions of god are both imaginary. The actual state of things on planet Earth indicates that God is imaginary by this measure—many human cultures imagine completely unique gods who have none of the commonality we would expect to see if God were real.

If God were imaginary, then within any of these religious groups we would expect people to be able to make up any claim for their god, and their god would never set the record straight. So within Christianity, we find some Christians claiming that God wants homosexuals to be stoned to death, while others claim that God wants homosexuals to receive loving treatment in every possible way. Both stances could exist within different sects of the same religion because the imaginary god is silent. Both diametrically opposed sides would vehemently argue that they are right and that they speak the truth. We see these kinds of arguments and disagreements in the news all the time, frequently erupting all the way to war between religious sects. If a god were real, he would settle these issues by speaking unambiguously to his followers, but this never happens.

If God were imaginary, we would expect that no prayer would ever be answered in a verifiable way. We would expect statistics around prayer events to exactly match the statistics of coincidence. If a prayer were made for something that's impossible, it would never happen. If a prayer were made for something possible, we would detect no statistical evidence that prayers are being answered. When scientists studied the effects of praying, there would be no evidence at all that prayer works and plenty of evidence that it does not. This is exactly what we find when we scientifically study prayer today.

We would expect no actual, unambiguous miracles to occur on the planet if God is imaginary. God would not spontaneously and instantly heal amputees, or people with cleft palates, or people with birth defects. This is in fact what we see on Earth today.

Even though many religions would declare that their gods had created the universe and Earth and all life on Earth at once, there would be gigantic amounts of evidence to the contrary if their gods were imaginary. In particular, there would be millions of fossils of millions of extinct species showing a steady progression from simple to complex over a period of hundreds of millions of years, and none of the religious traditions would mention any of this.

If God were imaginary, we would expect to see events happen at exactly the same statistical rates to believers and nonbelievers after controlling for confounding factors. So, for example, believers would not win the lottery any more often than nonbelievers, and no religion would be favored in lottery winnings. This is exactly the case today.

If God were real, we would expect scientific formulas to contain a factor for God. God would be answering prayers, performing miracles, changing weather patterns, intervening in gambling games, influencing the outcomes of medical protocols, etc. if He were real and answering prayers. If God were imaginary, He would not. And indeed, even though there are millions of scientific equations describing myriad aspects of the behavior of our universe, not one of those valid equations contains any factor for God.

If God were imaginary, we would expect physical laws on Earth—where the number of prayers is very high—to work identically to the way physical laws work on the moon or Mars, where no one is praying. This is in fact the way physical laws work.

If God were real and if God created the planet, we would expect a world designed by an all-loving, perfect, omniscient creator to be safe. On the other hand, we would expect a planet created randomly by nature to have all sorts of natural hazards—hurricanes, volcanoes, tornadoes, droughts, floods, monsoons, earthquakes, asteroid strikes, solar flares, tsunamis, ultraviolet radiation, cosmic rays, radon, poisonous plants, parasites, diseases, etc. The planet we see looks exactly like it was randomly created by nature and it kills millions of people every year.

At a larger scale, if the universe were randomly created by nature, we would expect the universe to be mostly uninhabitable to human beings. And in fact it is.

If God were real, and if God hated abortion like His believers claim He does, we would expect that there would be no miscarriages. If God exists, why would He allow natural miscarriages to destroy the sperm-egg fusions He had just created? Unfortunately, more than half of all conceptions end in natural miscarriages, also known as spontaneous abortions.

If God were imaginary, and if humans had evolved rather than being created by a perfect God, we would expect the human body to contain myriad flaws and problems. And in fact it does. Everything from body odor and dental plaque to arthritis and poor eyesight to heart attacks and cancer would be the norm if God were imaginary, where we would expect to see these many errors because of an evolutionary process. And that is how the human body actually works. There are hundreds of errors and problems to be found in the human body, rather than the perfection one would expect if the human body came from a perfect creator.

If the Bible came from a perfect, omniscient God, we would expect the Bible to be perfect, unambiguous, and filled with amazing insights. The Bible would be the most wonderful book ever created, far superior to any human example of writing. On the other hand, if the Bible was a mythical product of a prescientific culture, we would expect the Bible to be frequently at odds with scientific truth. We would expect it to contain nothing that prescientific culture wouldn't know. We would expect it to contain a great deal of contradiction, absurdity, and nonsense. Looking objectively at the Bible, we find no evidence of brilliance or perfection and thousands of markers for myth, contradiction, absurdity, and nonsense.

If God were imaginary, we would expect a great part of religion to be focused on money, since humans are interested in money even though a god who is omnipotent would not care about money at all. We would find religious people asking for money at every service, passing plates, building extravagant cathedrals, temples, and mega churches, hoarding money, etc., even in defiance to what their God prescribes in His holy books. So for example, if God were imaginary, we might expect to find the pope sitting on a gold throne with a gold staff in a gigantic palace within its own magnificent city-state that harbors vaults filled with gold. This is in fact what we see in our world.

We would expect an imaginary God in the Bible to direct humans to do things that God could easily do Himself if He were real. So for example, the Bible might instruct a group of people to go kill another group of people, even though an omnipotent God could easily do the killing Himself if He existed. This sort of bizarre contradiction is found throughout the Bible. In fact, the Bible itself is one of these contradictions—we wouldn't expect a real God to need human beings to write the Bible. With an imaginary God, that's exactly what we would expect.

If God is imaginary, we would expect many people to largely ignore what God tells them to do. So thousands of priests would rape tens of thousands of young boys and no response would come from God. Churches would amass great wealth in defiance of the teachings of their savior. Church leaders and publicly vociferous believers would be caught up in scandals. Hatred, demagoguery, violence, etc., against outsiders would occur even though God prescribes love. That is exactly what we see in our world today. Thousands of priests have raped tens of thousands of boys. The Catholic Church has amassed billions of dollars in real estate, gold, and other investments. Church scandals are so common as to be clichés. Religious wars and violence are a consistent part of human history.

If God is imaginary, we would expect diseases to ravage and kill millions of people throughout much of human history, but then science would advance and find cures. So the imaginary God would do nothing about smallpox for thousands of years, and then science would find a cure and smallpox would vanish, never to destroy the life of another human being. This is exactly what we see in our world today. If God were real and omniscient, we would expect that these diseases would not exist at all, or we would expect God to have cured these diseases long ago, or for God to write the cures in His Bible. The disease situation we find on Earth exactly matches what we would expect from an imaginary God.

When innocent people are suffering through natural disasters or being attacked by evil people, we would expect an imaginary God to do nothing to help them. So we would expect to see tsunamis and earthquakes killing thousands of people on a regular basis. And in fact we do see that, just like we would expect with an imaginary God.

This list could go on and on. What the list represents is a mountain of evidence indicating that God is imaginary, as summarized in this table:

INDICATOR	GOD IS REAL	GOD IS IMAGINARY
Visibility: If God were real, He would be visible, audible, and sensible like all other real beings. If imaginary, God would be invisible, insensible.	0	1
Ancient presence: If God were real, He would be active on Earth today. If God were imaginary, God might be extremely active in ancient tales, but completely inactive today.	0	1
Evidence: If God were real, we would expect to find evidence of all of these ancient deeds: stone tablets, floods, moved mountains, etc. If imaginary, we would expect there to be no evidence.	0	1
Alignment: If God were real, we would expect all religions and denominations to align on the one true God. If God were imaginary, we would expect humans to invent a thousand completely different gods.	0	1
Claims: If God were real, we would expect people's claims for God's will to all align. If God were imaginary, we would expect claims for God's will to be all over the map.	0	1
Prayer: If God were real, we would expect to see voluminous evidence that God answers prayers: in medical results, gambling halls, lottery winnings, weather patterns, etc. If God is imaginary, we would expect to see zero evidence for answered prayers.	0	1
Miracles: If God were real, we would expect to see documented, actual miracles occurring on Earth all the time. For example, amputated limbs would spontaneously and instantly regenerate. If imaginary, these miracles would never be seen.	0	1

	0	1
Age of Earth: If God were real, we would expect all scientific evidence to point toward a 6,000-year-old Earth. There would be no evidence for evolution. If God were imaginary, there would be millions of fossils showing a steady progression from simple to complex over a period of hundreds of millions of years, and none of the religious traditions would mention any of this.	0	1
Statistics: If God were real, we would expect lots of statistical evidence of His existence. If God were imaginary, we would expect to see events happen at exactly the same statistical rates to believers and nonbelievers after controlling for confounding factors.	0	1
Scientific formulas: If God were real, we would expect many scientific formulas to contain a factor for God. If God were imaginary, we would expect that none would.	0	1
Safety: If God were real and if God created the planet, we would expect a world designed by an all-loving, perfect, omniscient creator to be safe. If God were imaginary, we would expect a planet filled with natural hazards.	0	1
Universe: If God were real, we would expect the universe to be habitable. If God were imaginary, we would expect that most of the universe would be uninhabitable.	0	1
Miscarriages: If God were real, we would expect no miscarriages. If God were imaginary, we would see half of all conceptions ending in miscarriages.	0	1
Human Body: If God were real and perfect, and if God created man as described in the Bible, we would expect the human body to be perfect. If God were imaginary, we would expect to find myriad problems in the human body caused by its evolutionary origins.	0	1

Bible: If God were real, we would expect the Bible to be perfect, unambiguous, and filled with amazing insights. If God were imaginary, we would expect the Bible to be a book of mythology, filled with errors, contradictions, ambiguity, and nonsense without any scientific insight.	0	1
Money: If God were real, we would expect money to be unimportant to Him. If God were imaginary, we would expect a great part of religion to be focused on money.	0	1
Self-sufficiency: If God were real, we would expect Him to do everything Himself. If God were imaginary, we would expect that in the Bible, God directs humans to do things that God could easily do Himself if He were to exist.	0	1
Obedience: If God were real, we would expect all Christians to strive at all times to live flawless sinless lives of goodness in accordance with the Bible. If God were imaginary, we would expect many people to largely ignore what God tells them to do.	0	1
Obedience: It follows from the previous that if God were real, all Christians would religiously follow the Ten Commandments. If God were imaginary, we would expect the United States to be a nation where nearly every store is open on the Sabbath, the divorce rate amongst Christians is 50 percent, the number of Christians in prison is extremely high, etc.	0	1
Disease: If God were real, we would expect all diseases to have been wiped out by God millennia ago, because to do otherwise would be evil. If God were imaginary, we would expect humans armed with science to cure diseases.	0	1
TOTAL	0	20

When faced with all of this evidence, a believer will often become angry or defensive, or will resort to a remarkable dissertation of dissertation of rationalization, apologetics, and ad hoc reasoning. Those reactions do not change the facts, however. We can see the facts clearly by looking at all of the evidence and making rational determinations. The volumes of evidence demonstrating that God is imaginary, and the lack of any actual evidence indicating that God is real, means that God is imaginary. If God were real and matched his attributes described in the Bible, we would necessarily see the side effects of those attributes throughout our universe. Instead we see nothing of the sort.

20:

HOW COULD ANYONE SAY THAT GOD IS GOOD OR THAT GOD IS LOVE?

ONE OF THE ATTRIBUTES OF GOD THAT WE DISCUSSED IN CHAPTER 4 IS THE IDEA THAT "GOD IS GOOD." This attribute is important to believers for at least three reasons. First, the Bible clearly states that God is good, and that God is love. Therefore, in the minds of believers, this must be so—these are definitional attributes of God. Second, it's uncomfortable to imagine that the universe was created by an evil being, or that prayers are being answered by an evil being. Third, many Christians imagine that morality in the human realm can only exist if it rests on a foundation of goodness and love embodied in God.

For example, in his "Letter from Birmingham Jail," Reverend Martin Luther King, Jr. talks about Christian morality. He invokes the idea of just and unjust laws. Then he defines an unjust law as one that does not synchronize with the laws of God. Just laws, in King's thinking, impose both legal and moral obligations on citizens. With unjust laws, there is actually a moral obligation to disobey them. King quotes St. Augustine, who stated, "An unjust law is no law at all," echoing the thoughts of St. Aquinas.

Religious leaders like Rick Warren echo these sentiments, claiming that capitalism and other Western ideals are based on Judeo-Christian thinking that provides the moral foundation. The Catechism of the Catholic Church puts it this way: "The moral law is the work of divine Wisdom. Its biblical meaning can be defined as fatherly instruction, God's pedagogy."

Given these ideas, what would a critical thinker expect to find in the Bible? A critical thinker would expect the Bible, although clearly mythological (see Chapter 12), to consistently represent God as a good, moral, loving being. If God is good, then throughout the Bible, God should be doing good things at all times, and never participate in evil.

The strange thing that a critical thinker notices is that if time is taken to read the Bible, the mythical God portrayed in the Bible directly participates in many evil acts and practices. In fact, God is a monster at many points in the Bible. Here are a number of Bible passages that confirm this fact.

The most profound example is documented in Genesis (and discussed in Chapter 14). The evil of God in the myth of Noah's ark is summarized in Genesis 6:7:

> And the Lord said, I will destroy man whom I have created from
> the face of the earth; both man, and beast, and the creeping thing,
> and the fowls of the air; for it repenteth me that I have made them.

What are we to make of God's statement here? A critical thinker, understanding the definition of evil, sees things clearly: A being who participates in mass murder is evil, not good. Murder at the scale proposed in Genesis is so profound as to make God absolutely evil. The degree of evil represented here is compounded by the fact that God is supposedly omniscient. So when God created humans in this myth, He knew that He would later be killing them. The level to which this murder was premeditated is unprecedented, and this line of thinking applies to most of the evil acts in the Bible.

Another example: In the myth of Exodus, God kills every Egyptian firstborn, as described in Exodus 12:29–30:

> And it came to pass, that at midnight the Lord smote all the
> firstborn in the land of Egypt, from the firstborn of Pharaoh that
> sat on his throne unto the firstborn of the captive that was in the
> dungeon; and all the firstborn of cattle. And Pharaoh rose up in
> the night, he, and all his servants, and all the Egyptians; and there
> was a great cry in Egypt; for there was not a house where there was
> not one dead.

Killing innocent children is evil. There is no context in which it is not evil, especially when a hundred other non-evil options are available to an omnipotent, omniscient being.

God kills the entire Egyptian army in Exodus 14:28:

> And the waters returned, and covered the chariots, and the horsemen, and all the host of Pharaoh that came into the sea after them; there remained not so much as one of them.

God could have just as easily blocked the army long before they entered the parted sea—He had a hundred other options rather than murder. Instead, God resorts to murder on a massive scale. The good news is that this is a myth that never actually happened. The bad news is that the men who wrote this myth chose to portray their mythical God as an evil being rather than a good and loving one.

The Ten Commandments are a foundational element of Christian morality. They are defined in Exodus Chapter 20:

1. Thou shalt have no other gods before me.
2. Thou shalt not make unto thee any graven image.
3. Thou shalt not take the name of the Lord thy God in vain.
4. Remember the Sabbath day, to keep it holy.
5. Honor thy father and thy mother.
6. Thou shalt not kill.
7. Thou shalt not commit adultery.
8. Thou shalt not steal.
9. Thou shalt not bear false witness against thy neighbor.
10. Thou shalt not covet thy neighbor's house, thou shalt not covet thy neighbor's wife, nor his manservant, nor his maidservant, nor his ox, nor his ass, nor any thing that is thy neighbor's.

Many Christians post the Ten Commandments in their homes and churches, and they have also done quite a bit of work over the years to post the Ten Commandments in public venues.

Less well publicized are the prescribed punishments in the Bible for people who break the commandments. In Deuteronomy 17:5, the punishment for breaking the first commandment is: "Then shalt thou bring forth that man or that woman, which have committed that wicked thing and shalt stone them with stones, till they die." In Leviticus 24:16, the punishment for disobeying the third commandment is: "And he that blasphemeth the name of the Lord, he shall surely be put to death." In Exodus 31:15, the punishment for breaking the fourth commandment is also death: "Whosoever shall work in the Sabbath day, he shall surely be put to death." If you think about it, you'll realize that we would need to execute millions of Americans for working on the Sabbath if we followed the Bible's orders. If you are a rational person, you realize this notion is ridiculous. If this mythical God is good, loving, and moral, why would He demand such absurd punishments?

Note that Christians, while being quite enthusiastic about the commandments themselves, ignore the punishments. No one in the United States is put to death because they work on the Sabbath. Why would that be? It's because Christians understand the absurdity of the punishments. By ignoring the punishments, Christians are able to use doublethink to maintain their delusion that God is good.

In 2 Kings 2:23–24, forty-two boys are killed when a lesson or two in civility would have sufficed:

> And [Elisha] went up from thence unto Bethel: and as he was
> going up by the way, there came forth little children out of the city,
> and mocked him, and said unto him, Go up, thou bald head; go
> up, thou bald head. And he turned back, and looked on them, and
> cursed them in the name of the Lord. And there came forth two she
> bears out of the wood, and tare forty and two children of them.

In 2 Kings 19:35, 185,000 people die at the hand of God:

> And it came to pass that night, that the angel of the Lord went
> out, and smote in the camp of the Assyrians an hundred fourscore

and five thousand: and when they arose early in the morning, behold, they were all dead corpses.

Think about how many alternatives to mass murder are available to an omnipotent, omniscient being. Instead, God in this myth resorts to the absolute evil of murdering 185,000 people.

In the New Testament, there is an event known as the Massacre of the Innocents found in Matthew 2:13–16:

> And when they were departed, behold, the angel of the Lord appeareth to Joseph in a dream, saying, Arise, and take the young child and his mother, and flee into Egypt, and be thou there until I bring thee word: for Herod will seek the young child to destroy him. When he arose, he took the young child and his mother by night, and departed into Egypt. And was there until the death of Herod: that it might be fulfilled which was spoken of the Lord by the prophet, saying, Out of Egypt have I called my son. Then Herod, when he saw that he was mocked of the wise men, was exceeding wroth, and sent forth, and slew all the children that were in Bethlehem, and in all the coasts thereof, from two years old and under, according to the time which he had diligently inquired of the wise men.

Since God in this myth knew the massacre was going to happen, and took action on Earth because of it, he could have easily and omnipotently acted to prevent the massacre in a hundred different ways. But he did not do anything to avert the disaster, so thousands of babies died. This is certifiably evil.

In Exodus 32:27–29, God orders the death of 3,000 Israelites:

> And he said unto them, Thus saith the Lord God of Israel, Put every man his sword by his side, and go in and out from gate to gate throughout the camp, and slay every man his brother, and every man his companion, and every man his neighbor. And the children of Levi did according to the word of Moses: and there fell of the

people that day about three thousand men. For Moses had said, Consecrate yourselves today to the Lord, even every man upon his son, and upon his brother; that he may bestow upon you a blessing this day.

The Lord, according to this mythological passage, personally ordered all of these deaths.

In Isaiah 13:13–16, we find this description:

Therefore I will shake the heavens, and the earth shall remove out of her place, in the wrath of the Lord of hosts, and in the day of his fierce anger. And it shall be as the chased roe, and as a sheep that no man taketh up: they shall every man turn to his own people, and flee every one into his own land. Every one that is found shall be thrust through; and every one that is joined unto them shall fall by the sword. Their children also shall be dashed to pieces before their eyes; their houses shall be spoiled, and their wives ravished.

This is pure evil. The obvious question: What is something like this doing in the Bible if God is good and God is love? And there are many other passages like this one.

In Hosea 13:16, we find a similar description:

Samaria shall become desolate; for she hath rebelled against her God: they shall fall by the sword: their infants shall be dashed in pieces, and their women with child shall be ripped up.

The idea of ripping open pregnant women certainly qualifies as evil. In Numbers 31:15–18, we find:

And Moses said unto them, Have ye saved all the women alive? Behold, these caused the children of Israel, through the counsel of Balaam, to commit trespass against the Lord in the matter of Peor, and there was a plague among the congregation of the Lord. Now therefore kill every male among the little ones, and kill every woman that hath known man by lying with him. But all the women children, that have not known a man by lying with him, keep alive for yourselves.

Here, Moses, acting as an agent of God, specifies that thousands of male babies and children be killed, as well as thousands of women. Tens of thousands of men, women, and children were massacred.

In Deuteronomy 3:3–7, we find this description:

> So the Lord our God delivered into our hands Og also, the king of Bashan, and all his people: and we smote him until none was left to him remaining. And we took all his cities at that time, there was not a city which we took not from them, threescore cities, all the region of Argob, the kingdom of Og in Bashan. All these cities were fenced with high walls, gates, and bars; beside unwalled towns a great many. And we utterly destroyed them, as we did unto Sihon king of Heshbon, utterly destroying the men, women, and children, of every city. But all the cattle, and the spoil of the cities, we took for a prey to ourselves.

God here tells the people what to do, and it's easy to see that killing sixty cities worth of men, women, and children is absolutely evil. There is no other word to describe it.

What are we to make of this? Based on the examples we've seen here, how does God work? A critical thinker can look at the above passages rationally, without bias, and sees them for what they are. These are actions of an unquestionably evil being. There is no goodness or love demonstrated here.

A critical thinker can look across the Bible and find hundreds of other examples of evil: The God portrayed in the mythology of the Bible is a misogynist, an advocate for slavery, a racist, a homophobe, a being who demands genital mutilation, a being who requires animal and then human sacrifice for appeasement.

In addition, hell plays a prominent role in Christian mythology. God is the creator of this place of eternal torture, and there is no question that torture is evil.

Hell is a special example of evil. Hell is described by evangelical and fundamentalist Christians as a place of "everlasting conscious suffering in the lake of fire." Imagine that you are a being who claims to be omniscient, good, and loving, and who is able to create a universe from scratch. Only if you are absolutely evil would you create a place of "everlasting conscious suffering" in that universe, and then create people knowing that many of them would end up arriving in that hell. And according to Christian mythology, the majority of human beings end up in hell because the majority of human beings are not Christian. The entire notion is absurd because it's such an immense violation of goodness and morality. Every critical thinker can see that this God-being embodies evil at an unprecedented scale.

Wikipedia summarizes the concept of **love** as:

> Love is an emotion of a strong affection and personal attachment. Love is also said to be a virtue representing all of human kindness, compassion, and affection—"the unselfish loyal and benevolent concern for the good of another." Love may describe compassionate and affectionate actions toward other humans, one's self, or animals.

The dictionary defines **compassion** as:

> A feeling of deep sympathy and sorrow for another who is stricken by misfortune, accompanied by a strong desire to alleviate the suffering.

The question is: Is God good and is God love? How would a critical thinker approach this situation? A critical thinker would look at the evidence. In the many examples shown in this chapter, do we see in God evidence of kindness, compassion, or affection? Evidence of benevolent concern for the good of another? Compassionate or affectionate actions? Clearly not. The God described by the Bible is the polar opposite of love in so many cases. Any critical thinker—any rational person—recognizes that God is evil.

How might a believer try to rationalize all of this evil? There really is no way to rationalize it because God participates in so much evil in so many places in the Bible—God slaughters millions of people in the passages mentioned here in this chapter. It's difficult to imagine someone trying to rationalize or excuse the behavior of this mythical being in the face of all of this evidence, yet it happens every day through the process of doublethink as described in Chapter 9. The common response is for a believer to ignore all of the passages that define God to be evil.

But when confronted directly, a Christian might say, "The Lord works in mysterious ways. It's too complicated for people to understand." This explanation makes no sense to a critical thinker because it is incoherent. In the myth of Noah's ark, for example, God explains why he's killing millions of people and animals in a clear and transparent way. It's not that God's thinking in this myth is "mysterious," it's that it's absolutely evil (see Chapter 14). Killing millions of people is evil, especially when there are a hundred good alternatives that an omniscient, all-powerful being could use to solve the problem rather than resorting to mass murder. For rational people, there's no question that God is evil after reading the Bible's creation myth (Chapter 12) and the myth of Noah's ark (Chapter 14). God's massacres in the Bible and the idea of hell are repugnant to any rational person who considers them.

A critical thinker looks at all of the evil acts that God commits in the Bible and understands what they mean: The God of the Bible is not good or loving. God is the definition of evil.

So we look back in Chapter 4 and see these attributes of God:

6. God is all-loving and good.
7. God is perfectly moral and is a moral standard by which humans are judged.

There's no question that these two attributes are invalid. They have fallen because they have been proven false through direct evidence. There's no love demonstrated in the many examples presented in this chapter.

The dictionary defines the word **immoral** in this way:

> Not morally good or right; morally evil or wrong; conflicting with generally or traditionally held moral principles.

God is unquestionably immoral. Any critical thinker who examines the evidence can see that. This contradiction with two important attributes of God from Chapter 4 is another strong indicator that God is imaginary.

21:

DO YOU HAVE A SOUL?

HAVE YOU EVER TAKEN THE TIME TO STUDY BACTERIA AND HOW THEY WORK? Bacteria are the simplest living organisms that we find on Earth today, and therefore they are the easiest to understand. And even then, the complexity of these microscopic single-celled beings is utterly amazing.

A bacteria cell is a tiny, self-contained chemical machine. This machine is able to build its cell wall, absorb and digest food to gather energy from it, and excrete waste products. Bacteria can evolve—for example to become resistant to antibiotics or to adapt to a new food source. In some cases bacteria have tiny chemical motors that spin flagella to allow movement. Some can sense light. Some produce toxins that cause profound illnesses or death. And let's not forget that they can reproduce, sometimes in stunning quantities, if the conditions are right.

Bacteria do everything that they do by manufacturing copies of molecules that their chemical machines need to survive. The templates for these molecules are stored in their DNA. The DNA strand in a bacteria is a long string of genes, and each gene lets the bacteria manufacture a chemical that the bacteria needs. An Escherichia coli (also known as E. coli) bacteria cell has perhaps 5,000 genes, depending on the variety. By manufacturing 5,000 different chemicals that either float inside the cell wall or attach to the cell wall, the E. coli bacteria is able to live its life and reproduce.

That is not to say that E. coli are indestructible. There are many different ways to kill an E. coli cell. For example, enough ultraviolet radiation will damage the DNA strand and kill the cell—the cell becomes unable to manufacture essential molecules that it requires to sustain life, so it dies. An antibiotic can gum up one or more of the E. coli's 5,000 essential molecules, or the mechanism to produce it, and shut the cell down. A lack of food means that the cell can no longer derive the energy it needs to power its chemical reactions, causing it to die of starvation. There are toxic chemicals that break down the cell wall, causing the E. coli to split open and die.

So what do you suppose happens when an E. coli cell dies? The cell is a tiny bag filled with chemicals that spill into the surrounding water as the cell disintegrates. These spilled chemicals either disperse or get eaten by other organisms, and the E. coli cell disappears.

Does an E. coli cell have a "soul" that goes to "heaven" when the cell dies? To a critical thinker, this is a ridiculous question, and the answer is obvious: no. This would be something akin to asking if a battery goes to heaven when it dies. The reason we can answer no so easily lies in the fundamental nature of an E. coli's existence—an E. coli cell is a bag of chemicals that happen to work together in an interesting way. The chemicals are able to digest food molecules, move, and replicate themselves, which is fascinating. But it doesn't change the fact that they're chemicals reacting together to create a little chemical machine.

Does a bag of chemicals have a soul? No, clearly not. Souls are imaginary to begin with, as we will see in a moment. But even within Christian mythology, no believer imagines a heaven filled with the umpteen zillion dead bacteria cells that have populated Earth for hundreds of millions of years. Because bacteria are invisible to the human eye, there's no way for a human being to really imagine how many bacteria cells have existed throughout the earth's history. The number is absolutely staggering.

Looking to forms of life more advanced than the E. coli bacteria, there are millions of more complex organisms. There are tapeworms, ants, fruit flies, cockroaches, rattlesnakes, rats, and so on. The thing is, each of these creatures is just a more advanced, multicellular version of the basic chemical chassis found in an E. coli cell. Any animal is an intricate multicellular chemical machine, nothing more. Do any of these animals go to "heaven" when they die? Of course not. When they die, their chemicals disperse into the environment and the animals cease to exist. Even in Christian mythology, no theist imagines heaven filling with quintillions of everlasting tapeworms, fruit flies, mosquitoes, ticks, ants, cockroaches, rattlesnakes, rats, etc. that have populated planet Earth for millions of years.

If we scale the evolutionary tree, eventually we come to human beings. It's interesting to note that a human being shares about 60 percent of its genes with a fruit fly. In other words, if we look at the genes in a human being and compare them to the genes in a fruit fly, there is a fundamental set of genes that are identical, and it's more than half of the genes. This is because a human being is exactly the same kind of chemical machine as any other living thing.

Do fruit flies have souls? No. Do humans have souls, because they have more genes and bigger brains? No. How do we know this? Because chemical reactions are chemical reactions.

The idea that Christianity proposes goes something like this: There is a magical spirit thing called a "soul" that appears out of nowhere at conception and somehow attaches itself to and lives somewhere inside of a human body. But only inside human bodies—not inside yucky bodies like tapeworms, ticks, mosquitoes, and rats. But inside dogs too, and sometimes cats, and even ferrets and hamsters if they are pets, maybe—it depends on who it is who's describing souls. The soul lives inside the human body until the human dies, and then this magical spirit thing somehow magically transmits itself to some "other dimension" to be judged, and then it either goes to a wonderful magical place called "heaven," or to a different terrible magical place of eternal torture called "hell."

And don't forget the special case of the "rapture," where Christians believe that their actual physical naked bodies are somehow magically taken up into "heaven." So if a pilot is flying a jumbo jet during the "rapture," and the pilot is a good Christian, his naked body will completely vanish, leaving behind his clothes and a pilot-less airplane. This too is supposed to be taken seriously.

Just listening to these descriptions, critical thinkers can understand the absurdity. The idea of a soul is an imaginary notion that firmly sits in the realm of mythology. There is no more a chance that a human has a soul than a fruit fly or E. coli does, because humans, fruit flies, and E. coli cells are all related, and are nothing more than chemical machines.

Here's another way to look at it: According to many Christians, the human soul is magically installed at conception. Sperm and egg unite to become one complete human cell, and the soul magically appears out of nowhere, magically enters the mother's human body and magically attaches itself to the fertilized egg cell. Looking at it rationally and scientifically, a human cell is no different from any other animal cell in its chemical nature—it's just a collection of chemicals inside a cell wall. Yet, in Christian mythology, the human cell gets a soul.

There's a good chance that a newly fertilized human egg cell will die. More than 50 percent of pregnancies end in spontaneous abortions—that is, the natural death of the cell(s)—for a wide variety of natural reasons. So let's assume as critical thinkers that a newly united sperm and egg fails to implant and it dies. The woman never even knows she was pregnant because it happens so quickly. This dead cell is not so different from an E. coli cell. It's a small chemical machine, now dead due to lack of nutrients. So when the cell wall bursts and the chemicals disperse, is there some part of the cell that magically goes to "heaven?" And if so, what is it that goes there? This single cell—this bag of chemicals—is nothing but chemicals. What, exactly, is transmitted and where does it go?

Looking at this egg situation scientifically, the absurd nature of the soul concept is apparent.

It's when you look at it rationally like this that the true state of Christian mythology becomes clear. There is little difference between the idea of a soul and the sun diver story from Chapter 12. Both stories are absurd. The soul concept is yet another myth. We know that it's a myth—it comes from the book of mythology called the Bible.

This is what's so fascinating about religion. Two or three thousand years ago some men in a prescientific society dreamed up the mythology of a "soul." These are the same men who dreamed up the mythology of the Genesis creation story (Chapter 12), Noah's ark (Chapter 14), hell (Chapter 20), and so forth. The myth of the soul is no different from the rest of the myths in the Bible. It's a comforting idea, but fully mythological. When you die, the chemicals that make up your body will disperse and you will cease to exist, as with every other plant and animal in the biosphere.

One reason that Christians buy into the idea of souls and heaven is because most started hearing about the soul as toddlers and they never think about the concept rationally after that. If they would take the time to apply critical thinking skills, they would understand that the idea of a soul and the idea of heaven are myths. These notions are completely imaginary concepts, with no evidence to support them and plenty of evidence to the contrary. In addition, if Christians would take the time to look at life scientifically, they would understand that people, like all other animals, cease to exist when they die.

THINKING ABOUT THE LOGICAL RAMIFICATIONS OF A SOUL

If you read popular literature and Christian inspirational literature, you can find many stories of near-death experiences, heaven, and the afterlife. There are many people who claim to have died and then experienced an afterlife. They describe experiences that include: feeling their souls rising out of their bodies; being able to see and hear people in the room from positions floating in the air; being able to float through walls to other places; and being transmitted through a tunnel of light to experience the sights and sounds heaven. The ability to see, hear, and remember is universal in these stories.

A critical thinker listens to these stories and thinks about their logical ramifications. If a person's soul is able to rise, fly, think, see, and hear independently of the human body, then the hardware in the human body—things like the brain, eyes, and ears—are irrelevant to the human soul. If a soul can fly above the unconscious human body, and then see and hear people in the room, and travel to other places, then the implication is clear: Things like eyes, ears, and brains are not required for sensing or memory. Sensing and thinking have no ties to biological hardware in the human body.

So we must ask the logical question: Why does any person ever go blind or deaf? Why, if part of the brain is damaged in an accident, is there any loss of mental ability? How can a disease like Alzheimer's or a stroke turn a person into a mental vegetable? In these cases, why doesn't the soul, which according to Christian thought and literature must be independent of any biological hardware, take over to keep sight, hearing, and thought functioning perfectly? If a soul can see, hear, and think while floating on the ceiling of a hospital room while looking down at its body, that same soul should certainly be able to see, hear, and think while inside that body, regardless of the body's condition.

How does any religious believer deal with a logical contradiction like this? The only way is to invoke doublethink, as described in Chapter 9. The believer must devise some sort of illogical, ad hoc excuse to explain the contradiction, because a person with a soul should never go blind or deaf. For example, a believer might say something like: "A Christian can go blind while alive because the sight of the person's soul is only activated after death. But as soon as they die, they can see again." To which the logical response is, "Why is that? What evidence do you have to support what you're saying? If you research things like near-death experiences, you'll find that they can be explained and recreated through oxygen starvation and certain drugs that induce similar brain states to those of a dying person. And the visits to heaven are hallucinations or fabrications.

The fact is, there can be no thinking in human beings in the absence of the brain. There can be no sight in the absence of visual hardware connected to that brain, and no hearing in the absence of audio hardware connected to the brain. Therefore, when a human body dies, the brain hardware dies with it and the human being attached to that brain ceases to exist.

When you die, your chemical machine will shut down, the chemicals that comprise your body will disperse, and that is the end of you. This is true of all living things, from bacteria all the way up the chain. This is the reality of how life works. Creating a mythical story about an imaginary soul does not change reality.

It is fascinating to compare God with science. Imagine that we somehow expunged every bit of scientific knowledge from planet Earth; every scientific book, paper, and fact known to humankind disappears. What would happen next? A new group of scientists would go about their work and rediscover everything. They would rediscover all of the chemical elements and put them in a periodic table that would look identical to the one we have today. The only difference would be the names for the elements, since the names are arbitrary. They would recreate the equations for gravity, motion, energy, inertia, orbital mechanics, etc., and the equations would be identical to those we have today. They would rediscover the structure of DNA, the age of the universe, the existence of galaxies, the speed of light, relativity, evolution, and all the rest. The reason is because these are all fundamental things that become obvious to anyone who looks at the evidence available in nature. The scientific facts that scientists discover are woven into the fabric of reality for anyone to see and confirm.

Science catalogs reality, and science has no place for God because God is imaginary.

22:

UNDERSTANDING RELIGIOUS
SUPER-IRRATIONALITY

IN RALEIGH, NORTH CAROLINA, AS THIS BOOK GOES TO PRESS, THERE IS AN AD RUNNING ON THE RADIO FOR THE ANGEL COIN. The story the ad tells goes something like this. Back in 1793, a man named Augustine Dupré was about to be executed by guillotine in France. But in his pocket he had an Angel Coin. When Augustine said a prayer and rubbed the coin, a storm came up that delayed his execution, and later he was released. Since then, many other people have rubbed Angel Coins and experienced remarkable good luck just like Augustine did. Wouldn't you like to bring this same kind of amazing luck into your own life? Call the 800 number right now and order your very own solid silver Angel Coin today.

Listening to this ad, what do you think? Should you buy the Angel Coin and open your life to its powerful good luck field?

Hopefully, after reading this book, there's one thing that you now know for sure: Magical lucky coins do not have any effect whatsoever here in the real world that human beings inhabit. Rubbing a coin, or saying a prayer, has no effect on the events happening in our world.

But companies are still able to sell things like Angel Coins. Why? Because it's easy to create the illusion of effectiveness in the minds of people who are not critical thinkers. The fact that this ad is running tells us something. Ads on radio stations are expensive, especially in large metropolitan markets like Raleigh. The reason companies run ads is because the ads are working. If it costs $10,000 to run the ad, then the company is selling enough coins to make money in excess of that $10,000 cost. In other words, there are so many gullible people in our society that this company can profitably sell these lucky coins to them using a little story in a one-minute radio ad.

If you look back at the material we have covered in this book, you realize that religion is powered by exactly this same phenomenon. Little stories about God are told by millions of people and hundreds of thousands of churches every single day. We hear these stories all the time:

- "If you pray to God he will answer your prayers."
- "I had cancer, I prayed to God, and my cancer was completely cured—you should try praying too!"
- "I lost my car keys and I prayed to God. He showed me that they had fallen behind the coffee maker. I never would have found them without God's help. Pray to God now to find your lost dog."
- "If you give 10 percent of your income to our church, God will reward you with a hundredfold more!"
- "Bob gave a thousand dollars to the church and the next day his sick child was healed by God."
- "If you don't give money to God, you're going straight to hell when you die."

These statements all use the same techniques seen in the Angel Coin ad, and they work. People who are not critical thinkers turn to religion because of stories that they constantly hear from their friends, on the news, in magazine articles, on websites, from church members going door to door, etc. Religion, like the Angel Coin, works for people who cannot think critically and realize that the stories are untrue. The stories sound so convincing if no one ever analyzes them. So people say prayers, go to church, and put money in the offering plate.

Is God real or imaginary? It should be obvious to you by now that God is completely imaginary. If you are unable or unwilling to think critically, it can seem like God is real. It's easy to use faulty thinking patterns, poor evidence-gathering techniques, purposeful ignorance, and logical fallacies to create the illusion that God exists. But once you use critical thinking skills to analyze God, the illusion collapses.

In Chapter 4, we looked at the attributes of God. Then we started to examine them one by one to see whether they hold up to scrutiny. In every case we found that the pillars supporting the belief in God collapsed.

In Chapters 5 through 10, we looked at prayer from many different angles. What we found is that prayer does not work at all. To an uncritical thinker, it's easy to create the illusion that prayer works. Things like anecdotal evidence, confirmation bias, cherry-picking, the post hoc fallacy, doublethink, groupthink, the regression fallacy, and the placebo effect combine together to create a powerful and convincing illusion for people who don't think critically. But it's an illusion nonetheless, and provably so. To a critical thinker, it's obvious that the belief in prayer is a superstition.

In Chapter 12 and then again in Chapter 15, we looked at the Bible and asked a simple question: When we read the Bible as thoughtful people, do we see evidence that it's a book of mythology, like all of the other religious books and stories that human beings have imagined over the millennia? Or does the Bible look like the work of an omniscient, super-intelligent, perfect being with complete access to every knowable thing in our universe? The conclusion is obvious: The Bible is a book of mythology. And therefore, without question, God and Jesus are mythological beings just like every other imaginary God.

In Chapter 14 and then again in Chapter 20, we asked another simple question: When we look at the Bible, even though we understand it to be a book of mythology, do we see it portraying a being consistently filled with perfect goodness and pure love? Or do we instead witness a monster? We find that the God in the Bible is a monster. There are dozens of examples. The God of the Bible is unethical, immoral, evil, and often nonsensical.

Do God or Jesus appear to us when we ask them to? The Bible says they should, as discussed in Chapters 16 and 17, but they clearly do not.

Millions of people claim to have a personal relationship with God: They speak to God and God speaks to them. We can go to the bookstore or look on the Internet and find thousands and thousands of stories about these relationships. And yet it's easy to see that any relationship with God is an illusion, as discussed in Chapter 18. None of the logical side effects that should occur if an omniscient being were talking to people can be found in our world. It is easy to see that people who claim to have these relationships are hallucinating or fabricating them.

What would our world be like if God were real, and how would that compare to the appearance of our world if God were imaginary? What are the necessary side effects of the God described in the Bible? We looked at this question in Chapter 19 and found that our world looks exactly how we expect it to look given that God is imaginary.

And then there is the question of the everlasting soul that religion claims every human being possesses. It's easy to understand, as discussed in Chapter 21, that souls do not exist, nor do heaven or hell. These are all mythological ideas derived from a book of mythology.

Every attribute of God from Chapter 4 has been eliminated through contradiction with reality, clinical trials, examination of the voluminous evidence in the real world, and critical thinking. It's easy to understand that God is imaginary.

How does God work? God is a grand illusion powered by faulty thinking patterns, superstition, and suggestion. This illusion is easy to foist upon people who are unable to think critically, because they don't have the mental tools or the desire to understand the illusion.

Back in Chapter 1, we embarked on this journey together. Now we are here at the end of the journey. If you are a Christian, Muslim, Mormon, Hindu, Jew, etc., you now have a choice: Are you going to ignore critical thinking, compartmentalize your religion away from the intelligence you employ to live the rest of your life, and continue believing in a god or gods that are clearly imaginary? Or are you going to start thinking critically, acknowledge the reality of our world, and accept the truth of the human condition? God is imaginary, just like Santa, and it's easy to demonstrate it in many ways. Are you going to accept that reality or reject it?

If your plan is to continue claiming that God exists, what evidence will you use? Will you use your answered prayers? It's clear that the belief in answered prayers is a superstition. Will you use your "relationship" with God? We understand your relationship to be a hallucination, or even worse a fraudulent fabrication. Will you point to the Bible? We know that it is a book of mythology and the supernatural beings it portrays are mythological. Will you talk about God's morality, goodness, and love? It's easy to find many examples of God's monstrosity in the mythological book that describes him, and there are millions more examples of monstrosity here in the real world we inhabit. Will you defer to the beings themselves? Neither God nor Jesus ever materializes for us, even though they should. It's clear that God and Jesus are mythical, imaginary beings.

And yet, if you are a believer, you may remain strangely torn. Sometimes, when we dismantle a myth, we find that we actually liked the myth and wish it were true. You may cling to the notion of God even though there's clearly nothing there. If this is happening for you, it's likely for the reasons described in Chapter 13. You have so much invested in your worldview—things like life after death in heaven and the ability to reunite with loved ones are important to you. And you also have invested in so much fear—fear of things like hell and God's wrath—that you cannot release your grip on the delusion of religion. You cannot afford to look critically at your faith because the idea of heaven is so comforting, and the idea of hell so frightening, that you are unable to let go of them.

You may also find yourself wedded to the mythology, seemingly unable to break free. So try to apply rational thought to it. Do you, as an intelligent human being, actually believe that a god magically inseminated a virgin named Mary to create a corporeal copy of himself? Why would you believe a story like that? Note that stories of virgin births are not unique in any way. Even in today's modern world, close to 1 percent of young American women claim to have virgin conceptions. We obviously do not believe any of these stories—they are ridiculous—so why would anyone believe the Bible's mythological story of Mary from 2,000 years ago?

Even within the context of the Bible's mythology, why would a god do this? In the Bible's myth structure, Jesus is God. Therefore the myth's logic goes like this: An omniscient, omnipotent God impregnated Mary with Himself so that He Himself could grow up and be crucified, acting as a human sacrifice of Himself to Himself to atone for the alleged sins of human beings that He Himself designed and programmed from scratch in a universe He created Himself. Looking at this logic objectively, the level of nonsense here makes any rational mind spin. A critical thinker looks at this mythology with bewilderment because it's so silly. Yet Christian believers cling to this myth as though their lives depend on it.

The only way to understand it is to recognize that the belief in religious elements like these represents a special form of irrationality. We might call it religious super-irrationality. How else do we explain grown adults who firmly believe that an omnipotent god needs to sacrifice himself to himself? A Christian can see that the stories from Greek mythology, Mormonism, and Scientology suffer from this super-irrationality—it's obvious. But then something strange happens. Somehow a Christian is blind to his own super-irrationality.

The part where human sacrifice is involved is beyond the pale. As critical thinkers, it's unquestionable that human sacrifice is a barbaric, heinous ritual. But the notion of a god sacrificing himself to himself is indescribably irrational.

Think about the terminology that Christians frequently use to describe Jesus' death. This verse from 1 John 1:7 is typical:

The blood of Jesus Christ his Son cleanseth us from all sin.

> If there's one thing that a sane, rational person can say with certainty, it's this: When people start talking about human sacrifice and cleansing blood like it makes sense and it is a good thing, we know without question that we're dealing with deep, unhinged super-irrationality. Yet human sacrifice is the defining feature of Christianity. And the whole idea of substitutionary atonement that the sacrifice story embodies makes no sense whatsoever.

The myth itself makes no sense internally. Take it out of the myth framework and into the rational light of day and it's impossibly absurd. Yet there are billions of people who cling to this mythical story, along with the resurrection story, the creation story, Noah's ark, the rapture, and all the rest, as though they are literally true. People will actually fight wars about their beliefs if push comes to shove. As I write this, there is a war raging in Iraq pitting Sunni Muslims against Shiite Muslims, one small part of a long-running feud that started over one thousand years ago. This is the power that religious super-irrationality has over the human mind.

UNDERSTANDING RELIGIOUS SUPER-IRRATIONALITY

What's going on here? What is this super-irrationality that appears to be built into the human brain to handle religion? We can characterize religious super-irrationality by noting these defining attributes:

- A religious believer is willing to completely suspend rationality and believe in the mythology of her chosen religion. But this same person will remain rational and can easily reject the absurdity of other religions' mythologies. In other words, the irrationality is complete within one context, but it's selective to that single context.
- The chosen beliefs of a religious believer are extremely persistent and usually immune to evidence, discussion, common sense, questioning, rational thinking, etc., despite the fact that the believer can so easily see the irrationality in other religions.
- Religious believers think they and their beliefs are completely normal—that their super-irrational beliefs should be obvious to everyone and unquestionable. Yet they will laugh out loud at the beliefs in other religions, calling them absurd.
- When confronted about their super-irrational beliefs (e.g. "Come on—you believe a human body re-animated from the dead, complete with puncture holes, and then actually ascended into the sky? You can't possibly be serious."), the believers' response is often bitter anger or an astounding illogical spew of rationalization, apologetics, excuses, detailed nonsensical explanations, etc.

- A believer, especially if associated with a group of like-minded believers, will frequently shun, ostracize, and excoriate nonbelievers. In-group favoritism, out-group negativity, and tribalism can be extremely strong companions to religious faith. Out-group negativity can be so powerful in religious believers that it can escalate all the way to warfare. Religious wars have been a common fixture throughout human history.

How do we know that this religious super-irrationality is a malfunction in the human brain? There are several things that make this plain:

- Most importantly, the characteristics just described are bizarre. This sort of religious super-irrational behavior can appear inhuman to objective observers. Why would any adult believe absurd myths wholeheartedly, explode in anger when confronted with facts and reason, mistreat people who believe differently, etc.?
- Believers can be rational in other parts of their lives and when looking at the myths of other religions. The malfunction only applies to one's own religion.
- We see other examples of related irrationality in human beings. Take war as an example. To pick a specific case, think about the Battle of Gettysburg in the American Civil War. In this situation, we had fellow countrymen fighting each other, angered with each other to the point of murder, standing in lines on the battlefield, often within sight and earshot of the other side. Then they would raise their rifles and willfully slaughter each other. Approximately 50,000 men died in three days of fighting at Gettysburg. Why didn't these men look across the lines at one another, see the humanity in one another, lay down their rifles and conclude, "There must be a better way to solve this." Why would anyone consider the death of 50,000 people to be a viable, rational path? Yet wars are quite common throughout human history.

It's interesting to note that we observe similar super-irrational characteristics when looking at political alignments and beliefs. Political beliefs can be persistent, irrational, extremely strong, and anger-inducing. For example, you may have noticed that when a candidate is elected, the members of that candidate's political party see the actions of their candidate as nearly always right. But if the candidate from the opposing party is elected, that candidate is nearly always wrong, and often evil.

Even more interesting: The same events can be interpreted completely differently depending on which candidate is in office. So if gas prices are rising, the members of the president's party will say, "The president cannot control gasoline prices—oil is a global commodity with its prices controlled by market forces." The members of the other party will take the opposite position, loudly proclaiming that the president is fully responsible for rising gas prices. Then, when the opposing candidate gets elected, the two arguments will change sides. Party members will vehemently take up the opposite position of the one they held before. This bizarre behavior is continuously on display on political websites and in political debates. The irrationality and hypocrisy is obvious, and so strong, yet partisans seem to take no notice.

Why do these forms of irrationality and absurd behavior appear in both religion and politics? Perhaps because they are fueled by the same misfirings in the human brain. As a general rule, human beings are not very good at thinking unless they're trained to be critical thinkers. Many different faulty thinking processes and fallacies inhibit and pollute clear thinking, as described throughout this book, including:

- Confirmation bias
- Anecdotal evidence
- Placebo effect
- Superstitions
- Delusion
- Regression fallacy
- Post hoc fallacy
- Power of suggestion

- Groupthink
- Tribalism
- In-group favoritism
- Out-group negativity
- Doublethink

As human beings, we have to come to grips with the fact that evolution has imprinted our brains with a strong tendency toward super-irrationality in certain areas. This is the reason why every human being needs to learn to think critically, and to then apply critical thinking skills to every part of our decision-making process. Not only can mental clarity be clouded (sometimes completely obfuscated) with the super-irrationality involved with strongly felt issues like religion and politics, but we also have to deal with things like emotional response, anger, ego, favoritism, tribalism, and in-group and out-group biases that can ruin rational thinking.

The idea that political beliefs can be as irrational as religious beliefs should be a warning bell for all of us. Politics are vital in the modern world. Local and national governments make myriad important decisions that affect the lives of billions of people. The idea that the human decision-making apparatus can be so badly corrupted by super-irrationality should cause societies to demand trained critical thinkers in every government, corporate, and leadership position.

If you're a religious believer, you can learn about critical thinking and begin to acknowledge absurdity. Absurdity should be called out for what it is, as described in Chapters 11 and 12.

Now, as hard as it may be, you can turn this same critical thinking process upon your own beliefs and acknowledge their absurdity as well. Instead of relying upon mythology, you can make your own decisions using empirical evidence gathered by means of observation and experimentation. By using the techniques described in this book, it will be possible to:

- Understand that belief in prayer is a superstition.
- Understand that religious texts like the Bible and the Qur'an are books of myths.

- Understand that the Bible is not a source of moral guidance.
- Understand that the idea of a "soul" is a myth derived from a book of mythology.
- Understand that the "personal relationship" with God is a hoax.
- Understand with certainty that God and Jesus are as imaginary as Santa Claus.

Recognize religious super-irrationality for what it is, and then eliminate it from your thinking and your life.

Why is it important that you do this for yourself, and help other believers do it as well? Because religious and political super-irrationality is harmful to us as a species, especially in the United States. We need for every human being to be a critical thinker and to see reality clearly. Look again at the definition of critical thinking:

Disciplined thinking that is clear, rational, open-minded, and informed by evidence.

We are better off when we are in the habit of thinking critically in every part of our lives. As a society, we should confront irrationality constantly, especially in the political domain. We should expose irrationality of all types and eliminate it from the public sphere that determines the course of our civilization. We should educate people away from religion because religion acts as a huge reservoir of irrationality, superstition, and sloppy thinking that leaks detrimentally into many aspects of our society.

We should demand clear and rational thought in all parts of a modern, complex society. Decisions should be based on empirical evidence, experimental results, and critical thinking that indicates the best course of action rather than anecdotes, emotional whim, dogma, or political party lines. The more we succeed in thinking critically in all parts of our lives, the better our society will become.

23:

A BRIEF RESOURCE GUIDE FOR

RECOVERING BELIEVERS

IF YOU'RE A BELIEVER AND YOU TAKE THE MESSAGE OF THIS BOOK TO HEART, YOU'LL HAVE STARTED DOWN THE PATH TOWARD BECOMING A CRITICAL THINKER. You can then apply your critical thinking skills to your religious beliefs. You will see your religious super-irrationality collapse. It may seem like you are waking up from a bad dream. "How in the world did I ever believe all of that absurdity?" may be your reaction. You wake up in the real world, free of imaginary gods and all of the superstitions that go with them.

Once you arrive at that point, you are likely to feel one of several primary emotions:

1. Relief and freedom: This is a very common emotion for people to feel once they have lost their religion. If you have lived your life under the oppressive notion that a wrathful and vengeful god sits in heaven watching every single thing you do and reading every single thought inside your head, the realization that God is imaginary can be an amazing, uplifting, vitally freeing experience. It can change your life for the better in many different ways.

2. Anger and embarrassment: For some, the realization that God is imaginary can feel like a body blow, in the same way that losing a beloved spouse to an affair can feel like a body blow. "How could I have been so stupid? Why couldn't I see the signs? Who was I talking to during my 'relationship with God'—no one!

I was talking to myself!" This feeling will pass and, as with a cheating spouse, once the period of mourning is over, this often leads to a bright new life of freedom from irrationality.

3. Terror: For some, the collapse of faith creates a void. Even though you intellectually understand that God is imaginary, you may be terrified to stop praying, to stop talking to Him, lest He send a lightning bolt to zap you or a bus to run you over. This feeling usually passes as well, once you grasp and digest the reality of the situation. God is an imaginary being, so nothing happens when you stop praying to Him. Stop praying for a day or two and notice that everything in life works the same without prayer as it did with prayer. Realize that nothing bad will happen to you. There are billions of people who live their lives without believing in God. Stop fearing God and then see how free it feels to live life without the terror.

4. Sadness: For some, when faith collapses, several important things can collapse with it. If you felt you did have a relationship with God, even though you now see it was an illusion, you may miss it. If you felt you were going to meet up again with Aunt Sally and Grandpa Joe in the afterlife, the loss of that imaginary possibility can feel uncomfortable. Loss is frequently accompanied with mourning; this is a completely natural human response. Allow yourself to mourn and recover from your sadness, and then watch what happens as your mind embraces the benefits of reality.

Once you work through your feelings, you may then face a number of common questions. The collapse of religious faith can leave several gaps. Let's look at these gaps, along with their replacements.

PRAYER

One good example of a gap is prayer, because prayer plays an important role in religious life. What should you do in all of the situations where, as a religious person, you might have prayed? There are four types of prayer to consider:

1. Personal prayers of thanks: Gratitude is an essential process, recognized by psychologists to be an important element of happiness. Instead of praying to an imaginary God when you are grateful, however, it's more productive to thank those real people to whom you are grateful. For example, if you're grateful for surviving cancer, thank the doctors, nurses, and researchers who made your survival possible. If you're thankful to your spouse for doing you a favor, thank your spouse. If you're thankful for the food on your table, thank the person who earned the money and the company that wrote the paycheck. Also consider keeping a gratitude journal.

2. Personal prayers for strength, perseverance, insight, inner peace, etc.: Prayers of this type mimic two well-understood disciplines: meditation and self-talk. These two disciplines can be quite beneficial and are more effective when you eliminate your "imaginary friend" and practice them directly.

3. Prayers for others: When a friend or loved one gets sick, a common religious refrain is, "I'll pray for you." Since God is imaginary, that's identical to doing nothing. Instead of saying you will pray for your friend, an alternative is to actively help. Ask if there's anything you can do that would ease the burden of the illness. Could you take care of their kids, cook dinner, mow the lawn? You might make a donation to a related research charity in your friend's name. Perhaps you could organize mutual friends to visit regularly or provide a safety net. There

are many active things you can do to help rather than doing nothing with prayer.

4. Prayers at events: Imagine a sports event, graduation ceremony, awards banquet, wedding, or funeral. Or imagine a sports team about to go out for the big game. The preacher in the locker room says, "Let us bow our heads. Dear God, please keep these men safe today, and help them to…" We have all seen this. Instead, the coach could offer rational support. For example: "Thanks to each one of you for being here today for the game. Please be safe out on the field and keep an eye out for each other. Let's behave in a sportsmanlike way at all times and respect and honor the team we are playing…"

ETHICS

While religious irrationality breeds many examples of hypocrisy and contradiction, no example is more peculiar than the one suggesting that God is the source of morality. As we saw in Chapters 14 and 20, there are numerous examples in Christian mythology where God, rather than acting ethically, behaves in the most unethical, appalling, and heinous ways imaginable. And Christians exhibit no particular moral fortitude. The widespread child abuse among Catholic priests discussed in Chapter 5 is just one of thousands of egregious examples of overt Christian immorality.

A critical thinker looks at the Bible, understands that it's myth, and recognizes these ethical problems to be the work of the people who wrote the myths. It's telling that Christians in developed nations of the world reject misogyny and slavery even though the Bible fully supports both. Clearly, the mythological God-being is not the ultimate moral standard, even to Christians. If He were, Christians would do everything demanded of them by the Bible.

The fact is, human thinking is the source of all ethical behavior, for everyone. Since God is imaginary, this has always been the case. Using critical thinking skills, intelligent people derive a system of laws and ethics using logic and rational thought. In some areas of the law, things are crystal clear. Murder, for example, is easily understood to be evil and unethical by the vast majority of intelligent people without the need for any religion to stipulate it.

Murder represents the ultimate harm and injury, so it's evil. In addition, no intelligent person wishes to be murdered, and this wish can be empathetically extrapolated to all people. If I do not wish to be murdered—and by extrapolation, no human wishes to be murdered because it represents the ultimate existential threat—then I nor anyone else can be allowed to murder others. That is a general ethical precept that is easily derived from logic. The same logic can determine that there are certain exceptions—for example, extreme cases of self-defense.

Through a logical process like this one, all moral and ethical standards may be derived. And while not all areas of ethics are as clear-cut as murder, and some have multiple valid points of view, they can be negotiated easily by intelligent, compassionate people who are thinking critically. In these cases, ethical human beings work to find common ground and reach agreement.

MEANING

If, as a religious person, you have based your worldview on the idea of everlasting life and heaven, then the collapse of your religious beliefs may lead to the following question: What is the meaning of life? As a critical thinker, you grasp the magnitude of the universe and humanity's tiny place in it, and until you form a new worldview based on reason, it might be uncomfortable.

The universe is a place of unimaginable size. It contains hundreds of billions of galaxies, each of which can contain hundreds of billions of stars. Our own Milky Way galaxy is approximately 100,000 light-years across—itself an unimaginable statistic. Our galaxy contains approximately 300 billion stars, many of which have their own orbiting planets like our star the sun does. Our galaxy is just one out of hundreds of billions of galaxies. If you let that sink in, you realize how infinitesimally small planet Earth and the human race really are in the grand scheme of things.

In addition, humans are an accidental species—just one of the millions of species that have evolved and inhabited this planet over the course of hundreds of millions of years.

Given this scientific context, what is the meaning of our lives? I've written quite a bit about this elsewhere, and the fascinating thing is that the removal of all imaginary gods from humanity's collective thought space is actually quite helpful. It lets humanity see the reality of our situation clearly.

The common question is stated this way: What's the meaning of life? But that is not really the question at all. For each of us, as individuals, the question is: What's the meaning of each of our lives? What will you do with your existence, with your time alive on this planet? You get to create your own meaning—whatever you choose to be the meaning of your life. You are the designer of the life you choose to live. You have a nearly infinite pool of options, and each day you get to make the choices that guide your life.

For humanity as a whole, the question is: What will we do with our existence as a species? As far as we know, there's one intelligent species in the universe: humanity. But what if there's another highly advanced, intelligent species, and members of this species were to travel across many light-years of space to visit us? They would likely be astounded at how backward and savage we are.

Just to take the simplest possible example, the United States has thousands of nuclear warheads, each able to destroy a city. The Russians do too. China, England, France, Israel, India, and Pakistan have hundreds of their own. These weapons could destroy humanity many times over. Our best idea for controlling this existential threat to humanity is a doctrine called MAD—Mutually Assured Destruction. If just one bomb falls into the hands of terrorists and is detonated in a major city, the losses will be utterly catastrophic. The whole situation sounds like the plot of a terrible movie, but this is our reality.

Somewhere on the planet there is usually a war going on. There is also terrorism, dictatorships, political upheaval. Billions of people live in abject poverty because of shocking imbalances of wealth. In addition, the majority of people on the planet harbor super-irrational, usually unshakable beliefs in imaginary gods that clearly do not exist.

What would aliens make of such a situation? How would they evaluate us as a species? They might believe humans to be unhinged, possibly insane.

We should ask ourselves collectively: What will we do with our existence as a species? What if we, unified, worked together and got our house in order? What if we eliminated the nuclear weapons, the environmental degradation, the wars, the crime, the religion, the hatred—what if we decided to create heaven on Earth for every human being on the planet? In consciously doing this, as a species, we would give great meaning to all of our lives together. As we all become critical thinkers, and as we look at our situation as a species rationally, seeing the truth of our reality, this process of working together on common goals becomes easier.

ORIGINS

In Christian mythology, God creates the universe and life on Earth. There is no correlation between this mythology and reality. Looking at the real world, how do critical thinkers explain our origins?

The first thing to understand is that there are many things that were once attributed to gods. The list includes thunder, lightning, rain, rainbows, fertility, the seasons, tides, earthquakes, comets, eclipses, moon phases, etc. Today these phenomena are all understood scientifically, causing astrophysicist Neil deGrasse Tyson to famously say, "God is an ever-receding pocket of scientific ignorance that is getting smaller and smaller and smaller as time goes on."

Science has a complete explanation for the origin of our planet and the diversity of life that we see on it today, all based on mountains of evidence available to any observer who chooses to examine it. Take the time to learn about the science of planetary formation, the science of cosmology, and the science of evolution as a critical thinker. This whole area of research and understanding is fascinating and mind-expanding.

Science does not yet understand the origin of the universe, but invoking an imaginary god to explain it is rather silly. In every other case we have seen, there has been a natural explanation. It will be the same for the origin of the universe.

What if you simply cannot accept this? What if you think about the universe and conclude, "There's no way to explain the immensity of the universe without imagining a mystical origin—some unseen, unknowable intelligence—some prime mover or uncreated creator?" Then understand that with this explanation, you are defining a new God-being of your own, separate from the God/Jesus myth of the Bible.

The God/Jesus-being of the Bible is imaginary. So sit down and define your own new god or deity to act as the universe's creator. Then search for evidence to prove that this newly imagined god exists. As you work through this exercise, you'll realize that your only evidence for your new god is the universe. Then you will further realize that the universe is evidence that the universe exists, not evidence that your newly imagined god exists. There is no evidence linking the universe to any imagined god, including your newly imagined god, nor any evidence that your newly imagined god exists. And you're right back to the point of this book: All gods are imaginary.

The best course of action is to think about the universe scientifically, in the same way that scientists think about any scientific mystery. The cause of the extinction of the dinosaurs was a mystery for quite some time, and was then resolved through several key discoveries and insights. The structure and action of DNA was once a mystery that was eventually solved in the mid-twentieth century. We had no idea that there was such a thing as a galaxy until the 1920s, when powerful telescopes were developed that could see them. Similarly, no one had ever seen a bacteria cell until the microscope was invented. The origin of the universe will be unlocked in the same way. We simply aren't there yet. The solution, once discovered, will be fascinating, but based on what science has uncovered so far, it will not involve imaginary gods.

QUESTIONS YOU MAY BE ASKED

As you become a critical thinker and fully understand that God is imaginary, you will face questions and criticism if you make your new understanding known. Here are several of the most common questions and possible answers for you to consider as you create a new worldview.

- Q1: **"What, are you an atheist now?"** Earlier we talked about out-group negativity. It's a natural process associated with the super-irrationality of religion, and attaching a negative (to Christians) label to you is a way of putting you in the out-group. The "atheist" label, however, is interesting. A theist is someone who believes in an imaginary god. Therefore, an atheist is someone who does not believe in an imaginary god. This is a double negative that is unnecessary—nonbelief in imaginary beings is the default state for any intelligent person. This is why I and many others reject the atheist label. I'm not an atheist: I'm a normal, intelligent, rational human being. I'm a critical thinker who strives to see reality clearly and is free from the super-irrationality of religious believers. If religious people would like to talk with me about their irrationality, I'm happy to try to help them recover from their delusions. Each recovery that I can help facilitate makes our world a better place. I have many friends who believe in a variety of religious mythologies, and generally speaking, we have no need to discuss religion (or politics for that matter). Thomas Jefferson once said, "I never considered a difference of opinion in politics, in religion, in philosophy, as cause for withdrawing from a friend." Words to live by.

  Am I an atheist? No. Nor am I an aleprechaunist— that label would be just as silly. I'm a normal, rational human being who understands reality. There are no imaginary gods and no imaginary leprechauns. A theist, on the other hand, is a human being who believes in imaginary gods.

- Q2: **"What am I supposed to do with you now?"** Linus, of *Peanuts* fame, has a great quote: "There are three things I have learned never to discuss with people… religion, politics, and the Great Pumpkin." One answer to this question: Let's be friends, and in the interest of friendship, let's avoid talking about religion, politics, and the Great Pumpkin if need be.

- Q3: **"If you don't believe in God, where did all the beauty and order in nature come from?"** There is a famous quote from Francis Collins, a noted scientist who worked on the Human Genome Project and has served at the National Institutes of Health as its director, on his conversion to Christianity. He was in the Cascade Mountains, out on a hike, and he came upon something beautiful in nature: a waterfall frozen in place. This example of natural beauty turned him toward God. This is a common theme amongst Christians—that the beauty of nature in the form of flowers, sunsets, and frozen waterfalls is a testimony to God. This is a rather odd position that depends on confirmation bias. A frozen waterfall is caused by three natural processes: rainfall, gravity, and winter temperatures (which are caused by the inclination of the earth's axis and latitude). With too much rainfall, we get flooding—Hurricane Katrina in New Orleans being one example. Gravity helps cause tectonic plate motion, which can lead to earthquakes, tsunamis, and volcanic eruptions. The earth's inclination on its axis causes weather patterns that can include blizzards, droughts, monsoons, tornadoes, hurricanes, hailstorms, lightning strikes, etc. A rational person cannot look at the beauty of nature without also giving equal weight to all of the natural disasters that kill millions of people and cause massive suffering for billions more. When we evaluate natural phenomena based on empirical evidence and not by how it makes us feel, there's no reason to believe that it's an example of supernatural power, as in Collins' story.

- Q4: **"What happens when you die?"** When we die, we die. The chemical machinery that powers life stops functioning, and we cease to exist. The idea of the soul and an afterlife is mythology, just like everything else in the Bible. Chapter 21 has a good explanation of what happens when people die.

- Q5: **"Why don't you believe the Bible? It says right in the Bible that God exists, God created everything, and God wrote the Bible."** This statement represents a logical fallacy called circular reasoning. The dictionary defines **circular reasoning** as:

A use of reason in which the premises depends on or is equivalent to the conclusion; a method of false logic by which 'this is used to prove that, and that is used to prove this.'"

The ideas that "God wrote the Bible" and "The Bible says that God is real" create a circle. There would need to be independent evidence that God exists, but there is none (see Chapters 16, 17, and 18). The Bible is easily categorized as a book of mythology as discussed in Chapter 12. A book of myths is meaningless as evidence.

- Q6: **"You can't prove that God doesn't exist, so why don't you shut up you atheist idiot?!"** There is voluminous evidence demonstrating that God is imaginary, which is the point of this book. The super-irrationality of religion is a very interesting and disturbing part of the human condition, but it does not change reality. Believers will often tell you to shut up, so one option is to hand them a copy of this book, ask that they read it, and then have a discussion about it. It will be a fascinating conversation and one of two things will happen: Either you'll get to observe an example of impervious religious super-irrationality firsthand, or you will introduce someone to the beneficial process of critical thinking and help to free him from religion.

- Q7: **"How can you reject God? He created you!"** Rational people understand that it's not possible to reject (or hate) any imaginary being. It's also impossible for an imaginary being to create anything. And it's certain that the God of the Bible is imaginary. There's no question about this, as explained throughout this book.

- Q8: **"Where do you get your morality from without God?"** As discussed earlier in this chapter, intelligent people understand that morality and ethics come from rational thought, logic, and critical thinking. Simply by reading the Bible we can quickly understand that the mythological God worshipped by Christians is not a source of morality, not a source of morality (see Chapters 14 and 20).

- Q9: **"Why don't you ask God into your heart? I have a personal relationship with God, He talks to me and He is always by my side. I could never reject God."** A similar comment is "God saved my life—I could never reject Him after that day." It's an advanced form of irrationality in the first case (see Chapter 18), and post hoc reasoning in the second case (see Chapter 5). The simple reply is to ask that God authenticate Himself (see Chapters 15, 18). Or ask God or Jesus to appear in material form, as described in Chapters 16 and 17. If a person believes she is talking to God every day, ask her to ask God for authentication, and explain why this is important, as described in Chapter 18. The conversation should be interesting for both of you.

- Q10: **"Blasphemy is a terrible sin and you're a sinner. Do you realize you will face eternal torment in hell?"** One definition of the word "sin" is: "an immoral act

considered to be a transgression against divine law."
Since God is imaginary, there is no divine law and therefore it's impossible to sin. See also the next question.

- Q11: **"Have fun in hell with all of your atheist friends,
  you creep!"** Religious people, because of the tribalism
  and out-group negativity associated with religious
  super-irrationality, sometimes resort to attacks like
  this. They insist that their ethical and loving God
  will torture nonbelievers in a lake of fire for eternity,
  failing to see the multiple levels of contradiction and
  doublethink in what they're saying because they are
  unable to think critically. The interesting point is that
  a person who is free of religion is not threatened by an
  imaginary God or an imaginary hell. When we die, we
  die—that's the end of existence. Clinging to the myth
  of a soul and the myth of hell does not change reality.
  There's really nothing more to it than that. Ask God/
  Jesus to appear, and ask God to authenticate Himself,
  as explained in the previous question.

Imagine a world where everyone is a critical thinker—where decisions are made rationally, based on evidence, for the long-term benefit of all. In choosing to become a critical thinker, and in choosing to
abandon imaginary gods, you are helping humanity take a step in that
direction. The choice to become a critical thinker is a vital, important
inflection point in your development as a human being.

By thinking critically, you are able to see reality clearly, and therefore to understand and experience truth in your life. It's not necessarily
an easy road today—religious bigotry and hatred can be uncomfortable.
But as more and more people embrace reality, the power of religion
declines. One day the super-irrationality and delusion of religion will
subside and humanity will enter a new era. When that day comes, our
world will be a much better place.

What can you do to help speed up the process? You can form con-
nections with other critical thinkers, talk about our goals as a species,

and help elect politicians who are critical thinkers. You can help make the religious people around you aware of this book and the benefits of critical thinking in their lives. You can help people in your community understand that we're all better off when we're all thinking critically and clearly.

The faster we get to the point where every human being is a critical thinker, the better off we all are. Thank you for reading this book, sharing this book, and becoming a critical thinker yourself.

END NOTES

CHAPTER 1

Page 10: "There are many videos available" For example, http://youtu.be/ RDOuwMj7Xzo.

Page 13: "One part of the Bible" For example, Leviticus 24:13–16.

Page 13: "Parts of the Qur'an also" For example, Qur'an 2:191.

Page 15: "The dictionary defines truth in" Cited in dictionary.com, access date April 14, 2014.

Page 15: "There are billions of people" See dictionary.com's definition of "supernatural."

Page 15: "They cite numerous pieces of"

> Willard, Dallas. *Hearing God: Developing a Conversational Relationship with God* IVP Books; Updated and Expanded Edition (April 24, 2012)

> Blackaby, Henry T. and Blackaby, Richard. *When God Speaks: How to Recognize God's Voice and Respond in Obedience.* LifeWay Christian Resources (September 15, 1995)

> Blackaby, Henry T. and Blackaby, Richard. *Hearing God's Voice.* B&H Books (September 15, 2002)

Page 15: "Statistically speaking, if you live" "In U.S., 77% Identify as Christian," Gallup Inc., accessed April 14, 2014, http://www.gallup.com/poll/159548/ identify-christian.aspx.

CHAPTER 2

Page 22: "One substance that happens to": http://www.pbs.org/wnet/nature/ episodes/rhinoceros/rhino-horn-use-fact-vs-fiction/1178/.

Page 24: "Scientists call this second group" Dictionary.com Unabridged, Based on the Random House Dictionary, © Random House, Inc. 2014.

Page 24: "The placebo effect is defined" *The American Heritage® Medical Dictionary.* S.v. "placebo effect." Retrieved June 23, 2014, from http://medical dictionary.thefreedictionary.com/placebo+effect.

Page 25: "Therefore, we might next try" Dictionary.com Unabridged, Based on the Random House Dictionary, © Random House, Inc. 2014.

Page 26: "Thus the need for double-blind" Ibid.

Page 27: "First, we must ensure that" Ibid.

Page 28: "The effect of group size on" Statistical significance. Dictionary.com. *The American Heritage® New Dictionary of Cultural Literacy, Third Edition*. Houghton Mifflin Company, 2005. http://dictionary.reference.com/browse/statistical significance (accessed: April 14, 2014).

Page 31: "driving a magnificent wild animal" https://news.vice.com/article/china-outlaws-the-eating-of-tiger-penis-rhino-horn-and-other-endangered-animal-products

CHAPTER 3

Page 34: "In a post-mortem report published" Wapner, Jessica. "Did Alternative Medicine Extend or Abbreviate Steve Jobs's Life?", accessed June 23, 2014, http://www.scientificamerican.com/article.cfm?id=alternative-medicine-extend-abbreviate-steve-jobs-life.

Page 35: "The dictionary defines critical thinking" critical thinking. Dictionary.com. *Dictionary.com Unabridged*. Random House, Inc. http://dictionary.reference.com/browse/critical thinking (accessed: June 23, 2014).

Page 35: "It is likely that you" "Superstition." Merriam-Webster.com. Accessed June 23, 2014. http://www.merriam-webster.com/dictionary/superstition.

Page 36: "One source is anecdotal evidence" "Anecdotal evidence." http://dictionary.reference.com/browse/anecdotal

Page 37: "A story in *The Economist*" Buttonwood. "The Dangers of Anecdotal Evidence." *The Economist*, accessed June 23, 2014, http://www.economist.com/blogs/buttonwood/2012/09/economics-and-markets.

Page 38: "This type of thinking is" "Confirmation bias." Skepdic.com, accessed June 23, 2014, http://www.skepdic.com/confirmbias.html.

Page 38: "Now, as Linda goes through" "The Baader-Meinhof Phenomenon," Alan Bellows, accessed April 14, 2014, http://www.damninteresting.com/the-baader-meinhof-phenomenon/

Page 41: "Homeopathy is defined" *The American Heritage® Dictionary of the English Language, Fourth Edition*. S.v. "homeopathy." Retrieved June 23 2014 from http://www.thefreedictionary.com/homeopathy

Page 42: "For example, as many as" Wikipedia contributors, "The Regulation and Prevalence of Homeopathy," Wikipedia, The Free Encyclopedia," http://en.wikipedia.org/wiki/Regulation_and_prevalence_of_homeopathy, accessed June 23, 2014.

Page 42: "The common English word for" delusion. Dictionary.com. *Dictionary.com Unabridged*. Random House, Inc. http://dictionary.reference.com/browse/delusion (accessed: June 23, 2014).

Page 44: "homeopathy is a scam" http://www.the-scientist.com/?articles.view/articleNo/39703/title/Australia-Officially-Debunks-Homeopathy/, http://www.theguardian.com/world/2014/apr/08/homeopathy-is-bunk-study-says

CHAPTER 4

Page 50: "The one Supreme Being, the" god. Dictionary.com. Dictionary.com Unabridged. Random House, Inc. http://dictionary.reference.com/browse/god (accessed: September 02, 2014).

Page 50: "The sole Supreme Being, eternal" god. Dictionary.com. Collins English Dictionary - Complete & Unabridged 10th Edition. HarperCollins Publishers. http://dictionary.reference.com/browse/god (accessed: September 02, 2014).

Page 51: "A being conceived as the" god. Dictionary.com. Collins English Dictionary - Complete & Unabridged 10th Edition. HarperCollins Publishers. http://dictionary.reference.com/browse/god (accessed: September 02, 2014).

Page 51: "The perfect and all-powerful spirit" god. Dictionary.com. The American Heritage® Dictionary of Idioms by Christine Ammer. Houghton Mifflin Company. http://dictionary.reference.com/browse/god (accessed: September 02, 2014).

Page 51: "The Supreme Being and principal" Swinburne, R.G. "God" in Honderich, Ted. (ed)The Oxford Companion to Philosophy, Oxford University Press, 1995.

Page 51: "The Southern Baptist denomination is" "The Baptist Faith and Message." Southern Baptist Convention, accessed April 25, 2014, http://www.sbc.net/bfm/bfm2000.asp.

Page 52: "The Statement of Faith used" "Statement of Faith." Patrick Henry College, accessed April 25, 2014, http://www.phc.edu/statement_2.php.

Page 54: "According to polls, more than" "63% Believe Bible Literally True." Rasmussen Reports, accessed April 25, 2014, http://legacy.rasmussenreports.com/2005/Bible.htm;

Page 56: "More than half of adult" The Washington Times, accessed April 25, 2014, http://www.washingtontimes.com/news/2004/feb/16/20040216-113955-2061r/?page=all.

Page 57: "Frank Thilly writes in" Thilly, Frank. A History of Philosophy. H. Holt and Company, 1914.

CHAPTER 5

Page 61: "In either case, by definition" delusion. Dictionary.com. Dictionary.com Unabridged. Random House, Inc. http://dictionary.reference.com/browse/delusion (accessed: June 23, 2014).

Page 62: "It seems impossible to believe" Bishop Accountability, accessed April 25, 2014, http://www.bishop-accountability.org/AtAGlance/USCCB_Yearly_Data_on_Accused_Priests.htm.

Page 63: "The dictionary defines praying as" "Pray." Merriam-Webster.com. Merriam-Webster, n.d. Accessed June 23, 2014, http://www.merriam-webster.com/dictionary/pray.

Page 70: "A critical thinker might note" Dorland's Medical Dictionary for Health Consumers. S.v. "rationalization." Retrieved June 23, 2014 from http://medical-dictionary.thefreedictionary.com/rationalization; critical thinking. Dictionary.com. Dictionary.com Unabridged. Random House, Inc. http://dictionary.reference.com/browse/critical thinking (accessed: June 23, 2014).

Page 73: "The results were widely reported" Carey, Benedict."Long-awaited Study Questions the Power of Prayer,." *The New York Times*. March 31, 2006. http://www.nytimes.com/2006/03/31/health/31pray.html.

Page 74: "What you come to realize" superstition. Dictionary.com. *Dictionary.com Unabridged*. Random House, Inc. http://dictionary.reference.com/browse/superstition (accessed: June 23, 2014).

Page 75: "Christians and other believers are" *The American Heritage® Dictionary of the English Language, Fourth Edition*. S.v. "post hoc." Retrieved June 23 2014 from http://www.thefreedictionary.com/post+hoc

Page 79: "Groupthink fallacy is defined in" *The American Heritage® Dictionary of the English Language, Fourth Edition*. S.v. "groupthink." Retrieved June 23 2014 from http://www.thefreedictionary.com/groupthink

Page 79: "PsySR.org describes it this way" Psychologists for Social Responsibility. http://www.psysr.org/about/pubs_resources/groupthink%20overview.htm

Page 80: "Related phenomena include social proof" Wikipedia contributors, "social proof," *Wikipedia: The Free Encyclopedia*, http://en.wikipedia.org/wiki/Social_proof (accessed June 23, 2014).

CHAPTER 6

Page 83: "This type of study is" retrospective study. (n.d.) Mosby's Medical Dictionary, 8th edition. (2009). Retrieved June 30 2014 from http://medical-dictionary.thefreedictionary.com/retrospective+study

Page 84: "For example, in 1999 scientists" Karlson, E.W.1, Lee, I.M., Cook, N.R., Manson, J.E., Buring, J.E., Hennekens, C.H.

> "A retrospective cohort study of cigarette smoking and risk of rheumatoid arthritis in female health professionals." *Arthritis Rheum.* 1999 May:42(5):910–7.

Page 87: "The infant mortality rate in" "Faith Healing," Harriet Hall, http://www.sciencebasedmedicine.org/faith-healing-religious-freedom-vs-child-protection/.

Page 87: "The statistical study of prayer" http://ije.oxfordjournals.org/content/41/4/923.full, Fortnightly Review 1872;12:125–35.

Page 88: "It turns out that George" Shaw, George Bernard. *Androcles and the Lion*. N.p.: Project Gutenberg, n.d. N. pag. Web. 30 June 2014.

CHAPTER 7

Page 97: "The dictionary defines science in" "Science." Merriam-Webster.com. Accessed June 30, 2014. http://www.merriam-webster.com/dictionary/science.

Page 99: "In Raleigh, the headline was" *Raleigh News and Observer*, December 17, 2004.

Page 100: "The dictionary defines a miracle" The American Heritage® Dictionary of the English Language, Fourth Edition. S.v. "miracle." Retrieved June 30 2014 from http://www.thefreedictionary.com/miracle

CHAPTER 8

Page 107: "The truth that you should" "Coincidence." Merriam-Webster.com. Accessed June 30, 2014. http://www.merriam-webster.com/dictionary/coincidence.

Page 107: "Religious people often misinterpret what" There have been invalid experiments that demonstrated efficacy for prayer. Here is an excellent write-up about one of those invalid experiments: http://archive.wired.com/wired/archive/10.12/prayer.html.

CHAPTER 9

Page 117: "Meditation is a centuries-old" "Meditation." Merriam-Webster.com. Accessed June 30, 2014. http://www.merriam-webster.com/dictionary/meditation.

Page 117: "Self-talk is a common" self-talk. Dictionary.com. Collins English Dictionary - Complete & Unabridged 10th Edition. HarperCollins Publishers. http://dictionary.reference.com/browse/self-talk (accessed: June 30, 2014).

Page 117: "For example, the Mayo Clinic" "Meditation." The Mayo Clinic. http://www.mayoclinic.org/healthy-living/stress-management/in-depth/meditation/art-20045858

Page 118: "Rick Warren is one of" Warren, Rick, *A Purpose-Driven Life.* Grand Rapids, MI: Zondervan, 2002.

Page 119: "There is a process called" doublethink. Dictionary.com. Dictionary.com Unabridged. Random House, Inc. http://dictionary.reference.com/browse/doublethink (accessed: June 30, 2014).

Page 123: "Imagine that one hundred children" Wolff, Edward N. "Recent Trends in Household Wealth in the United States." Levy Institute. http://www.levyinstitute.org/pubs/wp_589.pdf, table 2 (accessed August 30, 2014).

CHAPTER 10

Page 128: "According to the SBC, in" Southern Baptist Convention, "The Baptist Faith and Message," http://www.sbc.net/bfm/bfm2000.asp.

CHAPTER 12

Page 140: "We can easily call these" absurd. Dictionary.com. Collins English Dictionary - Complete & Unabridged 10th Edition. HarperCollins Publishers. http://dictionary.reference.com/browse/absurd

Page 142: "The dictionary defines the word" myth. Dictionary.com. Dictionary.com. Unabridged. Random House, Inc. http://dictionary.reference.com/browse/myth

Page 144: "The statement of faith for" Southern Baptist Convention, "The Baptist Faith and Message." http://www.sbc.net/pdf/translate/basicEnglish/TheBaptistFaithAndMessage.pdf

Page 144: "Similarly, the Catholic Encyclopedia explains" Gigot, Francis E. "Bible: Collection of Writings Recognized as Divinely Inspired," TheOriginal Catholic Encyclopedia. http://oce.catholic.com/index.php?title=Bible

Page 145: "The dictionary defines the word" perfect. Dictionary.com. Dictionary. com Unabridged. Random House, Inc. http://dictionary.reference.com/browse/ perfect

Page 145: "Perfection is also defined as" "Perfect." Merriam-Webster.com. Accessed June 23, 2014. http://www.merriam-webster.com/dictionary/perfect.

Page 145: "An omniscient being is defined" "Omniscient." Merriam-Webster. com. Accessed June 23, 2014. http://www.merriam-webster.com/dictionary/ omniscient.

Page 146: "More than two billion people" Thompson, Gabriel. "Could You Survive on $2 a Day?" *Mother Jones.* December 13, 2010. http://www.motherjones.com/ politics/2012/12/extreme-poverty-unemployment-recession-economy-fresno

Page 146: "Or is it more likely" Page 140: Dex and Eutychus. "Who Wrote the Bible?" *The Straight Dope.* January 7, 2002. http://www.straightdope.com/columns/ read/1985/who-wrote-the-bible-part-1 "Arthropods and fish came first"

Page 151: "Arthropods and fish came first" Gould, Stephen Jay. *The Book of Life: An Illustrated History of the Evolution of Life on Earth.* W. W. Norton & Company; Second Edition (September 17, 2001)

Page 152: "All of this happens in" Wikipedia. "Ussher Chronicle." Last modified June 14, 2014. http://en.wikipedia.org/wiki/Ussher_chronology

Page 159: "The story is so silly" Gelman, Mark. "God Squad: Miracles happen, but don't sit and wait for them." *New Haven Register.* August 10, 2012. http://www. nhregister.com/general-news/20120810/god-squad-miracles-happen- but-dont-sit-and-wait-for-them

CHAPTER 13

Page 165: "For example, polls such as" "Most Americans take Bible stories literally." *The Washington Times.* February 16, 2004. http://m.washingtontimes.com/ news/2004/feb/16/20040216-113955-2061r/?page=all

Page 169: "There are approximately 350,000 religious" "Facts About American Religion." *Hartford Institute for Religion Research.* http://hirr.hartsem.edu/ research/fastfacts/fast_facts.html; http://www.statisticbrain.com/gas- station-statistics/ US Census Bureau. "Gas Station Statistics". *Statistic Brain.* January 1, 2014. http://www.statisticbrain.com/gas-station-statistics/

Page 169: "Tithe is defined in the" tithe. Dictionary.com. *Dictionary.com Unabridged.* Random House, Inc. http://dictionary.reference.com/browse/tithe

Page 169: "In addition there are large" Wikipedia. "Prosperity Theology." Last Modified June 20, 2014. http://en.wikipedia.org/wiki/Prosperity_theology

Page 169: "The church is a profitable" Ritchie, Joshua. "How Churches Invest their Money." *Mint Life.* https://www.mint.com/blog/investing/how-churches- invest-05172010/?doing_wp_cron=1399317208.7326059341430664062500

Page 170: "The majority of Americans never" U.S. Department of Commerce, Census Bureau, and ASC. "Number of persons 25 to 34 years old, percentage with a bachelor's or higher degree, and percentage distribution, by undergraduate field of study and selected student characteristics: 2012." *Institute of Education Sciences.* http://nces.ed.gov/programs/digest/d13/tables/dt13_104.60.asp

Page 170: "A surprising percentage of American" "High School Dropout Statistics." *Statistic Brain.* January 1, 2014. http://www.statisticbrain.com/high-school-dropout-statistics

Levin, Henry M., and Rouse, Cecilia E. "The True Costs of High School Dropouts." *The New York Times.* January 25, 2012 http://www.nytimes.com/2012/01/26/opinion/the-true-cost-of-high-school-dropouts.html?_r=0

Page 170: "Wikipedia defines compartmentalization in this" Wikipedia. "Compartmentalization (psychology)" Last Modified March 7, 2014. http://en.wikipedia.org/wiki/Compartmentalization_(psychology)

Page 170: "Cognitive dissonance is defined in" Wikipedia. "Cognitive Dissonance." Last Modified June 9, 2014. http://en.wikipedia.org/wiki/Cognitive_dissonance

CHAPTER 14

Page 178: "To come to that conclusion" love. Dictionary.com. *Dictionary.com Unabridged.* Random House, Inc. http://dictionary.reference.com/browse/love

Page 178: "Then look up the definition" evil. Dictionary.com. *Dictionary.com Unabridged.* Random House, Inc. http://dictionary.reference.com/browse/evil

CHAPTER 15

Page 184: "Approximately 7,000 languages and 40,000" Ciccarelli, David. "Languages and Dialects of the World. Guess How Many There Are." *Voices.* May 8, 2006. http://blogs.voices.com/videodaily/2006/05/languages_and_dialects_of_the.html

Page 186: "The so-called 'Wicked Bible,' published" Wikipedia. "Wicked Bible." Last modified June 2, 2014. http://en.wikipedia.org/wiki/Wicked_Bible

CHAPTER 17

Page 196: "In the Christian concept of" Catholic-Online. "The Blessed Trinity." Catholic Encyclopedia. http://www.catholic.org/encyclopedia/view.php?id=11699

CHAPTER 18

Page 201: "Rick Warren, who has sold" Warren, Rick. "How to Hear God Speak." *Purpose Driven.* http://www.purposedriven.co.uk/media/File/HowToHearGodSpeak.pdf

Page 201: "Michele Bachmann is one such" Roberts, Christine. "Michele Bachmann, GOP Congresswoman, on 2012 Presidential Race: I've Heard that calling." *New York Daily News.* May 31, 2011. http://www.nydailynews.com/news/politics/michele-bachmann-gop-congresswoman-2012-presidential-race-calling-article-1.142302

Page 201: "Herman Cain had a similar" Bazemore, John. "Cain Says God Persuaded Him to Run for President." *USA Today*. November 12, 2011. http://usatoday30.usatoday.com/news/politics/story/2011-11-12/herman-cain-god/51179242/1

Page 202: "Rick Perry experienced the same" Bulger, Matthew. "God Told Me to Run: Analyzing the Divine Calling to Run for President." American Humanist Association. http://americanhumanist.org/HNN/details/2012-03-god-told-me-to-run-analyzing-the-divine-calling-to-r

Page 202: "For example, Nabil Shaath, a" MacAskill, Ewen. "George Bush: God Told Me to End the Tyranny in Iraq." *The Guardian*. October 6, 2005. http://www.theguardian.com/world/2005/oct/07/iraq.usa

Page 202: "For example, people with schizophrenia" National Institute of Mental Health.. http://www.nimh.nih.gov/health/publications/schizophrenia/complete-index.shtml

Page 202: "Friendly voices, usually triggered by" Adams, William Lee. "In Your Head: Hearing Voices." *Psychology Today*. January 01, 2007. http://www.psychologytoday.com/articles/200701/in-your-head-hearing-voices

Page 202: "Voices caused by Third Man" Porter, Liz. "Mystery of the Third Man." *Age National*. June 28, 2009. http://www.theage.com.au/national/mystery-of-the-third-man-20090627-doj2.html

Page 203: "Hallucinations that might be brought" Lloyd, William C. "Hearing Voices." *HealthGrades*. August 23, 2013. http://www.localhealth.com/article/hearing-voices

Page 208: "The dictionary defines hallucination in" hallucination. Dictionary.com. *Dictionary.com Unabridged*. Random House, Inc. http://dictionary.reference.com/browse/hallucination

CHAPTER 19

Page 214: "Unfortunately, more than half of" Danielson, Krissi. "Miscarriage Statistics: Is It True That 70% of Pregnancies End in Miscarriage?" About.com September 26, 2008. http://miscarriage.about.com/od/pregnancyafterloss/f/70percent.htm

Page 215: "We would find religious people" http://www.cnn.com/interactive/2014/08/us/american-archbishops-lavish-homes/

CHAPTER 20

Page 223: "First, the Bible clearly states" For example, 1 John 4:8–16; 1 Timothy 4:4; Psalm 145:9; Psalm 100:5; Galatians 5:22.

Page 223: "For example, in his 'Letter'" King, Martin Luther Jr. "Letter From a Birmingham Jail." African Studies Center- UPenn. http://www.africa.upenn.edu/Articles_Gen/Letter_Birmingham.html

Page 223: "Religious leaders like Rick Warren" Rick, Warren and Hannity, Sean. *The Purpose of Divine Life*. Interview. Fox News. 2012. http://www.blackchristiannews.com/news/2012/11/watch-pastor-rick-warren-says-he-is-deeply-disappointed-in-some-things-obama-has-done.html

Page 223: "The Catechism of the Catholic" Catechism of the Catholic Church. "God's Salvation: Law and Grace." Catechism of the Catholic Church. http://www. vatican.va/archive/ccc_css/archive/catechism/p3s1c3a1.htm

Page 230: "Hell is described by evangelical" Bible Baptist Church. "Statement of Faith." http://www.bbcoakharbor.org/#/about-us/statement-of-faith

Page 230: "Wikipedia summarizes the concept of" Wikipedia. "Love." Last Modified June 24, 2014. http://en.wikipedia.org/wiki/Love

Page 230: "The dictionary defines compassion in" compassion. Dictionary.com. *Dictionary.com Unabridged*. Random House, Inc. http://dictionary.reference. com/browse/compassion

Page 232: "The dictionary defines the word" "Immoral." Merriam-Webster.com. Accessed June 23, 2014. http://www.merriam-webster.com/dictionary/immoral.

CHAPTER 21

Page 235: "That is not to say" Kaiser, Gary. "Using Antibiotics and Chemical Agents to Control Bacteria." Community College of Baltimore City. April 2014. http:// faculty.ccbcmd.edu/courses/bio141/lecguide/unit2/control/antibio.html

Page 237: "In other words, if we" Spencer, Geoff. "Background on Comparative Genomic Analysis." National Human Genome Research Institute. December 2002. http://www.genome.gov/10005835

Page 237: "But inside dogs too, and" Pacifici, Mimi. "The Pope Has Said: Animals Too Have Souls, Just Like Men." Dreamshore. January 1990. http://www. dreamshore.net/rococo/pope.html

　　Ross, Scott. "Do All Dogs Really Go To Heaven?" *The 700 Club* http:// www.cbn.com/700club/scottross/commentary/animals_souls. aspx

Page 237: "This too is supposed to" Hitchcock, Mark. *Could the Rapture Happen Today?* Multnomah Books (February 4, 2009)

Page 238: "According to many Christians, the" Wikipedia. "Ensoulment." Last Modified May 21, 2014. http://en.wikipedia.org/wiki/ Ensoulment#Christianity

CHAPTER 22

Page 243: "In Raleigh, North Carolina" http://www.ispot.tv/ad/7Tj7/govmint-com- angel-coin

Page 247: "close to 1 percent of young American women claim to have virgin conceptions" http://www.bmj.com/content/347/bmj.f7102

Page 248: "A special form of irrationality" http://ffrf.org/publications/ freethought-today/item/13184-the-evolutionary-psychology-of-religion

Page 253: "Look again at the definition" critical thinking. Dictionary.com. Dictionary.com Unabridged. Random House, Inc. http://dictionary.reference. com/browse/critical thinking

CHAPTER 23

Page 257: "For example, this YouTube video" https://www.youtube.com/watch?v=oHv6vTKD6lg

Page 257: "If you are thankful for" Marsh, Jason. "Tips for Keeping a Gratitude Journal." *Greater Good-The Science of Meaning.* November 17, 2011. http://greatergood.berkeley.edu/article/item/tips_for_keeping_a_gratitude_journal

Page 257: "Personal prayers for strength, perseverance" Mayo Clinic Staff. "Meditation: A Simple, Fast Way to Reduce Stress." May 5, 2014. http://www.mayoclinic.org/healthy-living/stress-management/in-depth/meditation/art-20045858; Mayo Clinic Staff. "Positive Thinking: Stop Negative Self-Talk to Reduce Stress." May 4, 2014. http://www.mayoclinic.org/healthy-living/stress-management/in-depth/positive-thinking/art-20043950

Page 261: "January 20, 2011 video interview with Roger Bingham from The Science Network (TSN)." http://www.youtube.com/watch?v=HooeZrC76so

Page 265: "The dictionary defines circular reasoning" Dictionary.com. *Dictionary.com's 21st Century Lexicon.* Dictionary.com, LLC. http://dictionary.reference.com/browse/Circular reasoning

Page 266: "One definition of the word" Oxford Dictionaries. Accessed June 24, 2014. http://www.oxforddictionaries.com/us/definition/american_english/sin

INDEX